Sky
High

Sky High

THE UNTOLD STORY OF IndiGo

Tarun Shukla

HARPER
BUSINESS

An Imprint of HarperCollins Publishers

First published in India by Harper Business 2024
An imprint of HarperCollins *Publishers*
4th Floor, Tower A, Building No. 10, Phase II, DLF Cyber City,
Gurugram, Haryana – 122002
www.harpercollins.co.in

2 4 6 8 10 9 7 5 3 1

Copyright © Tarun Shukla 2024

P-ISBN: 978-93-5699-912-1
E-ISBN: 978-93-5699-926-8

The views and opinions expressed in this book are the author's own and the facts are as reported by him, and the publishers are not in any way liable for the same.

Tarun Shukla asserts the moral right
to be identified as the author of this work.

All rights reserved. No part of this publication may be reproduced, stored in a retrieval system, or transmitted, in any form or by any means, electronic, mechanical, photocopying, recording or otherwise, without the prior permission of the publishers.

Typeset in 11.5/15.8 Minion Pro at
Manipal Technologies Limited, Manipal

Printed and bound at
Replika Press Pvt. Ltd.

This book is produced from independently certified FSC® paper to ensure responsible forest management.

*To my mother, Subhashini Shukla, a gifted painter,
who has always been my life's invisible tailwind.*

Contents

Foreword ix

Preface xiii

1. Project Golf — 1
2. The Big Deal — 21
3. Rakesh Gangwal — 37
4. Kapil Bhatia — 60
5. Rahul Bhatia — 70
6. The Cabin Crew — 95
7. Brand IndiGo — 118
8. Lobbying — 147
9. Headwinds — 178

What Next? 206

References 229

Foreword

When twenty-five-year-old Charles Augustus Lindbergh, one of the greatest aviators of all time, took off from New York on 20 May 1927 in his single-engine, single-seat plane *Spirit of St Louis* on a solo, non-stop flight across the Atlantic Ocean, and landed in Le Bourget airfield just outside Paris, covering a distance of 5,809 kilometres after 33.5 hours—flying blind through fog for several hours, navigating only by stars when visible, skimming over storm clouds at 10,000 feet—he changed the future of aviation forever.

It was one of the greatest human endeavours—remarkable for its indomitable spirit of adventure and courage.

What is less known though is that, to finance this enterprise, Lindbergh pitched in his modest savings of US$2,000 and raised a loan of US$15,000 to try to win the US$25,000 Orteig Prize money offered to the pilot from an Allied country who flies non-stop between New York City and Paris. In his attempt to win, Lindbergh had staked everything.

Six well-known aviators had already lost their lives in this endeavour.

Thus, Lindbergh was not only one of the most intrepid adventurers in the history of the world, but he was also, in a sense, a great entrepreneur.

Heroism and entrepreneurship are an obedience to a secret impulse of the soul. And aviation has always drawn great adventurers and entrepreneurs since the time of, and even before, the first successful flight by the Wright brothers in 1903.

Tarun Shukla is a journalist with an avid interest in aviation. He has covered that subject from various perspectives for more than a decade and a half in India. He has captured the incredibly successful story of IndiGo and the entrepreneurial spirit of its reclusive founders Rahul Bhatia and Rakesh Gangwal.

By most yardsticks and standards, IndiGo is a stunning success story. A blistering pace of growth, on-time performance, and profitability, to name just three. However, measured against the degree of difficulty in terms of the odds faced—antiquated Indian regulations combined with red tape that can choke and stifle even the most tenacious; an aviation compliance authority coupled with an aviation ministry out of step with each other and jointly out of tune with the times; with almost all sectors liberalized, the aviation sector alone in a 'time warp', still reeling under the Licence Raj; expensive infrastructure at airports that operate like a real estate cartel, devoid of rationale; an aviation regulator—with no teeth and limited scope of services under its ambit—that regulates a monopoly instead of regulating competition; a debilitating tax regime; in short, policies which hinder the expansion of the price-sensitive customer base at the bottom of the pyramid, what has been achieved is nothing short of stupendous.

Considering the overwhelming odds and impediments, the spectacular growth of IndiGo not only calls for a celebration of the Indian spirit but also demands an objective study. And Tarun has done a commendable job in fulfilling that need. That is, to write on aviation with all its complexity and technicalities, to get behind the façade of glamour and hype that surrounds it and sift facts from folklore and present the story on the making of an impressive and successful airline in the Indian context, in a way that appeals to the common people who are curious about aviation, and adds to the knowledge of aviation enthusiasts. This is no easy task, especially when the promoters of IndiGo are self-effacing and avoid the inquisitive press.

There is an additional handicap for a writer in bringing out a dispassionate and accurate account when the top management and the key people are secretive, for they fear the information may fall into the hands of the competition.

The task of bringing out a true account becomes more difficult when one is not given easy and open access to key documents; when credible rumours abound that, in India, to be able to get ahead of others and to be successful, especially in a tightly controlled industry like aviation, one has to be close to people in high places in the government and to the ruling party and indulge in questionable and unethical practices.

To assess the accomplishments of a business enterprise and their impact on society, one should view it from a fair distance to get a balanced and rounded view.

Nearly two decades hence, whatever has been accomplished by IndiGo, which was the last to launch during that era of new airline launches, is truly remarkable and needs to be captured to inspire other young entrepreneurs so that they can explore uncharted space and create and build a strong and vibrant India.

And Tarun has done an admirable job in recounting that story.

Captain G.R. Gopinath
Founder, Air Deccan, India's first low-cost airline

Preface

It was the winter of 2012, when Sukumar Ranganathan (then editor of *Mint* and later of the *Hindustan Times*) called me into his room on the sixteenth floor of HT House located in central Delhi. The orange-painted wall—the colour of *Mint*'s masthead and also of the newsroom walls—had a photograph of a leopard and various birds. Soft music played in the background as Ranganathan edited some story for the next day's edition. As I waited for him to finish, to my left I could see dozens of railway tracks heading out from New Delhi railway station. To my right, if it were not for the Ambadeep Building, I could have seen all the way up to India Gate in the distance.

These views aside, I was apprehensive about what was to come. In my several years at *Mint*, I had been hauled up often for creating some 'mischief' or the other by writing stories that upset the high and the mighty. I had received some legal stinkers too in my time.

These included, among others, lobbyist Deepak Talwar; his then 'friend' and minister of aviation, Praful Patel; another central cabinet minister Ajit Singh; entrenched bureaucrats; powerful law firms; honchos of two, now defunct, airlines—Vijay Mallya of Kingfisher Airlines and Naresh Goyal of Jet Airways.

While sometimes the pressure was directly on me, I knew Ranganathan too used to come under considerable pressure for clearing some of these stories—which he nevertheless did on most occasions. When they were outré, he would counsel me and ask if I had got the other side's views or not. These conversations were never easy, but to the point and sometimes curt.

After such meetings, I would typically lie low for a few days, writing regular news stories before returning to the hackles-raising stuff. Ranganathan had even issued instructions that only he would edit my stories and if he was busy, he would at least eyeball them quickly before releasing them on the new-age integrated content management software called Methode, from Eidos Media, where one could see who is writing what story, who is editing, the changes being made live across the newsroom. You could also see the newspaper pages getting designed for the next day and if your story got placed on the front page, it was your high for that day.

As a journalist, the fundamental question before me always has been—what is my job really? What is it that I must really do? The answer is simple: my duty is to make information public and increase public awareness.

My job is not to please or persecute, but to find ways to tell the truth and do the hard yards to collect documentary evidence (when possible) to back my claims.

Thankfully, in the nearly twenty years of my journalistic career (as of 2024)—first at *The Pioneer*, then the *Financial Express*, then *Mint*, and a fellowship in between that allowed me to work with *The Wall Street Journal* (WSJ) in Chicago, and from there to *The Economic Times*—I have been sued only once with even police officials being sent to arrest me, but thankfully, the case was closed soon after.

Mulling over some of this, as I sat there waiting to be 'counselled' for some story I may have filed, Ranganathan finally looked up from his computer and asked, 'Have you read the book *Nuts!*?'

I said 'no'. He advised me to read it. I said I would.

'It's a book about Southwest Airlines,' he added.

He then came straight to what was on his mind. 'Can you a write a book on IndiGo? Eighty thousand words, three months off, from tomorrow.'

I sat gawking, but said 'Sure, Sir', left the room and went back to my desk. My seat overlooked the revolving rooftop restaurant called Parikrama with Connaught Place as the backdrop. I sat there for a few minutes with my head spinning.

I was happy that the meeting had not ended in a homily. However, relief gave way to panic, as a sense of being out of my depth set in. I had once written a chapter on Indian aviation at the request of a German professor for a book published in the UK by Ashgate Publishing called *The Low Cost Carrier Worldwide*, but scripting an entire book on an airline? It was a different ballgame.

How did one go about writing a whole book?

I decided to read *Nuts!* in one go that same night. I recommend it to everyone interested in aviation. It is a fascinating story of how a low-cost airline changed air travel in the US forever.

The Indian scenario is different though. IndiGo was and is, even now, nothing close to the kind of an exuberant airline that Southwest was. For one, it did very few press conferences and public events. For another, it was also unlike the then government-run Air India with its unions, bureaucrats and ministers, all of whom could speak without fear of being sacked.

IndiGo, on the contrary, was an extremely closed airline. Its promoters, Delhi-based Rahul Bhatia and Miami-based Rakesh Gangwal, were super reclusive. Few knew how they really operated, what was on their minds, or what they were doing that made IndiGo grow so well, taking it from a good to a better place all the time.

The only thing the airline was happy to announce in its early years was its results. It also sometimes relished cheap thrills—like announcing a profit of Rs 787 crore for 2012–13, when Air India was inducting its brand-new Boeing Dreamliner 787 planes. You could call it a coincidence, but IndiGo, which flew only smaller, narrow-body planes, perhaps wanted to convey that its fleet may not have the wide-body Dreamliners, but it was profitable unlike all the other carriers (at that time).

Since it was not a listed airline then, its president Aditya Ghosh would call me discreetly and tell me the airline had filed its results with the aviation regulator—the Directorate General of Civil Aviation (DGCA)—and I could perhaps access it and write a piece without bringing him into the picture. For me it was a story; I would do what was necessary.

Mint had been started in alliance with *WSJ*. In Ghosh's mind, we were perhaps the best brand to get IndiGo's profits story out.

By 2011, IndiGo held nearly 20 per cent of the market share, though Jet Airways was the largest with a market share of around 26 per cent. Kingfisher Airlines had captured 18 per cent, Air India hung on to 16 per cent, SpiceJet was at 14 per cent and Go First was at about 6 per cent.

Nevertheless, IndiGo was still not considered part of the big league. Jet's Naresh Goyal and Kingfisher's Vijay Mallya ruled the Indian skies and the public mindscape. At least, that was the impression. Whether it was the World Economic Forum (WEF)'s Indian summits, or the HT Leadership Summit, Mallya and Goyal would be the most sought-after people on the dais. IndiGo's Bhatia and Gangwal were nowhere to be seen in public. It was hard to find a picture of Gangwal—and it still is.

In the capital, at aviation ministry meetings with all the promoters, Bhatia would sometimes make a rare appearance, sit close to the door and sneak out as soon as the meeting ended. The media waiting outside ran only after Mallya and Goyal for comments. If you reached out to Bhatia, he would smile and merely point to Mallya and Goyal indicating the 'big guys' are over there.

IndiGo was thus a complete black hole for a journalist those days.

Despite my tracking the sector, I had a rather hard time to start the legwork for the book. Despite multiple requests, IndiGo did not give any meetings with its promoters or its senior officials.

What made things more difficult, which I realized eventually, was that even senior IndiGo officials were provided information strictly on a need-to-know basis. It was, therefore, difficult to adequately map the airline. Even some very senior officials were ignorant, for example, that a large aircraft order was being planned by their airline, until fifteen minutes before it was actually placed.

Therefore, I spent weeks researching the promoters and drawing concentric circles around them and mapping where they came from. I tracked down their family members, business associates and met hundreds of people over the next few months. After all, when something is difficult to find, it makes the hunt even more interesting. In my case, this became a story I just had to crack.

Six months into it and based on many of these interviews, I started to send questions to Bhatia and Gangwal, repeatedly requesting them for an appointment. Gradually Bhatia thawed, first meeting me in his office and then at his farmhouse in Chhatarpur in Delhi. I ended up meeting Gangwal too and found my conversations with him fascinating as well.

The three months my editor had given me became many more months. When the first draft went for editing, it took forever. In the meantime, I got a fellowship and left for the US in 2015. In the Alfred Friendly Press Partners journalism fellowship at the

Missouri School of Journalism I also got a chance to report for *WSJ* from Chicago, which gave me a new kind of exposure.

The book, still not ready, was at the back of my mind. I had spent a lot of time on it and felt it should see the light of day.

After I returned from the US and settled in, I got another challenging opportunity—to move to *The Economic Times*' new long-form journalism offering, based on the lines of *The New Yorker*, called ET Prime and to work with another set of inspiring editors including Shishir Prasad, Deepak Ajwani, Javed Syed and Sruthijith K.K.

IndiGo now was no more the 'teenager' of 2012, but a big daddy. It had slain the competition. The 'King of Good Times', Vijay Mallya, now bankrupt, had fled to London—ironically on his bitter rival Jet Airways' flight—and was being referred to as an 'absconder' and a 'wilful defaulter' for saddling (mostly) the public sector banks with Kingfisher Airlines' debt.

Jet Airways too was sinking fast, but Goyal refused to give up control of the airline. He eventually took the twenty-five-year-old Jet Airways down with him in 2019. Nearly 16,000 proud employees were rendered jobless, in shock, and depressed with no surety they would get their salary dues and gratuity after years of hard work.

Goyal, however, could not flee India like Mallya did. Reminiscent of a dramatic Indian movie, the Emirates flight he was on and already on the runway, was called back by the Narendra Modi-led BJP government. Goyal, who had built his empire largely under the rule of the Congress government, saw his and his wife Anita Goyal's passports impounded. They now face investigations over money laundering. Goyal was also jailed.

With nearly Rs 70,000-crore (US$8.4 billion approx.) annual revenues, a 350-plus aircraft fleet, market valuation of around Rs

1.3 lakh crore (US$15 billion approx.), this has left IndiGo as India's largest airline (based on domestic market share) and the world's ninth largest airline (based on overall capacity and frequency deployment). No other Indian airline has come close to matching these numbers since Indian aviation really took off in 1932 with J.R.D. Tata's Air India.

What does IndiGo do so differently and right? Why do others fall behind or fall by the wayside, while IndiGo grows from strength to strength? Why has the airline done well despite the nearly twenty-five-year-long friendship (the same as Jet Airways' lifetime) of its promoters Bhatia and Gangwal breaking down beyond repair? How will the airline be without Gangwal? How will it face a rival with deep pockets—Tata and Singapore Airlines-backed Air India?

These questions fascinated me and despite the odds I faced, I decided to revisit the entire book because the story still needed to be told. IndiGo is now to Indian aviation what Android is to mobiles. Currently, every second Indian domestic air passenger flies on an IndiGo aircraft.

My multiple meetings over the years with Bhatia and Gangwal, and interviews with over 300 people have helped me weave this fascinating story of patience, planning and persistence that has created a monster air travel network in India of over 2,000 daily flights that few could have dreamt of in 2005.

I hope you will enjoy this journey with me as much as I did researching and writing it over several years. I would also be very happy to hear from you on Twitter/X (@shukla_tarun), LinkedIn or via email at tarunsmail@gmail.com.

Warm wishes and happy flying.

1
Project Golf

London-based Bhupendra Kansagra landed in India in 1998 after word spread that a British Airways' consulting firm Speedwing was planning to revive India's defunct airline, ModiLuft. Speedwing had prepared a business plan and, perhaps to instil confidence, had kept all the top management positions for British Airways executives.

'In their presentation they explained how there was immense scope in India for air travel. We were convinced,' said Kansagra, who has roots in Africa, is among the richest Asians in the UK and runs the investment firm Solai Holdings Ltd.

Satish Kumar Modi or S.K. Modi had launched ModiLuft in May 1993 in technical partnership with Lufthansa. But after three years, the German airline had terminated their agreement with ModiLuft claiming Modi had defaulted on lease payments for its four aircraft. The airline was grounded and went into a messy litigation.

However, the airline's licence had not been revoked and soon after, the process to restart it was started with a new set of investors. While looking to raise US$17.5 million in equity and US$17.5 million in debt, Modi had met Kansagra through Khandwala Securities, a merchant-banking firm in Mumbai. Speedwing's offer was via a subscription agreement through a US-based company.

Already convinced, Kansagra did not spend a lot of time on Modi and agreed to put in US$4 million out of the US$17.5 million of equity and waited for more funds to be raised from other international investors. ModiLuft had a lot of creditors; credit settlement was a pre-condition for US companies. Therefore, raising further equity was delayed. Investors, who had already put money into the escrow account, were tired of waiting and began to withdraw.

By early 2000, close to US$15 million from the amount raised was gone. If Kansagra had also pulled out, the project would have collapsed. Eventually, Kansagra started talking to Modi and increased his investment from US$4 million to US$7 million, and then to US$15million.

In October 2000, Kansagra sent money from the US to India, converted it into equity and took 56 per cent shareholding of Royal Holdings Pvt. Ltd, which owned the ModiLuft brand. The process to restart ModiLuft gathered some momentum once again.

There was division of work now—Modi was to handle the Indian side of the challenges associated with ModiLuft, including settlements with creditors and government-owned airports and oil companies that he was more familiar with than Kansagra; the latter was to handle financing.

Soon enough, Kansagra roped in Allied Boston Bank in San Francisco, an offshore bank licenced by the Republic of Palau. However, this took a nasty turn. By the end of the year, it became clear that the bank was conducting business without authorization. Running the bank was another way of stealing people's money, Kansagra recalled in one of the many interviews with me including at the coffee shop of Gurugram's Leela Ambience Hotel.

In 2001, the local courts barred the bank from conducting any business. Now ModiLuft had equity but no debt, and its business plan required an element of debt according to Speedwing. On the Indian side, Kansagra was hoping against hope that the airline's creditors would be happy to receive at least some money back (instead of losing it all should the airline's debt be written off entirely) and allow it to fly again.

By December 2000, the firm had also leased an aircraft and issued letters of intent to lease more because under the then Indian regulations, an airline was required to have at least five aircraft within six months of launching the operations. The launch date was optimistically set for April 2001. The airline also started to recruit staff for the incoming fleet.

By February 2001, Kansagra and Modi started panicking as there was no debt, no sign of government clearance, and 500 people were already on the payroll. Also, no creditor settlement was forthcoming with the state-run Indian Oil (IOCL) and Bharat Petroleum Corporation Ltd (BPCL). They insisted that they be paid all their dues in exchange for the approval to let the airline fly again. Without that, the government was not prepared to clear the airline's take-off.

'The Indian government was a complete nightmare,' Kansagra recalls. 'All the creditors were very bitter towards Mr Modi, because I think he must have told them that he would be doing the financial closing soon and might have given excuses like he would come and settle next week, and so on. So, he had no credibility left. And they thought we were all the same gang, you know. So, there was great hostility that we didn't budget for.'

This could not go on. Matters reached a tipping point and the time for niceties was over. The investor duo exploded in a verbal duel, Kansagra recalls. There was an acrimonious meeting in London, where it was decided that Modi will either do his part or quit as the chairman.

Around the same time, Kansagra met Rahul Bhatia at his home in south Delhi's Chhatarpur area. Bhatia, from a travel agency background himself, had been introduced to Kansagra through one of the British Airways' marketing executives.

Bhatia and Kansagra then formed an alliance where they agreed that Bhatia would do the ground handling and sales for Royal Airways and perhaps in an indication of his local clout, Bhatia also told Kansagra, 'If you run into any trouble with Mr Modi, come back to me.'

It would appear that Bhatia was not wrong in his judgement about Modi.

Kansagra soon got wind of the fact that instead of getting government clearances, Modi, behind Kansagra's back, had been trying discreetly to wrest control of the company. Kansagra held 56 per cent and was the finance signatory. There was Rs 80 crore, or whatever was left of it, sitting in the bank, and Modi wanted to change the signatories. Kansagra swiftly got an injunction from the courts against any such move.

This issue escalated into a bitter battle and, in late 2001, resulted in Modi's removal as chairman of Royal Airways. In September 2001, the 9/11 terrorist attacks on the twin towers of the World Trade Center shook the world. Share prices of airlines and aircraft manufacturers plummeted. Bankruptcy loomed and, worldwide, tens of thousands of layoffs were announced in the weeks following the attacks.

The US government came to the aid of its airlines, with US$10 billion in loan guarantees, along with US$5 billion as short-term assistance. Some argued later that the negative financial effects following the 9/11 attacks only hastened an industry reorganization that would have happened sooner or later in any case.

Many airlines, including US Airways, which filed for bankruptcy after the attacks, were in financial difficulties prior to 9/11. Other airlines also had overstretched financial positions in the 1990s, having negotiated plump wage contracts with unions and purchased new aircraft. The downward dive in passenger demand post 9/11 forced them to tighten their belts, renegotiate contracts and sack staff.

In November 2001, British Airways abandoned Royal Airways, saying that it needed to focus on its own survival, rather than launch other airlines through consultancy. Royal Airways, to be launched as a two-class—business and economy—airline in January 2002, massively downsized its 500 staffers.

'That false start cost US$10–12million,' says Kansagra.

Around the world, the aviation industry's focus had shifted from expansion to survival. Royal retained a few trusted employees, led by Siddhanth Sharma, Sanjay Kumar, Vineet Mittal, O.P. Ahuja and I.P. Singh, in the faint hope that something might still work out.

From 2002 onwards, Kansagra and Rahul Bhatia deepened their ties.

'He said let's try and do these things together—that's how we started deploying consultants. He recommended some from Europe. One came from Ryanair. We did a lot of work with him,' says Kansagra.

Sometime in 2003, Royal Airways had reached settlement with the government. By the end of 2003, Rakesh Gangwal, Bhatia's friend, got involved in the efforts to restart Royal Airways. Gangwal worked from Atlanta and Washington, having moved on from US Airways. He recruited the first chief executive officer (CEO) for Royal Airways, Mark Winders, who stayed with the airline for a year till late 2005. Jason Bitter was to be the chief operations officer (COO). Sanjay Kumar and Vineet Mittal were sent to London to study various low-fare airlines, particularly easyJet.

This team too prepared a detailed business plan for Royal Airways but before it could raise funds, investment banker Morgan Stanley wanted the plan to be approved by a UK-based consulting firm, Aviation Economics, run by two ex-Ryanair staff. The firm liked the project plan and cleared it swiftly.

This April 2004 plan, a copy of which I have reviewed, was headlined 'Come, fly with us' and noted that the majority shares (56 per cent) of Royal Airways was owned by Royal Holdings Service Ltd, a Nevada-registered company.

Its promoters, the London-based Kansagra family, had significant business interests in Kenya, Tanzania, Sudan, Nigeria and the UK, where they had a luxury hotel in the heart of London. Kansagra was listed as a director on the board of Royal Airways and was to play an active role in reviving the airline.

Rahul Bhatia—listed as Managing Director, InterGlobe Enterprises Ltd—was to assist Kansagra, and had agreed to become a member of the board of directors. Rakesh Gangwal, listed as an experienced and respected professional in the aviation sector, was to provide guidance to the Royal Airways management team on the low-cost business model, help in recruiting experienced industry professionals, and continue as an advisor to the airline even after its launch. Gangwal was then chairman of Worldspan, an e-commerce provider for the travel trade.

Finally, the presentation identified InterGlobe as a leading travel group that offered air transport management services to the airline industry, including sales and marketing operations, route management, and airport services to fourteen airlines. InterGlobe delivered sales in excess of US$200 million annually, had twenty-one offices in fifteen cities and had 350 trained and experienced industry professionals in India.

It also had a firm called Galileo India, with eighteen offices and 400 agents in 119 cities, and was stated to have pioneered automated ticketing for domestic airlines in India. The pitch gave an excellent insight into the state of Indian aviation then and was built around the upcoming economic growth.

Indian general elections were held from 20 April to 10 May 2004. The presentation was made shortly before the elections and predicted, post-election, a friendlier policy regime. The BJP-led government had come out with India Shining campaign which backfired and instead brought the Congress-led UPA government to power which then lasted for two terms.

The presentation expected aviation norms to be liberalized to allow 49 per cent foreign investment in scheduled airlines (although that did not happen until 2012). While airlines were required to follow route guidelines entailing compulsory services to commercially non-viable routes for connectivity, the presentation expected it to be abolished. It also expected that the government would provide explicit subsidy support for essential but economical services (this too came true really only over a decade later in 2016, when the regional connectivity scheme *Ude Desh ka Aam Naagrik* or UDAN was introduced by the government).

Among the domestic operators, only the state-run Indian Airlines was allowed to fly international routes and provide ground handling to other airlines.

The government-owned oil companies such as Indian Oil Corporation and BPCL enjoyed a monopoly over the supply of jet fuel. That too was expected to be opened up. Mukesh Ambani's

Reliance Industries did finally come into the jet fuel business after many years, but is still not a dominant player.

Other changes anticipated in the presentation were: lowering of sales tax on jet fuel, other aviation-related taxes, and airport charges. Privatization of Indian Airlines and Air India was also on the cards. The bids for Delhi and Mumbai airports had been called for 18 February 2004 by the then BJP-led government, it noted.

The taxes on jet fuel have indeed been reduced by many states since then, but a key aviation hub like Delhi still has a higher rate. Air India privatization that led to the airline going back to its founder—Tata Group—finally came through in 2021, though Delhi and Mumbai airports were indeed privatized in 2006 by the new Congress-led UPA government.

Having painted a fairly rosy picture, the presentation moved on to the benefits of operating a low-cost airline in India. It noted that the model had flourished across international markets at a time when full-service airlines were reeling under huge losses. Post 9/11, making drastic changes in the fare structure of a full-service airline was difficult, if not impossible. Further, a full-service airline fleet had multiple aircraft types; emphasis on service and traditional reservation systems; and the bulk of the sales was dominated by commission-based travel agents.

On the other hand, for new a low-cost carrier (LCC) start-up, the post-9/11 world presented a sweet deal—the lease rentals for planes were at rock bottom, ensuring a competitive edge for the new operator. Also, a typical LCC had a fleet made up of just one aircraft type, offered a single-class configuration (usually only economy), no seat allocation and no interline transfers. It offered no in-flight freebies such as free meals or beverages, but sold such services in-flight, generating additional revenue.

The distribution system of a LCC made extensive use of online bookings and call centres generating substantial savings in commission costs and maintenance of ticketing outlets. In sum it offered an undiluted focus on the basic activity—getting passengers to their destination quickly, safely and on time—though without any pampering.

The presentation pointed out that following the success of the first LCC, Southwest Airlines in the US, many others had followed—jetBlue in the US, easyJet in the UK, Ryanair in Ireland, Virgin Blue (now Virgin Australia) in Australia, and AirAsia in Malaysia. The LCC model was bound to succeed as much in India as it had elsewhere in the world.

Financially, it said, it was a win-win scenario; early investors would only gain, not lose.

In February 2000, jetBlue had begun operations; its IPO and listing took place in April 2002 and the share price peaked in October 2003, fetching four times the IPO price. Its operational revenue stood at US$635 million in 2002, with a net profit of US$55 million.

Ryanair, launched in 1995, went in for an IPO in 1997. The presentation stated that during 2001–03, the airline's revenues had grown from €467 million to €843, its net profit soaring from €104 million to €150 million. Its share price had risen by more than 500 per cent since its listing in 1997. Similarly, AirAsia commenced operations in December 2001 and in June 2003, three new financial partners invested, valuing the company at US$100 million, and it was expected to go public with an IPO size of US$200 million in late 2004.

The presentation noted that early-stage financial sponsors had exited LCC projects through highly successful capital market transactions. There was a case, therefore, for the growing Indian market to adopt this new-age model.

Several operators had taken to the skies when the aviation sector in India was opened up to private players in the 1990s—NEPC Airlines and its subsidiary, Skyline NEPC; Jet Airways; Air Sahara; East West Airlines; and ModiLuft.

Many of these had failed and shut down, leaving few to fulfil the growing needs of the sector. Air India, for example, covered forty-four destinations with two Boeing 747s and seventeen Airbus A330s, reporting a profit of US$30 million and operating revenue of US$1.3 billion, for the year ending March 2003.

Indian Airlines—with a fleet of fifty-two aircraft, fifty destinations, a 40 per cent market share and exclusivity over ground handling—enjoyed a competitive advantage over private players in the domestic sector. In the year ending March 2003, it reported a total turnover of US$195 million and a net loss of US$43 million. There was thus the possibility to squeeze more airlines into the system.

Market-wise too, LCCs had been successful in locations where air travel was either underserved or overpriced, incumbent carriers were weak, and where the airline had a focused business plan that increased productivity and efficiency without compromising on safety.

Added to this, the ability and advantage of creating a sustainable low-cost base, coupled with factors such as economic growth and changes in regulatory structure, meant that the chances of replicating the LCC success stories from elsewhere was high.

India fitted well into that matrix, the presentation noted. It was an extremely price-sensitive market and more people could take to the skies if tickets became cheaper. There was also great potential due to the under-penetration of air travel, long distances and long travel hours by road and rail, all of which meant that middle- and upper-middle class passengers might switch to air travel if the pricing was reasonable. Besides, strong growth in the industry and service sectors further improved the growth prospects of air travel. The corporate sector, a significant segment, could also shift patronage to a LCC if safety and punctuality were guaranteed.

It predicted average flight occupancy of 64 per cent in the first year, which would increase to 75 per cent by the fourth year on metro routes, and 74 per cent on non-metro routes. The average fare was calculated as Rs 4,104 for the first year for metro routes, and Rs 5,136 for non-metro routes, which would go down to Rs 3,627 and Rs 4,341 by the fourth year. This would be 40 per cent cheaper than Jet Airways' economy fares at that time.

Railway traffic was assumed to grow at a historic annual average rate of 2 per cent, while air traffic was assumed to grow at 6 per cent starting from 2004. Market stimulation or cheap fares were assumed as nil in the first year for all routes, and in later years a two-tiered approach was to be adopted. For routes with matured traffic, such as Mumbai–Delhi, a stimulation of around 5 per cent was envisaged for the first year and in other routes, stimulation of around 10 per cent was proposed.

In terms of possible competitor response, the presentation noted that state-run Indian Airlines would react with tactical prices. However, it was burdened by bureaucracy, inefficiency and legacy airline issues such as overstaffing and unionized workforce, and was under government obligation to service uneconomical routes.

Naresh Goyal's Jet Airways would also resort to tactical pricing, with an emphasis on its product, service, fleet network and loyalty. On the flip side, it had aircraft leased at pre-9/11 prices, high service costs, inefficiencies due to a fleet with multiple aircraft types, all of which increased costs.

Subrata Roy's Air Sahara was seen as an airline that would react sharply on key competitive routes, but was burdened by a mixed fleet, high maintenance costs, disorganized and inconsistent policies, and a high-cost base, with no concern over losses.

Capt. G.R. Gopinath's LCC, Air Deccan, started in 2003—emerging on the scene and operating only short flights—was seen as key competition. It too had a mixed fleet—both Airbus and ATRs. The presentation hoped that this airline which was to be called Aasaan (erstwhile ModiLuft) would take off before Air Deccan became firmly entrenched.

How soon would fresh competition come in? The licences of the 1990s' start-up airlines such as Archana Airways, NEPC Airlines, Damania Airways and East West Airlines had expired. While Crown Air, registered by lobbyist Niira Radia, did hold a valid licence, no new permissions had been given after 1996 except to Air Deccan.

Let alone new licences, the no-objection certificate (NOC) for Kansagra to refloat the airline was denied repeatedly, while he went around seeking US$35 million in investments. He held long roadshows at the Oberoi in Mumbai. Jeh Wadia (son of Nusli Wadia who owns Britannia Industries and Bombay Dyeing) had come for the presentations. According to a source who prefers to remain anonymous, Jeh had reportedly said, 'I am looking to start my own airline, looking at Air Deccan and this one.'

Eventually, Jeh did not invest and launched his own airline named GoAir (renamed Go First and has ceased operations from May 2023). Shortly thereafter, for some reason or the other, two prospective investments of US$35 million from German and Saudi investors fizzled out. The money never reached the bank.

'The story did not sell,' the source reported. Jet Airways was believed to have had a hand in that. Jet was going for its IPO shortly and it had injected doubts into the investment banking circles on the chances of success of a low-cost airline in India. Jet claimed that there were no secondary airports in India, the fuel cost was the same, there were no parking spaces and airport slots and so on. A close confidante of Naresh Goyal was said to be the driver of this whisper campaign.

'*Aap kaise karoge? Sab toh hamare paas hai.* You will lose on business traffic, you don't have any morning flight slots,' this confidante once told my source.

In between, Aasaan was pitched to then chief minister of Andhra Pradesh, Chandra Babu Naidu, who, to encourage the state's growth, was looking to launch an airline with Hyderabad as the hub. He had expressed the state's willingness to take a 4–5 per cent stake and allot plenty of landing slots in Hyderabad.

The name Aasaan had been chosen because it meant 'facile' and was quite a popular word in Hyderabad. However, it had a connotation of 'easy lay' too. Someone did not like the state investing in this airline and scuttled it, Kansagra said. 'It had a very funny sexual connotation. That wasn't going to go very far when Andhra pulled out.'

It was time to look for another name. 'We were looking for a domain name that was available with the dotcom extension, because that was the beginning of the era of [online] technology,' he recalled.

In an internal discussion, Jason Bitter, the COO of the soon to be re-renamed airline, suddenly sprang the name 'SpiceJet' on the rest. While some saw a stereotypical Western mindset of an exotic India behind the name, it turned out to be acceptable to all, also because the domain name was available.

The twist and turns for ModiLuft turned Royal Airways turned Aasaan turned SpiceJet did not end here though. Bhatia was torn between continuing to support SpiceJet, 'which had a lot of baggage, legacy claims, litigation [with former promoter Modi], shareholders, creditors—a mess,' and starting his own airline. He chose the latter and applied to the civil aviation ministry for a permit.

'I was very upset,' Kansagra recalled.

Indeed, through a Right to Information (RTI) query, I found out that InterGlobe Aviation Pvt. Ltd had filed an application to get a no objection certificate (NOC) from the aviation ministry on 14 January 2004. He received the NOC three months later relatively swiftly on 15 April 2004 from the BJP government's civil aviation ministry led by minister Rajiv Pratap Rudy.

Galileo India Pvt. Ltd (a Bhatia company) was to hold 75 per cent of the new company's shares, InterGlobe Enterprises 24.96 per cent, and Kapil Bhatia and his son Rahul Bhatia 0.02 per cent each. Its authorized capital was Rs 31 crore and subscribed capital Rs 30 crore. Kapil and his son Rahul Bhatia were to be the only directors on the airline's board.

The company had stated in its initial submission to the ministry that it would start operations with Boeing 737–800 aircraft, of which five would be acquired at the beginning, and two each would be acquired in the third, fourth and the fifth year.

'But they were not issuing licences in those days, because Naresh Goyal was reasonably in control and so he didn't let the floodgates open,' recalls Kansagra, remembering the shock.

Indeed, Goyal made life difficult for every new entrant. 'Sometimes we blame politicians but often it is businessmen who are more dangerous than politicians. People who are already entrenched in the business would have reached there because of the reforms. But they forget how they got there in the first place, and they do not want others to enter,' Capt. G.R. Gopinath said of the challenges he faced during his Air Deccan days and added, 'Naresh Goyal was very smart in cosying up to politicians. He lobbied openly against me.'

How did he still manage to land the Air Deccan licence?

'I got it because my relations with BJP were stronger than Naresh Goyal's lobbying against me,' was his reply.

Gopinath ran a company called Deccan Charters for helicopters from 1997. His services were used by many politicians. Karnataka's south Bengaluru MP and a senior BJP leader Ananth Kumar often stayed at Gopinath's house. Kumar had introduced him to Venkaiah Naidu, another senior BJP leader who later became India's vice president after Prime Minister Narendra Modi came to power in 2014.

They all had liked the idea of starting a LCC, but the project was not taking off. Naidu and Gopinath had met Prime Minister Atal Bihari Vajpayee in 2002.

'*Aam aadmi ka airline shuru kar rahe hain*, like a Ganesha please remove all the obstacles in my way,' Gopinath recalled telling Vajpayee.

Vajpayee was quick this time. '*Aap jao, aage badho* … there will be no obstacles in your way,' he promised Gopinath.

Air Deccan was started a few months later in 2003 with Rs 5 crore of borrowed money. 'And none of them took a single penny from me,' Gopinath added. But that was only half the battle won, because while the BJP-led ministry allowed him to take off, when the government changed a year later and the Congress-led UPA government came to power, he faced a fresh set of challenges.

When Air Deccan was about to receive its first Airbus—A320 from Toulouse, Gopinath got a call from the deputy director of the directorate general of civil aviation (DGCA), P.K. Chattopadhyay, who asked him to send the aircraft back. It had already landed in Dubai for refuelling and in a few hours, it was to enter Indian airspace.

Chattopadhyay asked questions that should have preceded the DGCA permission for import of the aircraft. He wanted to know when Air Deccan did not have its own parking space, where would it park the aircraft.

When Gopinath replied that he would park it in Nagaland if he had to, Chattopadhyay had another follow-up question—where would he maintain the imported planes? Gopinath said he had a letter of engineering support from Air India. Chattopadhyay shocked Gopinath by saying that the support has been withdrawn unilaterally.

'Then someone else will do it,' he told him and in anger added, 'the plane is on its way and whoever is doing all this will pay for it.'

The A320 finally landed in Bengaluru and Chattopadhyay, a 'nice guy', was later asked by Capt. Gopinath why he had behaved so differently that day.

'DG Satinder Singh was standing in front of me,' he said indicating he was only doing his job as per directions from above.

Aviation has always been a heavily lobbied sector in India.

K. Roy Paul, the then secretary in the ministry of civil aviation, says there may have been another angle as to why only Air Deccan and then Bhatia got their licences.

The ministry had become entrenched in controversies over the last few years.

For one, when the same BJP-led government tried to sell a 40 per cent stake in Air India, the Tatas and Singapore Airlines were forced to pull out because of an orchestrated opposition and lobbying by many including politicians such as Sharad Pawar and Praful Patel, who were reportedly close to Naresh Goyal.

Around the same time, lobbyist Niira Radia, perceived as close to then aviation minister Ananth Kumar, had tried to start an airline named Crown Air, but ran into headwinds on the grounds of opaque funding.

'I was keen that the bad name the ministry had received because of Tata and Singapore Airlines should go away,' Paul, now retired and living in Kerala, said, 'I wrote in an internal note then that it should be open to anyone who applies for it, and government should not take selective decisions.'

It helped that Bhatia was not a notable name then and perhaps his licence went largely unnoticed by Goyal. 'Bhatia used to come, not that there was no lobbying for or against him, but he was not that important. Naresh Goyal was more important,' Paul said.

Whatever else may have happened, InterGlobe managed to obtain a newly minted licence, which he named Project Golf—possibly because both he and his father Kapil loved the sport. Rahul Bhatia then suggested that Kansagra should come on board without bringing in any equity and abandon his start-up.

'Yes, he did invite me to join his company. But it became difficult. I didn't want to abandon the 24,999 shareholders I had. We felt it was probably easier for him to just do it on his own,' Kansagra says. 'I said, you do your thing and hopefully you will make it to the other end. It's like in a river—he is carrying me on his back and the current is strong. Either we both will sink, or he drops me, and makes it to the bank. At least he lives, and I am gone; or may be both of us will be gone.'

Anyone else in Kansagra's position might have packed his bags and left after hearing this. However, airlines have this charm that keeps the promoters hooked. Kansagra went back to seeking funds again.

Kansagra recalled, 'I had thought that if I try, I may perhaps be able to raise funds. I went to whomever I had links with, to see if they would fund me. Subrata Roy was the most high-profile among those I approached. Others were looking at it only from the point of view of investment alone without involvement in management, but rather casually. Subrata was in the business and wanted to do an LCC, and I went to pitch to him. It didn't meet his standards, whatever they were.'

Then came Ajay Singh who had been the officer on special duty (OSD) attached to the late Pramod Mahajan. Though the BJP was now out of power, Singh was looking to keep himself 'busy'. Kansagra says, 'He was involved with the ministry of telecommunications, when Pramod Mahajan was the minister, in stimulating the mobile phone industry. He knew stimulation and he said he would put up some money. That's how we joined hands, did the rechristening as SpiceJet Ltd, bought aircraft, and the rest is history, I guess.'

Both struck a deal, got funds and ModiLuft finally flew as SpiceJet between Delhi and Mumbai in May 2005, nearly a decade since it was grounded as ModiLuft. However, it seems Kansagra and Singh did not get along well. 'We got together to launch SpiceJet. The day we parted, we went our separate ways. His mindset and my mindset were different even while we worked together. By the end of it, there was not a lot left. Maybe it had to with our eating habits—he doesn't drink, he doesn't eat meat. I drink, I eat everything,' said Kansagra.

Although he was not inclined to elaborate on what led to the parting of ways, some prodding brought out that it may have had something to do with an episode similar to the one SpiceJet has been having with another of its former promoters, Sun TV's Kalanithi Maran. Kansagra had sold the airline to Maran in 2010, and then it was re-sold to Ajay Singh for a token amount of Rs 2 in 2015.

'It saddens me to hear the horror stories coming out on SpiceJet,' Kansagra said, referring to the airline's cash-strapped situation from 2022 that had led to show-cause notices, defaults, safety violations and litigations.

'It is a challenge for Ajay to raise funds when the litigation with Maran is on. I wish he had given them the shares they were promised. This would have been avoided. There is enough water in the sea, you can't drink it all. Live and let live,' he said. 'And that's why I said we have a different way of working.'

However, Bhatia and Kansagra's eating habits appear to be in sync. 'Rahul is a great businessman and very focused. I spent many nights at his lovely home, very hospitable. I wish he gets to the 500 aircraft fleet. He will get them delivered, I am telling you. He gets the best people that money can buy and stays true to the model.'

But didn't he say he was very upset with Bhatia when he decided to get his own airline licence when they were together trying to start SpiceJet?

'It is all relative, isn't it?' he asked and added, 'He did what he had to. But he did offer me a stake and he did not short-change me. I would say he would have been a better partner.' Perhaps that is why when Kansagra is in town and dining at Bhatia's China Club restaurant in Gurugram, he often checks if Bhatia is around and asks him to join in.

And to circle back, while the vastly experienced British Airways may have abandoned SpiceJet early, Kansagra's persistence paid off and he went back to London bagging $10 million (around Rs 80 crore in 2023) in profit from selling the same airline.

Does he regret that he did not take the 5 per cent stake that Bhatia was giving him in IndiGo then? Because, nearly twenty years later, that 5 per cent is worth Rs 6,500 crore as IndiGo is now valued at around Rs 1.3 lakh crore or US$15 billion in 2024.

'I would have been rich,' he interjects, 'I have no regrets. It is what it is.'

2
The Big Deal

Nearly three decades ago, Boeing was doing exactly what it is doing today—trying to ensure it was ahead of Airbus in securing aircraft orders globally.

In India, Boeing had an unusually good run during the 1990s–2000s after a newly launched and inducted Airbus A320 plane crashed at a golf course in Bengaluru in February 1990, killing over ninety people out of the 146 on board. Indian Airlines (now Air India) was the only A320 customer then. For over a decade Airbus lost out to Boeing although the Indian government allowed the A320 to fly again a few months after that crash.

The airlines of the '90s—Jet Airways, Air Sahara, Damania Airways, East West Airlines, etc.—all took off with leased Boeing airplanes.

To preserve its dominance, those days, Boeing indulged in a few gimmicks. They flew down instructor engineers from the US, billeted them at Hyatt Regency and Centaur hotels in New Delhi, and started to train engineers including those retiring from Indian Airlines—the only carrier using Airbus aircraft—on Boeing planes for three months, free of cost. They threw in a free daily lunch for all who enrolled.

These classes went on for around four years from 1993 onwards. And Boeing trained nearly 300–400 engineers.

But as they say, there are no free lunches.

'This was the reason not a single Airbus plane was taken by any private carrier till 2000s whereas the privatization occurred in 1993,' said Dinesh Keskar, Boeing's senior vice president of sales for the Asia-Pacific. To start an airline and get DGCA approval, one of the critical prerequisites was the availability of trained engineers in their rolls.

This overture extended to Keskar inviting Naresh Goyal and Pervez Damania to give graduation-day speeches and meet the trainees. This instilled confidence in the engineers and created a bridge with the operators.

Nevertheless, the training was only one of the reasons why Boeings became the aircraft of choice.

Keskar, despite being a very senior official maintained one-on-one relationships with not merely ministers, US ambassadors to India, and board members, but even with the support staff in the ministry and the airlines. His success as a vendor was no surprise.

'Every time someone bought a plane, I had to call the bureaucrats to clear the purchase, even though the demand wasn't that high then,' he told me. Keskar said he sold around 2,500 planes worth US$300 billion in Asia during his tenure. Of this, around 400 planes worth US$30 billion at sticker prices were in India alone. During his sales pitch he also used to cite Boeing's local India base as another reason why customers should opt for the American manufacturer.

Air India had a large maintenance base in Mumbai for Boeing aircraft. It had added Boeing 747s to its fleet when Ratan Tata was on its board. Boeing had stationed its own staff in Mumbai and Delhi to help airlines get grounded aircraft quickly back in the air. In the '90s, when an Air France 747 had an accident during take-off at Delhi and suffered 70 per cent damage, Boeing set up a hangar at the Delhi airport and made it airworthy in six months.

But Boeing's dominance of Indian skies ended in a decade. 'IndiGo changed all that,' Keskar said, referring to the airline that ordered 100 Airbus aircraft in one shot. 'I would have never imagined that IndiGo will get as big as it has now.'

It did not happen overnight. In early 2000, with no genuine airline customers in hand, Airbus's vice president for India, Nigel Harwood, recalls he saw anyone who showed the slightest inclination to buy a plane. Some were rather colourful characters. An airline requires deep pockets not merely to start, but to fund the early losses. Aircraft order advances was a huge outgo.

If an aircraft had a sticker price of say US$50 million, for instance, the pre-delivery payments (PDP) themselves were quite significant. Airbus would not build a plane with small change as advance. The initial payment was a minimum US$1 million per aircraft. On big ticket orders, this could be significantly lower. However, the next tranche would fall due as soon as the aircraft went into production.

Furthermore, a new player would be put under the lens; balance sheets would be audited by one of the Big Five international audit firms, so that Airbus could satisfy themselves that the party meant business and had the wherewithal.

'When you get to that point where you realize you have to sign this piece of paper and you have to send a cheque to Airbus for this amount, a lot of people shy away,' says Harwood. 'It was difficult to evaluate who was real and who was not, and quite often Airbus found they (the potential clients) were not real.'

So, when the request came to meet with InterGlobe Enterprises' Rahul Bhatia, an unknown player during those days, Harwood decided to meet him too. 'When he came in, it was like a big gorilla walking in. I was like, holy moly! He was in a white kurta-pyjama, was extremely courteous, and I could not make out if I was talking to the owner of the company or an employee. I was thinking, has this guy been sent in? And then he gave me his business card that said managing director. I realized he was the right guy,' recalls Harwood who now is the executive vice president of the aircraft leasing firm Air Castle based in Singapore.

Rahul Bhatia does not believe in a formal dress code and is more comfortable in knee-length shorts even for professional meetings. As one person recalled, in a meeting where Bhatia had arrived before them at Hyatt Regency, Delhi, the delegates realized that he was wearing shorts only when he got up to leave after the meeting.

Harwood reported to the Airbus headquarters at Toulouse that there was, indeed, a customer named InterGlobe looking to order their aircraft. The number of planes needed was not specified at that time, but the background of the firm seemed 'okay'.

Bhatia suggested that they follow up this meeting with another one in Washington where another of his friends (and later his co-founder) Rakesh Gangwal was based. Harwood was reluctant because the prospect was not taken seriously by even the Airbus COO, New York-born John Leahy, who had a reputation as one of the world's best aircraft salesman. He was reported to be a good friend of Rakesh Gangwal.

'I know Rakesh,' Harwood recalls Leahy saying, 'I didn't know he had an angle in India on this. I am prepared to meet him, but to be honest with you Rakesh is long gone from India. He is happily settled in the US, so chances are this is not really going anywhere.'

That together with the fact that InterGlobe wasn't really at Tata Group level company gave Toulouse the feeling this was another fishing expedition. 'There was no credibility. Someone ordering 100 planes in India was just nonsense. At the end of the day, it was a company that had never experienced anything like this before. It was so low-key an organization that nobody had ever considered it [would start an airline],' says Harwood.

The meeting with Gangwal was exhausting. Gangwal handed over to Harwood a wish list 'longer than his arm' to take to Toulouse. Gangwal and Bhatia said they were thinking of twenty to thirty aircraft, and later spoke of buying forty to fifty. While planning the airline, they could see growth coming in and thus revised the order a few times.

Finally, Airbus headquarters started to engage. Yet the final number—an order for 100 aircraft, a US$6 billion deal at list prices then—was kept a secret by Gangwal and Bhatia even from the manufacturer. They wanted to gauge how things changed according to the size of their order.

'Rakesh has a way of negotiating that I have never seen before. He will ask for a point, when you eventually concede that point, he will move the goalpost and say if you have conceded that much, you can go a little further. So, you are always struggling to satisfy him in terms of the negotiation,' says Harwood. 'The point they had in their favour was that they knew they could play us against Boeing. So, the moment you said no, they said okay, we are going to talk to Boeing. They were always doing that.'

Was Boeing really in the game? That was a big mystery. Also, one always wonders when Boeing had such a grip over India, how did it let the IndiGo order slip through the cracks?

I have heard a story of how Keskar, who rose through the ranks in Boeing, had met Gangwal once in Atlanta. Gangwal did not even extend basic courtesies when he entered the room and ticked him off.

'Rakesh was a nobody at that time,' Keskar shot back when I put this to him. 'He wanted terms and conditions that were not the norm then. They wanted to pay overtime for the airplane with very little down payment. They wanted Boeing to carry the risk. And 100-plane deals were not the norm then; it was 30–40 planes typically. I never met him again.'

The meeting with Bhatia too went nowhere. 'I only had one meeting with him at his restaurant, China Club. He took me there. We talked and I offered them ten airplanes, that's it.'

Airbus was clearly hungrier than Boeing because it seemed to have gone out of its way to support Gangwal in what he wanted. When you buy an Airbus plane, for example, it comes without the engine, avionics and seats, among other things. Only the airframe or the outer skeleton is made by Airbus and the rest is outsourced. So, Airbus will quote, say, US$50 million as the sticker price of an aircraft, where US$42 million is for the airframe, US$5 million for the engines, and avionics, seats and everything else costs US$3 million.

Now, a buyer could say he does not want to spend that US$3 million and will spend only US$2 million, in which case the price will come down to US$49 million per aircraft. Or the buyer could say the configuration is not good enough and he wants in-flight entertainment. So, the price could go up by US$3 million to US$53 million. Airbus knows that if the price is roughly around US$50 million, most people will overspend on add-ons. Gangwal, however, opted for the first scenario and set about bringing even that number down.

Airbus typically gives its customers a list of vendors who fit the aircraft, along with their quoted prices. Gangwal refused to go through Airbus and asked for the contact details of all the manufacturers. 'If you put a glass on that aircraft, Rakesh would say, "Let me see if I can get that for nine cents instead of ten cents." And that's what he would do. And that's what they did. Rakesh went to each supplier on his own and negotiated with them directly,' recalls Harwood.

Gangwal had anticipated, correctly, that vendors would bend over backwards to do anything to secure a deal for 100 aircraft. Such high volumes meant sustained business for over ten years for every one of them, from seat makers, light suppliers, galley fitters and carpet makers, to engine suppliers, avionics companies and so on. Also, unlike Boeing, which has only one choice of engine, Airbus provided Gangwal with the opportunity to drive two engine-makers to the wall—General Electric (GE) and International Aero Engines (IAE).

Once the deal was largely thrashed out, the two sides met again to sign the term sheet—a near-surety that the order was almost done. Time to take it easy, perhaps? Not so for Gangwal. For this documentation, Airbus had booked a conference room in Washington. At lunch, the Airbus executives—some of whom had flown in from France—wanted to take a break and step out. Gangwal walked out thinking he was being taken to a room next door to grab some sandwiches. Instead, he saw a fleet of cars ready to take him to a fancy restaurant. Nothing doing, said Gangwal and started walking out of the hotel stating, 'You guys follow me.'

'We went to Chipotle and Aditya Ghosh was explaining to the French how that place works … here is a burrito … you have various ingredients, and you have to pick and choose. It was less than eight dollars those days,' Gangwal recounted, recalling the 'lunch'. Chipotle is a quick-service Mexican joint popular across US cities, much like McDonald's, and is also closer to the Indian palate, especially if you are vegetarian like Gangwal. There is obviously no fine dining in there and often the second question the staff invariably asks you—after you have selected what you want—is always, 'For here?' (are you eating it here?) or is it 'To go?'

'One of the French guys took it (the burrito) and sat down,' recalls Gangwal, 'I said no. We are not wasting time here. We will eat while we are working. Lunch time is not dinner when you can relax and enjoy.' He ensured all the burritos were 'to go', much to the disappointment of the Airbus team. It must have been an awkward moment. The news of this made its way to Airbus headquarters in France as well. Gangwal couldn't care less.

When Gangwal was somewhat satisfied with the term sheet, he flew to Paris and then boarded a private jet with Bhatia and Harwood from Paris to Toulouse, for a meeting with Airbus' top brass—Noël Forgeard and John Leahy. Even on this short flight, just in case he could still extract something more from Airbus, Gangwal did not lose the opportunity to fill Harwood's ears with how he was still being wooed by Boeing. It was never over with him till the contract was signed.

Thanks to IndiGo, which placed this order for 100 planes, Airbus finally could smile at that year's Paris Air Show. Of the total 155 aircraft orders from India in 2005, 135 were for Airbus and only 20 for Boeing. While Air Deccan had taken some Airbus planes to start national routes, the jinx on Airbus had finally been broken by IndiGo's big plane deal.

The Deal of the Century

Yet, of all the deals that Harwood made with various airlines during those years, including Air Deccan, Vijay Mallya's Kingfisher Airlines, Jeh Wadia's GoAir, and Indian Airlines, it is the IndiGo deal that he and Airbus are ever cagey about.

In industry circles, especially the aircraft lessor community, word was that Airbus sold the planes very cheap as they hadn't seen any orders coming in for many years from India and because of depressed global air travel demand after the 9/11 terrorist attacks.

According to two people who are aware of the deal, the planes cost newbie IndiGo around US$26 million each when the planes were being sold to even loyal customers at around US$35 million.

When probed, Harwood becomes defensive about it. 'If it was a bad deal, they (Airbus) wouldn't have done it. There are controls in place, like there are in any company. An individual can only go so far. I had the ability to negotiate up to a point, then it had to go to John Leahy, then to Noël Forgeard. If Noël signed it, then it was within his approval process and that's why it happened. It was an aggressive deal, but why shouldn't it be for 100 aircraft?'

The deal, however, was not only about price alone. It was also about how many pilots and engineers Airbus would support IndiGo with, favourably worded maintenance contracts, delivery pipeline flexibility and what spares they would receive, among other things. Consequently, IndiGo could put an aircraft in the air much cheaper than anybody else in India.

The former Airbus executive vice president Kiran Rao, who worked the Indian market too during those years and later almost became Airbus's global COO, agreed the deal had a 'different price'.

'By taking them seriously, I mean we gave them good, early and plentiful slots in the production line that enabled them to get a steady supply of airplanes. We gave them a good contract, rather they negotiated it with us,' Rao says. 'And not only us, but they negotiated very well with all the suppliers too. They had every engine contract, for example, worked out for parts and supports and everything was planned for. So, when you say IndiGo's success can be attributed to Airbus, it is not. It's just that they knew what to ask for, and how to ask for it,' he says, adding, 'If you go to the market to buy twenty mangoes or 100 mangoes, of course you get a different price.'

When Airbus Fell Out with Air Deccan

Just before IndiGo's entry, Kiran Rao had convinced Air Deccan—which, in 2003, had started operations with ATR turboprops for regional routes—to take a few leased Airbus planes and start national flights.

'The biggest challenge for Airbus was to continue to believe in the India story,' Rao agrees, recalling those years. 'This is where I give my boss the credit, because John Leahy always knew something would happen in India. He just didn't know when. He kept me focused on the job, whereas a lot of bosses would have pulled out and said, forget it, nothing is happening, go do something else. Dinesh (Keskar, Boeing India chief) had got the Jet Airways' contract, so Boeing was happy. From Airbus' point of view, ten years without an order was a long time.'

Air Deccan was a breakthrough. 'With Capt. Gopinath, you knew the guy had a spark, and you knew he was going to do what he was going to do,' Rao says. 'Up to that point, there were a lot of people who would say they would start airlines, but didn't have the plan or the character to do so.'

So, Airbus tried to ensure that Gopinath could fly bigger planes. For example, it was difficult to buy an aircraft in India then, as Indian banks would not finance them. Airbus gave an undertaking, a kind of a security guarantee, to the banks that if something were to happen to Air Deccan, it would repay the money to the banks.

But this first-love soured quickly when Gangwal's IndiGo debuted. 'They negotiated a fantastic deal on the aircraft,' Gopinath says, 'probably the best deal in the world. That guy had twenty years in aviation, and you can't become the president of a full-service airline being brown [in the US]. You really have to be outstanding. Even though we had paid Airbus the money early, it took us one year to get the aircraft. In their case, Airbus gave them the aircraft on the very first day they started.'

The otherwise genial Gopinath went ballistic when Airbus started to delay his planes and IndiGo kept expanding. 'I still remember they had all come to my office in Bengaluru for some documentation. One of them said he wanted a masala dosa and someone else wanted something else. Lunch had been ordered when I asked them to get out of my office. I was so upset that they did not give me the aircraft and superseded me with IndiGo. They didn't know what to do and left without having lunch.'

Yet, when the Airbus aircraft started to arrive, Air Deccan went on to grab a sizeable chunk of the Indian skies, even though it too had its own teething problems. The spunky start-up finally succumbed to financial woes and was bought out by Vijay Mallya, who grabbed it merely so that Kingfisher Airlines could fly international routes. India allowed only airlines with a minimum five years of domestic operations to fly abroad. Kingfisher did not have enough years. By merging Kingfisher into Deccan, and retaining the Kingfisher Airlines brand, Mallya met this requirement and started flights to London earlier than otherwise possible.

However, a few years later, Kingfisher Airlines went bankrupt. Mallya, in the eyes of the Indian government, is a wilful defaulter and absconder. He fled to London in 2016 while the creditor banks were approaching the courts to impose a travel ban on him. Ironically, he flew on his arch-rival Naresh Goyal's Jet Airways flight, lugging all of seven heavy bags.

Jet Airways collapsed later, and Goyal is now being investigated for money laundering. He too tried to follow Mallya's footsteps by fleeing on an Emirates flight to Dubai in 2019, but this time his flight was called back from the runway by the government.

Both he and his wife Anita—during the last two decades India's first aviation family, as it were—were embarrassingly off-loaded. Naresh Goyal went into judicial custody and has sought bail on medical grounds, while his wife had already been granted bail at the time of writing this. The two, however, cannot leave India.

Negotiating Styles

Why did Kingfisher not get it right?

'I have negotiated with Gopinath, Wadia, Mallya, Goyal and Bhatia, and I can honestly tell you the most professional among all of them was InterGlobe,' says Harwood, 'because they just knew what they wanted and the reason for this was Rakesh. He would say, "I have done this a hundred times, young man, I will tell you how I will structure this deal."'

Mallya, in stark contrast to Gangwal's forensic style, negotiated his aircraft deals on his yacht named *Indian Empress* while it was anchored in Monaco. 'You sit on his boat, have a glass of champagne, talk about the number of aircraft, and three glasses later, it becomes thirty [aircraft]. Vijay is larger than life and loves to negotiate in a personal setting,' Harwood says. 'The difference between him and Bhatia is that Bhatia is all about doing it professionally—let's have a meeting, let's sit around the table, let's have an agenda, let's minute everything, let's follow it up, etc. But

Vijay is about sitting on a boat in Monaco, having a few drinks, building a personal relationship, and then talking business.'

Mallya would also be surrounded by many of his loyalists and advisors from his liquor business, United Breweries group, when the deal was being framed. 'Ravi Nedungadi (a long-time aide of Mallya and CFO of his liquor business who passed away in 2022) would be there, as would be several of his friends who would float in and out of the discussions aboard this 311-foot-long yacht, then go off to sunbathe while he carried on with the discussions,' recalls Harwood. 'Someone would walk in and say let's have dinner now, and despite being at an important point in the negotiations, he would stop for dinner. I have to say, if you ever want to negotiate in style and pure class, that's the way to do it. Mallya's belief was that if he could get you on board, put his arm around you, and manage you, you would do a good thing for him.'

And that's how he negotiated his deals.

'We have sat at his homes in Goa, San Francisco and Mumbai. You worked with what his schedules were and what he required. His and InterGlobe's were two completely different styles. I am not saying one is right or wrong,' says Harwood, 'Just that they are completely different. If asked to bet on one of them, though, you would have to bet on the professional one. What's happened with Kingfisher is extremely sad, though. When it started, it had the potential of becoming the Emirates of India. I have to say, that's what it was for the first six months, and then the cracks started to appear. It's extremely sad and nobody would wish that upon Vijay, but he is a smart cookie despite the trouble he is in.'

IndiGo gained significantly from Kingfisher's exit, expanding its footprint. One of the key reasons for Kingfisher's death was also a badly worded contract with its engine makers. When Pratt and Whitney engines started developing snags in 2010, Kingfisher planes started getting grounded for repairs while IndiGo's contracts ensured they were getting paid for those snags by the engine maker.

Such contracts helped IndiGo a lot even though they may have bruised some of its vendors. For example, former CEO of GE India and country head, GE Commercial Aviation Services (GECAS), T.P. Chopra, financed aircraft deals worth more than US$1 billion in 2005 and 2006 but with IndiGo, he revealed, GECAS started on a very bad note. Why? Gangwal.

'Rakesh knew everyone in GE, including then vice-chairman, David Calhoun, and my boss Henry Hubschman, for twenty years. I remember he had said a long time ago that he would start an airline in India, buy lots of planes and work with GE. GE aircraft engines and GECAS, which finances aircrafts, are completely different arms of the big world of GE. So, the engine guys started talking to the airline about engine sales, and we (GECAS) talked about aircraft financing,' said Chopra. These were the engines for the 100-plane order.

The negotiation was going so well that GE was sure it would close the deal soon. But a few months later, IndiGo bolted and decided to go with the rival International Aero Engines (IAE) engines.

'That obviously left a fairly bad taste in the engine manufacturer's side,' adds Chopra, 'Especially since they had come through the vice-chairman. That was in bad taste—placing a big order, and then going to somebody else. I think we backed off from the aircraft financing discussions for a long time, about nine months, not because of acrimony, but because we were upset that we had lost the deal.'

However, Chopra remained in touch with the other promoter Rahul Bhatia.

'About eight weeks before the delivery of the first plane, I asked him about the financing of their first few planes. Bhatia said it would be difficult, being last minute and because they were already way down the road with the Royal Bank of Scotland. I told him to give us a chance, we will make it happen. We took off. Some guys in Ireland, Riyaz Peer Mohamed (then CFO), Aditya Ghosh (then InterGlobe Enterprises' legal counsel who later became IndiGo president), and us, we cut the deal down in four to six weeks. The process was crunched to weeks instead of months; otherwise, they would have closed it with the Royal Bank of Scotland anyway. We financed the first six planes for IndiGo. The rest is history.'

If you look at the history of Indian aviation, however, it is full of financially distressed airlines, crying for funding. Most Indian airlines have had almost no cash in the bank (often because the promoters have siphoned off money and bought farmhouses and London flats with it) and are always making losses while IndiGo, which has lower costs than its rivals, has over US$2 billion in free cash—and growing.

In 2022, as the effects of Covid-19 were waning, IndiGo, who had lost nearly US$1.5 billion during this black swan event, did not ask for any government credit line unlike SpiceJet and even the Nusli Wadia-owned Go First.

Gangwal's foresight and acumen has given IndiGo an additional source of revenue. IndiGo buys a plane at a discounted price of, say, Rs 100 crore apiece in bulk. This plane starts getting built in the factory a few months before the date of delivery. Closer to the delivery date the airline, when it has to make the full payment, it sells the plane to an aircraft leasing company for, say, Rs 172 crore. It leases back the same plane for six years or more. This gives the airline around Rs 72 crore in the bank every time an aircraft is delivered. IndiGo, according to a person who has worked on their deals, makes around US$10–12 million per plane or roughly Rs 80 crore in this fashion—the reason for them continuing to take delivery of new planes during the pandemic when most of their fleet was grounded.

In an industry where the oil price and US dollar exchange rates can break your back fairly quickly, this money is a godsend, not just during pandemics but in normal times too. It becomes the airline's cushion, enabling it to meet financial emergencies and expand aggressively, and increasing its capacity to bear losses, especially on newer routes. As IndiGo grows, however, it will gradually start looking at owning its planes like Air India because it does not need the up front cash anymore with enough on the books and the business itself throwing up profits every year.

IndiGo is, therefore, a story of smart financing and placing big bets so much so that it has been dubbed an aircraft trading company.

It now has a fleet of over 350 and nearly 1,000 aircraft on order. Harwood clearly did the right thing by agreeing to meet Bhatia two decades ago.

3

Rakesh Gangwal

It was a sunny Washington summer day in 2004, when people love to queue up to pick freshly prepared meals from docked food trucks alongside the capital's manicured parks. However, Airbus India head Nigel Harwood, IndiGo's Rakesh Gangwal and Rahul Bhatia were inside an upmarket Italian restaurant negotiating an aircraft order.

When the meal, ended, Harwood excused himself to go to the washroom. Bhatia called for the bill and reached for his wallet, but Gangwal stayed his hand, 'Not us, he will pay.'

Harwood, who had flown down especially for this meeting, paid for the meal. With that Italian meal, which may have cost around US$300, Gangwal laid the foundation of a cost-focused budget start-up called IndiGo—an airline, which would go on to become a US$15 billion (around Rs 1.3 lakh crore in current rates), enterprise nearly two decades later.

Born in 1953 in Kolkata into a Marwari family, Gangwal, now in his seventies, has his roots in Jaipur. The Marwaris typically hails from the Marwar–Shekhawati–Jaipur region of Rajasthan. They are a small closely knit community but control many big businesses in India much like the Jewish community does in the US (Facebook, Google, Goldman Sachs, Dell, etc.). Kumar Mangalam Birla of Aditya Birla Group, Rahul Bajaj of Bajaj Auto, Subhash Chandra of

Zee Group, Harsh Goenka of CEAT Tyres are among such notable Marwari-businessmen.

'Most Indians know him (Marwaris) as the furtive shopkeeper around the corner,' former head of Procter & Gamble in India, Gurcharan Das, wrote in a foreword for a book titled *The Marwaris*. 'Like the Jew in old Europe, he is the moneylender of last resort, who charges extortionate interest and dispossesses widows of their land and jewellery when the loan is not repaid. Or he is perceived as the ruthless tycoon who did not stop at anything, including the pre-empting of licences during the hypocritical forty years of the Licence Raj ... The question is, what made them so spectacularly successful?'

Das concludes that it is partly to do with how the community sticks together. For instance, when a Marwari travels on business, the wife and children are taken care of by the joint family. The travelling businessman finds good Marwari food at the basa, charity outlets run by the Marwari community.

When a Marwari needs money, he takes a loan from another Marwari trader on the understanding that it is payable whenever asked for; he also reciprocates when the other person needs help. Interest is adjusted at the end of the year. Sons and nephews become trainees to other Marwari traders, where they learn business skills—sort of an MBA.

The Marwaris are also risk-takers and migrate to wherever business takes them. During the British Raj when Calcutta (now Kolkata) presented profitable trade opportunities, they moved there as brokers and agents to the British. Profits in speculating on cotton, jute and hessian made them rich and helped them found industries later.

Marwaris are also socially conservative and took to English education much later than many other communities.

Gangwal too has several of these characteristics. His family probably moved to Kolkata during the British times, where he studied at the all-boys Indian Certificate of Secondary Education (ICSE) board affiliated Don Bosco School and then earned a B.Tech. in mechanical engineering from Indian Institute of Technology, Kanpur.

He worked for Phillips India for two years and at twenty-four, he left for the US for an MBA at Wharton Business School.

He married Shobha, with whom he had a daughter named Parul. She is, as Gangwal puts it, 'the glue' of the family. Parul studied at Washington International School and graduated in economics from the University of Virginia, worked with Morgan Stanley and Salesforce. She is a trained classical dancer, and an investor in the Minnesota-based firm Wheelhouse Venture Capital that owns and manages commercial real estate properties and also invests in startups including those in India.

A vegetarian fond of green chillies and Cuban cigars, Rakesh Gangwal has a Spartan lifestyle. He dresses simply—often in blue jeans and a white shirt, and sometimes carries a small bag. You could mistake him for a pharmaceutical salesperson. He hates to be photographed, dislikes attention; there are barely half a dozen photographs of him online.

His views on the media are not very charitable—a newspaper is not even worth the fish it is used to wrap the next day—as I understand from people who have been associated with him. I, however, was fortunate enough to have hit it off well with him, perhaps because I genuinely enjoyed learning about the industry. Whenever we spoke, for me, it was a master class in aviation.

Gangwal claims to be an agnostic. He named his first firm Caelum Investments, perhaps a reflection of how he sees himself.

Caelum is a faint constellation in the southern sky and means burin—an engraving, chisel-like tool—in Latin.

After obtaining his MBA, he joined Ford Motors and followed it with a stint at the consulting firm Booz Allen Hamilton for four years where the pharmaceutical giant Eli Lilly was his client. He grew close to them, sensed a business opportunity, and returned to India in 1984.

Gangwal decided to set up a capsule manufacturing plant with technology from Eli Lilly and sell them to major pharmaceutical firms such as Glaxo, Merck and others. Eli Lilly undertook to buy 60–70 per cent of his production at market rates; the rest could be sold in India. They would supply the machinery as well. Back then, India ran a trade deficit. This would have brought in a lot of dollars, Gangwal thought that the government would love it.

However, those were the days of the Licence Raj. The endeavour turned out to be a nightmare. Indira Gandhi was the Prime Minister till late 1984 and after her unfortunate assassination, her son Rajiv Gandhi became Prime Minister in December 1984.

Gangwal spent days together in government offices seeking permissions for his factory. Clerks would ask for duplicate copies of forms; and kept asking for more, till they sat down to find faults in them. 'You kept filling government forms forever,' he recalls. In the meanwhile, the existent manufacturers, who would have been hit badly by Gangwal's new project, did everything they could to scuttle it, including filing various complaints and making sure nothing moved.

After more than eight months of attempting to start a new factory in his home country, Gangwal gave up and went back to the US. Booz Allen took him back and handed him the United Airlines account, his first brush with airplanes. Airplanes have dominated his life ever since. Much like Eli Lilly, United Airlines too was impressed with Gangwal's guidance. They later hired him and made him a manager for strategic planning in the airline.

During his eleven years with United, he steadily rose through the ranks to become senior vice president of planning. He got along very well with Stephen M. Wolf, United's chairman and CEO (1987–1994), who became Gangwal's mentor. When Wolf left United in 1995 to join Air France as advisor, Gangwal too followed him to Paris, as vice president, planning and development.

In 1996, Wolf returned to the US as chairman and CEO of US Airways. Gangwal, now forty-five, followed him. He took over as CEO of US Airways, while Wolf decided to continue only as chairman. Gangwal's task was to bring in efficiencies and cut costs, while Wolf pursued 'global visions', spending several days in a month hammering new aircraft deals.

Gangawal's rise to heading a US airline was not easy though. It is best captured in what he said to *Washingtonian* in 2007 in an article that talked about how many Indian–Americans came to the US with big hopes and only a few dollars in their pockets but thanks to hard work—and often lucrative government contracting—became millionaires and made their presence felt in both politics and business.

'As a first-generation immigrant there is a deeper hunger. When I first came here, we did not have the same social fabric or support. You had to quickly become self-reliant. The second generation doesn't have the same hunger. There is no fear. This is their country,' Gangwal said, adding that children born in America to Indian parents are more 'comfortable in their skin'.

In 1996, at the time Gangwal joined it, US Airways was in poor health and was being pummelled in surveys. It had 400 aircraft and 2,100 daily flights. Things were so bad that Gangwal told the employees, 'Either we do it, or we perish', referring to the cost-cutting exercise started by himself and Wolf.

Gradually, under Gangwal, the airline's seat occupancy went up from 64.7 per cent in 1995 to 72.7 per cent in 1998 and operating profit from US$322 million to US$1.01 billion. Debt fell from US$2.8 billion to US$2 billion. US Airways bought 400 new planes from Airbus to replace its ageing fleet.

Gangwal also launched a LCC, MetroJet, under the full-service US Airways umbrella. It was meant to challenge the popularity of the LCCs led by Southwest Airlines, which were eating into the traffic of legacy airlines such as US Airways.

MetroJet was a no-frills, low-cost operation that concentrated primarily on the American east coast's leisure destinations such as Florida and New England and the focus was to increase aircraft utilization, charge for meals and assign seats to passengers at the gates.

Within ten months of operation, the airline was serving twenty-one cities and Gangwal was so enthused that he even told the employees that MetroJet was 'spectacularly successful'. But unfortunately, what MetroJet did was to cannibalize its parent US Airways' traffic and did not improve the loss-making airline's fortunes. The older aircraft it used from the US Airways fleet were not as fuel efficient and labour costs were high. It could not challenge the efficient and more-loved Southwest Airlines. MetroJet shut down after the 9/11 attacks.

After showing some early signs of recovery, the US Airways turnaround didn't go anywhere. In 2002, Gangwal resigned two months after 9/11 saying he planned to pursue interests in private equity. Wolf followed suit a few months later, retiring to pursue private equity as well.

Both exits also became very controversial. Months before he left, Gangwal had told analysts that the extensive cost-cutting, large infusion of regional jets into the fleet and into the carrier's commuter affiliates was the only way to profits.

The labour unions had accepted as many as three pay cuts at US Airways, but it turned out on their exit that Gangwal and Wolf enjoyed high severance payouts while they were chopping staff salaries. In 2001, Wolf left with US$15 million when he stepped down as chairman. Gangwal too received US$15 million. Reports said that in the previous year, Gangwal had drawn US$675,000 as salary and US$7.5 million in other compensations, making him one of the industry's highest-paid executives. This invited a lot of bad press in the US.

Interestingly, MetroJet was not the only budget carrier that Gangwal had raised and failed. Gangwal had launched another LCC named Shuttle when he was at United Airlines in 1994. Shuttle had been based out of San Francisco. This was the era of the dotcom boom. Shuttle was profitable but was mired in labour and operational problems exacerbated by a high-frequency schedule. Flights were often delayed and cancelled. After 9/11, when travel demand fell, the airline was canned by United Airlines and its fleet folded into the main airline.

When asked, Gangwal did admit to these failures and the bad press. 'MetroJet, yes it was not a success. It was launched to defend our turf in the south coast not just from Southwest Airlines. We got caught up with new union rules, pilots did not sign up, flight attendants refused, engineers refused, they changed their mind. So, it died. That's a lesson in life—till everybody has signed up, never start anything. U2 [Shuttle] was way, way back. And that also did not work out.' He said, however, it was a lesson learnt.

'Failure does not scare me. How do you go from the average state to become exceptional? And you can do that by learning from failures. I am not going to cry over it. I will dwell on it. I have failed and see how I can avoid the scenario the next time. I have learned success is easy if you can fix the failures,' he says.

Gangwal also said that after US Airways he had made up his mind to not touch the airline business. 'In the US, compensation has to be reported. So, they did. First, when MetroJet failed, we put in a merger agreement where United [Airlines] would buy US Airways. I had made up my mind I was going to leave. I had told myself I want to get out of the industry. It's a very difficult business to run, and profitably. Too many things go wrong. The justice department in July [2001] shut down the merger due to antirust reasons. I told the board I have made up my mind to leave. The board said, look why don't you wait till the end of the year from what was then August ... and we shall get a new CEO. I said it's not about money, I just want to do something else. Somehow, I got talked into staying till the end of the year. Then 9/11 happened and it was a debacle. We parked 112 planes; 12,000 employees; and I walked out of the door without knowing what I would do in life. I mean enough was enough.'

He also defended taking the compensation when other employees took pay cuts. 'In terms of money contractually, once the deal had failed—US and United merger was shot down—we had a contractual right, both Wolf and me, that within a certain period after the deal failing, we both were each entitled to US$25 million—a lot of money. Of course, I was going to take it,' he says.

'But once 9/11 happened, it was a mess, and we were asking employees to take a pay cut. On top of that, the government was giving bailout to the industry till it stabilized. Then that became a very complicated issue. How do you take US$25 million when all this is going on? Nobody really cared afterwards. But I gave it up. A lot of US press wrote about it—US$15 million was the pension plan, US$25 million was on if you do the deal with United and US. The press had picked up this US$25 million and then it was decided there's no taking it,' he says.

Still, Wolf and Gangwal's $15 million payment was made by US Airways, which said it was 'part of the agreements that were negotiated to bring these executives to the company'. This riled the employees with the spokesman for pilots, Roy Freundlich, terming it as unfair. 'We modified our contracts to help the airline survive,' he told *The Washington Post*, referring to the $646 million concessions in pay, benefit and work-rule that the pilots agreed to a year before. 'What the company is saying to us now is that they're going to honour management contracts with three individuals who received US$35 million while thousands of pilots sacrificed much, if not all, of their pay. It's completely unfair, inexcusable and incomprehensible.'

Once the 9/11 slow-down and the controversies subsided, Gangwal joined Worldspan, a reservation system for travel agents implemented in early 1990 by Delta Air Lines, Northwest Airlines and Trans World Airlines (TWA). In mid-2003, when Gangwal was its CEO, Worldspan was sold to Citigroup Venture Capital and Ontario Teachers' Pension Fund.

The US exposure played a vital role in Gangwal's outlook to corporate life and his next adventure. For example, Gangwal was fed up with the US's presentation-driven meetings. When he started IndiGo, he conducted the meetings differently. Gangwal asked the attendees not to waste time on presentations and demanded summaries in three or four bullet points. Many of the top-level meetings happened mid-way in Paris. Gangwal would fly down from the US and the IndiGo leadership from Gurugram. These all-day meetings started early, exhausting everyone.

Gangwal focused on the agenda and ensured no deviation. His questions were always sharp—'Tell me the economics, tell me the logic.' And once he shared his take on the matter, he left it with a caveat: 'Don't go with what I say. Don't say later I told you that's why you did it. Do your own diligence.'

He can often embarrass the person in the room. One of his favourite statements even during the IndiGo days was, 'I don't agree with you. You don't know what you are talking about.' This was one of the reasons why nobody ventured to voice their opinions, because, as one of the executives puts it, 'His expectations were very high. If I spoke up, he might find fault in that also. So, it's better to keep quiet.'

Rahul Bhatia was present at many of these meetings, but rarely spoke. However, he is known to smile and sometimes wink, while Gangwal was 'butchering' people in his own way. 'In those days there was something going on between the two of them. Like a bad cop and a good cop,' the executive spoke of the years before 2019, when their personal relationship was not splintered.

Whenever Gangwal came to Gurugram for reviews, he drew up a list of broad points he wanted to discuss—crew productivity, network challenges, ground time drags, OTP problems, manpower issues—and would send the list in advance to those whom he wanted to meet. If you ask Gangwal about all this, he laughs, 'Why the fear? I never discipline anybody, but I ask a lot of questions.'

He held clear views on the various departments. 'The marketing team will come with a hundred ideas. You will say no to ninety-eight of them, but you will end up accepting two of them, because they came with a hundred ideas. It is like creating an elephant in the room. If you have people in marketing and strategy, chase them away. Don't depend so much on marketing people.' Indeed, IndiGo kept only a skeleton staff for this department for most of the time Gangwal was there.

Gangwal focused much on aircraft financing and knew how to drive the AF Team hard. For example, if he knew a task needed five days to complete, he would give a three-day deadline. So, the staff—separated by different time zones as IndiGo was in Gurugram and Gangwal was in Washington then—worked day and night to meet his demands.

In a way, he was a master panic creator. In his time, he created many crises, leaving the staff to struggle to meet his expectations. 'On top of it, you can't make mistakes, you have to do what you have to do within those hours,' says an executive who has worked with him closely.

He instilled extremely tight cost controls at the airline, reflected in the cumbersome budgeting process. The airline CFO and team would make the first budget draft and then filter it down to each department for their comments. Every head of department had to justify with elaboration if costs were going up for the department. If a valid justification was not given, the budget got chopped off. The final budget used to be approved by Gangwal and every expense had to be budgeted for.

In 2005, at the time of its launch, IndiGo gave out offer letters to pilots. Pilots do not come cheap. They were also being given a joining bonus to move to a new start-up like IndiGo. They were to join in March but the airline was to launch only in August. Because there were no planes yet, CEO Bruce Ashby put his foot down stating he had no money to pay them. He told the operations head, Capt. Shakti Lumba, who had hired these pilots, to ask them to go work somewhere else and come back after the aircraft was delivered.

During the initial months, Gangwal had given Ashby permission to spend only US$1 million. It was difficult to tell pilots to go join another airline and come back after a few months. It was embarrassing and Lumba wrote to Rahul Bhatia that he should shut down the airline if they did not have enough money. Rahul replied, '*Rakesh ko bata*.' So Lumba wrote to Gangwal saying he was told the airline had money and that's why he had quit Air India and joined them, according to Lumba.

'But your CEO now says there is no money to pay pilots; so, I suggest we don't start the airline because this is not a taxi service.' Soon enough, Ashby called Lumba and informed him that Gangwal had released another US$1 million. The pilots could join and the company would be happy to pay them.

In those days, cost-control measures bordered on the bizarre. The IndiGo office was initially very small; there were even fights for seating space. Gangwal said they couldn't have more seating space; this was all they had, so everybody had to make do. It became almost suffocating as more people joined. But nothing was done. Eventually, additional seats were made available.

'Rakesh was a very tough taskmaster,' says an executive. He is tough inasmuch as he expects people to accept the consequences of their ideas and actions. For example, if someone threw up an idea at an engineering department meeting, Gangwal informed the person about the various possible repercussions. It was then up to that person to take a call. If the decision proved wrong, Gangwal was unsparing. The questions that Gangwal asked, the points he made—played a critical role in making people look ahead. The culture of foresight that Gangwal had brought helped IndiGo avoid many pitfalls later.

Perhaps this is one of the reasons for IndiGo taking forever to make changes in its product. IndiGo aircraft, for example, were not equipped with ovens; they never served hot meals or beverages. They did not provide any reading material on board initially. When SpiceJet started serving hot meals and tea and coffee, IndiGo realized they had stolen a march over IndiGo, as corporate travellers want morning coffee or tea.

IndiGo held endless meetings, and conducted all sorts of surveys internally, tested tea and coffee service on board, before implementing it, after much delay.

It even toyed with the idea of an on-board magazine for a long time but canned it because it did not make economic sense. In Gangwal's view, a 180-seater aircraft would carry as many magazines as possible. With multiple daily departures, lakhs of magazines would be required. The additional weight would cause more fuel burn and so increase costs. Also, who would place the magazines on board? IndiGo's cabin crew was already short of time due to handling cash for on-board food and merchandise sales. It would be extra work.

Passengers may rip off pages or take it home as a free gift from an airline which otherwise gives almost nothing for free (even water comes in small paper cups, that too, often when asked for). A torn magazine would reflect poorly on the airline's image, which meant the magazines would have to be replaced every three days. What would be the cost of additional print runs? It was likely that the advertising revenues received from the magazines would not be able to cover the printing and distribution costs.

Once the fleet size reached 100 planes, it was decided to launch a watered-down version of an in-flight magazine. Named *Hello 6E*, it had an IndiGo employee on the cover, no reading material, mostly products to sell, and was packed with advertisements.

Advertisers pay a premium once the captive audience becomes large enough. Soon enough, the magazine became a small profit centre for the airline. It still is. In 2019, when the airline went aggressive on international routes, it was forced to emulate other international airlines—by offering a full-fledged in-flight magazine for passengers to kill time on long routes. IndiGo does not provide in-flight entertainment on most of its aircraft (though it is now working on having its own offering), unlike its full-service rivals such as Air India, Emirates, Qatar Airways and Etihad Airways that fly on the same routes.

Gangwal felt that there was no need to pamper the customer with extras. 'A piano on the plane may make it look fancy, but does it add to profitability? New ideas are a dime a dozen, but commercially worth little. It's like a disease—get excited and introduce frills from lounges to frequent fliers to everything else—then never recover the costs incurred,' was his opinion.

Most people, he believed, love a short flight, and the first thing a passenger wants to do when the aircraft lands is to make a quick exit. No one likes to remain inside an aircraft any more than it is needed.

Gangwal's reclusive nature and successes have also given rise to tall tales that border on urban legends. One had a bartender in the US jumping on the counter with half a lemon in hand and announcing that whoever squeezed out even one drop of juice from this lemon after the bouncer had finished squeezing, would get free drinks that night. None of the US Airways executives came forward, but Gangwal went up nonchalantly and squeezed five drops out of the lemon—the master of extracting the last bit of value out of anything. While he won't deny the 'extracting' skill in real life, Gangwal laughed off this story, saying it was an old chestnut in the US, and people just changed the name of the person each time.

Another story was that in the chaotic moments after the 9/11 crashes, when airlines were undecided about what was to be done with their already airborne flights, Gangwal, as the CEO, directed all US Airways flights to land on an as-is basis, even before the US regulator Federal Aviation Authority (FAA) shut the US airspace and ordered airborne aircraft over the continental US to land. Gangwal's decision, apparently, was not taken out of fear or in panic. It was pure pragmatism and opportunism. He wanted to occupy all available parking bays because he knew instinctively that none would be left once everyone else decided to abort their flights.

This story could be true, because the FAA did take time in issuing its order. The FAA alerted the United States Air Force (USAF) at 8.40 a.m. that American Airlines Flight 11, that had taken off from Boston at 7.59 a.m. for Los Angeles, had been hijacked. Flight 11 crashed into the twin towers at 9.03 a.m. Five minutes later, the FAA banned all take-offs to New York City or flights through the airspace around the city.

At 9.42 a.m., one hour from the first event, the FAA grounded all flights over or bound for the continental US. Over the next two-and-a-half hours, some 3,300 commercial flights and 1,200 private planes were guided to land at airports in Canada and the US. 'Gangwal's ability of looking at strategy is unique. His understanding of the international business scenario, and attention to detail is phenomenal,' one of the IndiGo executives said.

When Vijay Mallya's Kingfisher Airlines was shutting down, Gangwal insisted that IndiGo take as many slots as possible at Mumbai airport that became available as a result. So, IndiGo moved many of its existing flights out of the network and placed them in all the slots that Mumbai airport gave them at that time.

Gangwal knew a second airport would not come up for many years in Mumbai, and slots at the already constrained airport—

India's financial capital—would be worth their weight in gold in the future. Airlines have grandfather rights on slots, so once they have a slot, they can use it for any flight they want. Mumbai slots would also ensure cornering the premium and high-yielding corporate traffic making the flights and the overall network more profitable.

Similarly, when IndiGo started its international operations in 2011 with a flight to Dubai, Gangwal directed the airline to capture all the bilaterals (the number of flights allowed between two countries) that were left, as the next negotiation between the governments for more landing rights could take years.

Therefore, IndiGo mounted flights from wherever it could to Dubai. Indeed, the Dubai bilaterals have not really been expanded as sought by Middle Eastern airlines since then, despite tremendous pressure from cash-rich Dubai.

Gangwal's reaction was also possibly prompted by a controversial report in 2011 by the comptroller and auditor general (CAG) that pulled up former aviation minister Praful Patel for giving windfall rights in the preceding years to Dubai at the cost of hurting Air India. The rights were given so freely that it later became a popular joke that Emirates and not Air India had become the national carrier of India, flying significant traffic to its hub in Dubai and forward to US and Europe among other regions.

In 2022, aviation minister Jyotiraditya Madhavrao Scindia agreed that Dubai as a hub and not, say, Delhi was a big concern for India. 'In the case of one or two countries, there certainly is that pressure that you're talking about. But my only effort is to make sure that our airlines—and that effort is bearing fruit now—combined with the long-haul fleet acquisition plans of our airlines, whether it is SpiceJet, or IndiGo, or Air India or Vistara and ... wet lease plans of a number of our airlines and the window

I have given by increasing the wet-lease period,' he told me in an interview in November 2022 on whether he plans to give in to the pressure from Emirates Airlines, Qatar Airways, Etihad Airways, etc., for more rights. 'I do not like the fact that today, India's hubs are lying outside our country. This is something of a huge concern for me ... And I think we need to create a domestic hub as well. I'm looking into it.'

With Gangwal, grabbing all the resources within reach was followed by another ploy. 'Gangwal's strategy is to kill anyone possible on the way and once you have the market share, dominate it,' says a US airline investor who did not want to be named and who once had conversations with him on starting an airline. 'His reading of the market was correct. He understands the math behind the airways, not only in terms of operational costs. If in your cost of capital, you have an advantage and market control in terms of ticket price too, then others will have to follow you. You are going to make others bleed. And you will eventually render the other players irrelevant. There is no looking back.'

IndiGo has indeed been criticized for bringing in so many planes, that rivals have become extremely nervous. When you bring so much capacity and you have the lowest cost and so much money in the bank, you can drive out many airlines from the routes and become a near-monopolistic player.

Just before the pandemic struck in 2020, in an IndiGo leadership meeting, Rakesh Gangwal was asked what should be done on a Delhi–Bengaluru route where IndiGo had the largest inventory but there were so many other flights too. To fill flights, the airline would have to drop fares but then yields would drop too.

'He said—Welcome to the world of airlines. This is a daily fight and something that jetBlue and Southwest too go through. He gave a fantastic perspective of the overall market and then said, don't exit the market, just keep at it, and others will exit,' someone present in the meeting recalled.

Gangwal plays down the charges. 'Not true. I truly believe in good competition and profitable airlines. India needs at least three very successful airlines, maybe four. But beyond four it's not possible. Two full-service and two low-cost airlines, but healthy and profitable and growing and meeting the demand of the various segments of the business.' According to him, this is the best scenario.

'It is not possible to kill airlines,' he says. 'If you start doing that, you will lose a lot of money. Many airlines which try to do that (kill other airlines) get into very serious financial trouble, because then your objective has changed. Instead of building a network, building an airline, you are trying to do the competitive [play]. And that is not a good idea.'

But IndiGo has been dominating and beating frequencies on any station it opens. And many airlines have been forced to vacate some routes too. 'We want to build high frequencies in city pairs in a particular station. For instance, let's say we want to fly to a lot of places out of Kolkata so that a Kolkata customer will say "I should be flying with them", because it's always what he or she sees. That's the strategy. Not because of competition,' Gangwal says.

For IndiGo, keeping its costs lowest is also critical for other reasons. 'We will have [a] cost advantage. That's absolutely a given. What you do with that cost advantage? It allows you to add more capacity and bring the fares down because, as we are adding capacity, we have to fill the seats and if we don't fill the seats then we are in big trouble. It's like a virtuous cycle—you add capacity, you continue to bring your costs down and bring fares down which generates demand. If we don't bring fares down, we will not generate demand and then all these planes that we are taking, it doesn't make sense [to fly them empty],' says Gangwal. 'If we are not able to bring fares down, we will not be able to absorb that kind of capacity. It's part of the business strategy to bring fares down. Other airlines are dropping fares because they need cash to pay their bills. It's not for making profits.'

Despite Gangwal's rebuttal of the allegation, it is widely felt in the industry that IndiGo goes after its competition hard and the lowest common denominator with highest costs dies, one by one. The collapse of Kingfisher Airlines, Jet Airways and Go First are cases in point. Even when SpiceJet almost went belly up in 2014, IndiGo expanded its footprint quickly.

Gangwal's vision led to IndiGo becoming a launch customer when it booked the next generation fuel-efficient Airbus' A320neo planes. Having been in the business for a long time, Gangwal was sure that a new plane would be launched in a few years.

He was waiting for it. In fact, he had been prodding Airbus to bring better technology. In a business where margins are 2 or 3 per cent, a cost saving of about 12–15 per cent thanks to a more fuel-efficient aircraft is a game changer. After its historic 100-aircraft order, everyone had thought that IndiGo was all set for a decade, but the airline surprised everyone with an unexpected order for another 180 planes in 2011, of the A320neo.

This time it was Airbus executive vice president Kiran Rao who negotiated this 180-aircraft deal at Gangwal's home in the US. Gangwal perhaps knew that he did not have so many levers this time to crack a really good deal like the one he did with the first 100 planes—there was no 9/11 and Airbus had got a strong foothold in India by now.

Yet, the discussions got so tense that at one point Rao lost his cool and left the room and called up one of his close friends to complain about Gangwal, 'I am exasperated. What is he made of?'

Rao recalls, 'My friend joked, "He is a Marwari from Kolkata. They used to deal with the East India Company."'

Weeks went by and then the action shifted to the Paris Air Show where the order was to be finally sealed. 'We were to sign it at the Paris Air Show. It was a Wednesday, the signing ceremony was at two o'clock in the afternoon, and I was still on the phone with Rakesh at noon. He was yet to agree to the deal. I was called for a VIP lunch at the Airbus chalet. I said to my boss, look, I have not finished yet, but my boss said you have to be here because you can't leave an empty seat at the table. So, I continued to negotiate with Rakesh on my Blackberry, holding it under the table. At 1.45 p.m., Rakesh said no, I need to speak with John Leahy and Tom Enders because I am not happy (Leahy was then Airbus number two as COO, and Enders was the president). I said Rakesh, right, that's it, enough is enough. It's all fine. I am going to hang up the phone now.'

YouTube has a video of the signing of this deal in the Paris Air Show. Leahy, Enders and Rahul Bhatia are seen clapping while a smiling Gangwal appears to have just ended his speech. Another big order had been closed.

'He does that to everybody,' says Rao, 'nothing special for me. Rakesh can be very cutting in his negotiating style, but once it's all over, you become long-term best of friends and partners for the future. I can probably write a book on how to work with him in aviation. What you know when you negotiate with Gangwal is that he knows more than you about what you can do and can't do. He is a good friend, and we have had some great times together, but we have also had some difficult times where I had to try and find ways of accommodating what he needs and what he wants.'

In this deal, the airline inducted the A321neo—a stretched version of the A320neo—that seats 222 (up to 244, depending on density) passengers, that is, at least thirty-six more seats than the A320neo. In effect, with every five A321neos, IndiGo will add one extra A320neo to its fleet in terms of capacity.

'Indian airports are constrained,' notes Gangwal. 'Mumbai airport is constrained, and to add capacity you cannot add more frequencies, so the next best is gauge up. But from the pilots and maintenance points of view, it's the same plane. Just a bigger fuselage. So, you can put more seats.'

This is a huge advantage because not only are A321neos bigger, they can also replace older A320s at the congested Mumbai and Delhi airports to allow for more capacity—and more metro-route dominance. It can also fly longer distances so that IndiGo can tap into places like Hong Kong, which it earlier could not do otherwise.

It has also ordered another version of this aircraft—A321XLRs, which it hopes to deploy in the European routes. It is beyond the range of the current fleet that flies to the Middle East and Southeast Asia. This version, with an expected range of eleven hours non-stop, is anticipated to be delivered in 2025.

Gangwal claimed that the idea to place big orders was not merely to command good discounts but to stay invested in the long-term growth story of India. 'I had told Rahul that the only way it will work is, we are going to think long term, and we are going to build a massive network,' says Gangwal. 'And Rahul was very much in line with that vision. And that is why we placed these orders ten to fifteen years out. Nobody does it. The vision is to have an air transportation network that India can be proud of forever. And in my lifetime, I will accomplish that. We will have a massive air network in India.'

IndiGo has around 60 per cent share of the domestic Indian market within 19 years of its inception. This is double the market share of its closest rival, the now Tatas-backed Air India group.

'Very simply, when we started, we had high hopes and aspirations of what we wanted to do but those were aspirations, visions, plans. Now the comfort level and confidence is fundamentally different. Now it's up to us to execute and do it. And I feel very good about it, very comfortable about it. That little bit of uncertainty which may have existed ten years ago, it's all gone. Now it's all about how big and how successful and how fantastic we can make IndiGo. That's what this is about,' he had told me in one of the conversations before the Covid-19 pandemic struck and before the two promoters got into a legal fight and Gangwal decided to exit the airline.

He had also said then that he had no intention of selling out. 'Absolutely. Absolutely, without any doubt. The fun has just started. The hard part is behind us. Now is the time to have fun,' he had said, adding, 'We don't want to be the best airline in India. We want to be the best airline in the world in the low-cost arena. We don't want anyone to be better than us anywhere in the world. That's the goal. Ryanair is massive, Southwest has been there for long. Five years ago had I said IndiGo will become the largest domestic carrier in India, you would have laughed. But watch, in ten years, how big we will be. Just watch. Maybe by 2025 we will become a very massive airline, a very massive airline.'

Unfortunately, by 2025, Gangwal will be seventy-two and is likely to have sold most of his stake in IndiGo as he announced in 2022 after a bitter legal battle with Bhatia that he will sell his stake over the next 'five years plus'. In sharp contrast to his earlier averment he has now said, 'It's only natural to think someday about diversifying one's holdings.'

Nevertheless, the CEO who left US Airways with US$15 million, will exit IndiGo two decades later as an investor with almost US$4 billion in his pocket—the next waypoint in his journey that started from Kolkata and took him to Kanpur, Philadelphia, Chicago, Paris, Washington and then to Gurugram.

Life for him has now mostly shifted to sunny—and arguably tax-friendly—Miami where he bought a US$30 million (around Rs 200 crore then) beach mansion in 2014–15, the same year the airline paid the highest-ever dividend of Rs 1,500 crore each to its two promoters, just before the IPO in the next fiscal. The mansion is located on an island called Indian Creek, one of the most exclusive and wealthiest places in the world, with a population of just eighty-six and forty-one homes as of 2010. This elite village's past and present residents include Donald Trump's daughter Ivanka Trump, Amazon founder Jeff Bezos, singer–dancer Beyoncé, and Spanish music icon Enrique Iglesias.

As for Nigel Harwood, he says he did not mind paying for that Italian meal in Washington. 'He likes to pretend he is the boss. It is part of his mind games,' Harwood laughs, when reminded of Gangwal insisting that he should pay for the meal. 'But it was a good dinner that got me the 100-plane deal. And because of it I got a bonus from Airbus that year. It was money well spent.'

4
Kapil Bhatia

In the 1970s, foreign travel in India was not as easy as it is today. It was also very expensive. While firms such as SITA World Travel were bringing group tours to India then, there was nobody really taking Indians outside.

Kapil Bhatia thought this was a great opportunity to tap and he started working on outbound tours perhaps for the first time. To begin with, he prepared a detailed seven-day itinerary for Southeast Asia, the cheapest foreign destination even then, that covered Delhi–Bangkok, Bangkok–Penang, Penang–Kuala Lumpur, Kuala Lumpur–Singapore, Singapore–Bangkok and Bangkok–Delhi legs. The group members were charged Rs 1,604 per person and named Exotic Enchanters. They were packed on to a Thai Airways flight and allotted frugal, low-budget hotels to stay in and given five Singapore dollars daily for lunch and dinner.

Kapil Bhatia himself went on this tour. While the idea was sound, the accounts later showed that this was a loss-making proposition. So, the second group was sent on the same trip but at a revised rate of Rs 2,200. There were enough takers still. It was the beginning of group tours out of India.

In many ways, the enterprising Kapil Bhatia laid the seeds for InterGlobe Enterprises, but he did not become as high-profile as his risk-taking son, Rahul Bhatia, who now owns the crown jewel, IndiGo.

'Kapil was our senior, he is a pioneer of [the] travel business,' says Balbir Mayal, chairman of Delhi's New Airways Travels, a former president of Travel Agents Association of India and someone who has known the family for the past fifty years through their highs and lows.

How did Kapil Bhatia really begin his professional journey? Bhatia had migrated from Pakistan's Rawalpindi after India's partition in 1947 when he was around fifteen years old. The harrowing and bloody tragedy had uprooted and bankrupted people, who had to flee, leaving behind their homes, farms and other belongings.

Bhatia, now ninety-one, lost his father very early in life and therefore grew up in an extended family and a single-mother environment. Perhaps given his oratory and excellence in making presentations his first job was that of a teacher. He also worked in the Indonesian embassy, Ambassador Travels and as a sales manager for Thai Airways in his early days.

He desired to start something of his own but had no money. He then languished for some time. Somewhere along the way, he met and convinced a businessman named J.K. Singhal to invest in his idea. Singhal in turn knew M. Mahajan (whose family now runs diagnostic firm Mahajan Imaging) who together with L.C. Garg, Kailash Chand, Surinder Arya, O.P. Kalra, Raj Narain Kalra, and S.R. Gupta, contributed Rs 20,000 each to build a corpus of Rs 2 lakh to start this new travel business, according to Vipin Singhal, the late J.K. Singhal's son.

They called their company Delhi Express, a joint venture of ten people in 1965, with its first office housed on the ground floor of

Hotel Janpath. Kapil Bhatia was the managing director and ran the show, while the other directors were silent investor–partners.

The first big opportunity identified was in Punjab, the main source of migration to Canada and the UK then. People were willing to pay through their nose to go abroad. Bhatia worked hard and became the general sales agent (GSA) of Syrian Arab Airlines. Syrian, at that time, flew once a week between Delhi–Damascus–London.

'That was the start of Delhi Express,' says Vipin Singhal. Initially, when major airlines such as Air France came to India in the 1960s, they set up plush offices, often in Delhi's Connaught Place. The smaller airlines, however, did not have the wherewithal to set up full-fledged offices across India. They appointed GSAs. Typically, the GSA sells all of the airline's products in a region and in return receives commissions.

Becoming a GSA those days was equivalent to getting some big government licence. Those who worked in this industry remember how it also had a murky side—GSAs also had to lobby with politicians and the government for permission for flights into India. The politicians and bureaucrats had to be kept 'happy'. However, a GSA appointment meant a lot of money because commissions were high.

Since there were only two or three major families in such travel trade then, including Bhatia, this also made them very powerful in their own right. Bhatia, for example, was very close to Arun Nehru, a member of the Nehru-Gandhi family who was brought into politics by Indira Gandhi. He later rose to become a key advisor to Rajiv Gandhi in 1981 after Sanjay Gandhi's death in 1980. Rajiv Gandhi was India's Prime Minister from 1984 to 1989 and Nehru was often referred to by businessmen as 'decisive' and a 'one-window clearance' person.

Mayal on the other hand was in the other camp. He was close to Sanjay Gandhi who was very powerful when Indira Gandhi was the Prime Minister. Mayal had known Sanjay, a Doon School pass out, through a common friend and another Doon School pass-out Akbar Ahmad, also known as Dumpy.

'I was stronger than Kapil in many ways in politics around 1977,' he added.

He then laughed regretfully and said, 'We didn't get to see power because Nehru came up after [the] 1980s. If Sanjay had been there, I would have been a minister or bigger in business. Kapil Bhatia was very strong in Congress.'

A person who had worked with Kapil Bhatia recalled, that after Emergency was imposed by Indira Gandhi and a non-Congress government came in, travelling abroad had become tough for the 'first family'. The new government was not keen for them to fly abroad but Bhatia not only risked the government's ire and booked Rajiv to travel abroad on Syrian Airlines but also booked Indira Gandhi to fly to London for an international award. Given the pushback Gandhi got for imposing Emergency in India and her ouster soon after, this international recognition must have been very important for her to remove the 'stain'.

'When Indira Gandhi was out of power, the tickets used to be issued to the family by Mr Bhatia,' Mayal says. 'I was there.'

While the politician–businessman nexus is not always apparent, I have seen a couple of instances that bore out the closeness between Arun Nehru and the Bhatias.

At the Italian restaurant Tonino in south Delhi, I have seen Rahul Bhatia having an elaborate brunch with what looked like two families at a corner table. Out of the usual journalistic curiosity, I checked with the restaurant manager who the other gentleman was. He said he was Arun Nehru, who was like Bhatia a regular here. Similarly, when Nehru, sixty-nine, fell ill in 2013 and was admitted to Fortis Hospital in Gurugram, Rahul Bhatia made several trips to the hospital and had placed his close aides on watch to keep him updated about Nehru's health all the time. He was deeply disturbed when Arun Nehru passed away, according to a person who was aware of these developments but asked not to be named.

Political contacts in fact were required even by Seth Chand, who is said to have got the first GSA in India for Iraq Air. He was said to be close to the politically powerful, erstwhile royal family of Amarinder Singh, also from the Congress then. Among Chand's many relatives was the mother of Naresh Goyal, the founder of the now bankrupt Jet Airways. Goyal was the youngest of four brothers in the family, and Goyal's mother requested Chand to take Goyal under his tutelage. Goyal too went to learn the ropes of the trade through this association.

In many ways, Goyal's and Kapil and Rahul Bhatia's stories have many parallels. They both started out as travel agents in Connaught Place (CP) in New Delhi and they both worked for others before starting their own GSAs.

'I used to meet Mr Goyal at the Air France office in CP. We had to go there and get the tickets. You gave a voucher, and they gave you a receipt. Naresh Goyal used to walk from his office in CP to Air France. He knew who the Syrian people were, who Iraqis were … Iraqi [flight] was also a once-a-week operation. I remember Mr Goyal wearing simple pants and shirt. He was very low profile, but always smart to talk to. I never found him in T-shirts; always in formal clothes. Much later, when he started his own GSA, he started wearing suits. At that time, in 1972–73, he also took the GSA for Air France independently. Since then, he grew phenomenally. At that time, he was representing sixteen or seventeen airlines as GSA, through Jet Air,' Singhal recalls.

In 1969, Kapil Bhatia became the GSA for Air France in Uttar Pradesh, while Naresh Goyal's firm had the same GSA for Punjab. Delhi Express became the GSA for Thai Airways, Scandinavian and many other airlines. Branches opened up in many locations—

Jalandhar, followed by Chandigarh, Kanpur, Lucknow, Jaipur, Hyderabad, Calcutta, Patna, Bangalore and Madras.

Kapil Bhatia could sense the potential of the airline business but chose to stay in the travel trade, as he feared airlines were a loss-making, risky business. Goyal, on the other hand, decided to start Jet Airways. During these conversations I discovered that Kapil Bhatia even gave money to Naresh Goyal to start Jet Airways. However, after attending the first few meetings, he told Goyal they would not be able to get along as their ways of 'approaching life' were different.

'I don't want to get into something that I don't enjoy,' was what he told him, a person close to Bhatia recalled. To Goyal's credit, he amicably gave back the money Bhatia had invested in Jet Airways. Bhatia was much more polished, jovial, and maintains relations even when he does not need to. He still often sends ties or Scotch whisky from his foreign travels to many people including InterGlobe employees whom he knows well. He does not need to, says one such recipient who did not want to be named. However, it is always a surprise when a gift or two lands at his table with small notes from Bhatia senior. Similarly, Bhatia's annual Diwali parties were also well-attended. He would even stand at the door, personally welcoming all his employees as if they were all his family members, and everyone was given gifts.

'The joke still is that if you see people laughing and giggling in a corner, you know Kapil Bhatia is in their midst, but if you see a corner with only one or two people standing and chatting quietly, you know one of them must be Rahul Bhatia,' said another official who has worked with them for many years.

Both father and son, though, crack jokes. This perhaps helps break the ice easily. They also have another habit in common, says Mayal. They both dip their biscuits in tea before eating them. Also, while Kapil Bhatia enjoys his gin in the afternoon and Scotch in the evening, Rahul is not a great drinker and drinks only wine once in a while.

But Kapil Bhatia can be rough when he is in the boardroom and rip the management apart for mistakes committed. However, once out of the meeting, none of that shows. And when it is time to drink, you are not allowed to talk shop at all. This culture has kept many of his employees together for years, and their eyes on the ball.

In the early days, life was, however, not all jokes and liquor, when Kapil Bhatia would ride a bicycle from Rajinder Nagar, where the family stayed in a rented house, to Hotel Janpath. It took some time before he could move to a scooter and bring his son, Rahul, and wife to the office in Connaught Place, as it had an air-conditioner. By the 1970s he had moved to south Delhi's leafy Anand Niketan and built a house there. The scooter had also given way to an Ambassador car, perhaps also because Bhatias are tall, and it was bigger than the only other car available then—the Premier Padmini.

By the late 1980s, more airlines were looking to make inroads into India. One of the world's largest airlines, United Airlines, also wanted Indian traffic. In the meantime, tragedy had struck Delhi Express as its co-founder V.K. Singhal passed away. His next generation wanted to take over the reins. While Kapil Bhatia had run the show so far and was the public face of the company, the new blood perhaps did not want to remain in the background and one day, Vipin asked him to leave the company.

'Kapil was in a terrible shape; he was so broken. We used to meet for coffee then and he would pour his heart out,' Mayal recalls.

Bhatia then started his own firm called InterGlobe Enterprises in 1989.

'When United visited the offices of Delhi Express, they thought this was the best company to work with. Rahul took United around at that time,' Vipin Singhal recalls. 'Rahul etched the GSA agreement of United with InterGlobe. That was the twist,' he says, implying that the GSA should have gone to Delhi Express, as its offices were shown to United Airlines' executives, and not the offices of InterGlobe, which perhaps as a start-up had nothing to show for.

United was a big trophy. 'InterGlobe was wholly owned by the Bhatias,' says Singhal. 'Whatever GSAs were there, they managed to transfer them to InterGlobe. Nobody was left in Delhi Express.'

Given that most of the airline relationships were that of Kapil Bhatia, this was no surprise. There was also a rush by staff members to join his firm, as one executive who worked there put it, 'He was a very popular leader.'

Mayal said he even held mediation meetings between Rahul Bhatia and Vipin Singhal at the Oberoi Hotel in Delhi many times during those years but too much water had flown under the bridge by then. The situation had become too toxic.

'I hold Vipin totally responsible for this,' he said.

When I put all this to him, Rahul Bhatia remembered the events with bitterness. According to him, in 1988, 50 per cent of the initial owners of the company had passed away, which essentially meant that the new generation had become actively involved. As it happens in life, he said, when new people come in, they have their own sets of objectives and aspirations, and that was the 'beginning of the end of the company'.

When the new ownership of Delhi Express removed Kapil Bhatia from Delhi Express, Rahul Bhatia recalled, a fierce legal battle ensued. For the first two or three years, the banks that had a relationship with Delhi Express were not supportive of their new company, InterGlobe.

The only bank that came to their rescue was Bank of Tokyo. However, despite their good intentions, that institution could only take so much exposure. So virtually every two weeks, the

Bhatias used to be at the doors of Bank of Tokyo with a begging bowl, looking for money. This went on for three to four years. As InterGlobe started to get more business, the pressure eased and things settled down by the mid-nineties. Rahul Bhatia says he doesn't know where Delhi Express is now, but even today his father owns 10 per cent of that company—but it's history now, and not relevant.

Vipin Singhal too seemed bitter about the feud but was unusually full of admiration for Kapil Bhatia. They still meet, he says, but only at public functions. 'Mr Bhatia is a gem of a person—lively and articulate. He has a certain charisma. You must meet him,' Singhal said in the small travel agency office which could barely fit in three people. It is in sharp contrast to InterGlobe's travel and hotel empire, housed often in the company's own swanky towers in Gurugram and other local offices.

Mayal said Kapil and son are both very fond of each other and have breakfast together daily and discuss everything. 'Though Kapil was a pioneer and the key brain, he praises his son a lot. He says because of him I am what I am today,' Mayal says, 'And even now when we discuss those dark Delhi Express days, I tell him that in hindsight it was a blessing in disguise or else you would have remained a worker for life and IndiGo would not have happened.'

At InterGlobe's brand relaunch party in 2011 at the Imperial Hotel in Delhi, steps away from where Bhatia started his travel career and Delhi Express, Bhatia senior was very happy at how things had turned out.

InterGlobe had become a US$1 billion company by then and was launching a new logo, moving away from an archaic pyramid shaped 1989 logo which used the letters IG with another pyramid on top of it, to a more minimalist logo that used six different sized (and coloured) spokes connected together.

This was created by London brand consultancy Circus and Mumbai-based design agency Grandmother India. 'My main business,' Kapil Bhatia said in a rare public speech there, 'was to represent the GSAs of various international airlines in the country. After struggling afresh, all those airlines came back to me. It was destiny—things kept improving till we got established. We now have a large number of airlines; we have other verticals of businesses which are successfully running.'

He went on, perhaps recalling the removal from Delhi Express, 'I am happy to say that if my character didn't shine the brightest during adversity, I would be a forgotten man. Today, by the grace of God and the good wishes of my friends, I am a satisfied and happy man.'

On that day, InterGlobe had sixty-one offices across forty-four cities globally and 8,500 employees. Delhi Express was but a faded memory. He appeared to be gratified.

Uncharacteristically, Rahul also agreed to go through a photoshoot by my Mint colleague Ramesh Pathania even as I interviewed him—the only interview he gave that day.

As for the Exotic Enchanters group that Kapil Bhatia started, one of the reasons for such group trips becoming popular was not the fleshpots of Thailand etc. perhaps, but also because the travellers had themselves worked out a business angle. They would buy black- and- white televisions, a big novelty then, from Singapore at cheap prices, and sell them in India for Rs 1,000, recovering a bulk of the cost of their trip.

During his life, Bhatia clearly made business work for himself and for many others too.

5
Rahul Bhatia

Just after IndiGo crossed the 200-aircraft mark in 2019, I asked Rahul Bhatia a rather awkward question.

Did he think he would become as successful as he was then?

Not just the fleet-size, IndiGo had touched a market share of around 50 per cent and was already the most valued Indian airline with a market capitalization of around Rs 60,000 crore. In contrast, India's longest-run private airline Jet Airways, at its peak, was worth only Rs 12,000 crore.

'*Yeh toh kehna mushkil hota hai*,' he said then and took me back to his 2005 aircraft order. Both he and Gangwal were planning to order only fifty Airbus A320 planes with fifty as an option which was to be converted into a firm order later, he revealed. But last minute, they went all in and decided to make it a firm 100-plane order, taking a well-considered punt on India's growth story. To date, he said, it remains the single-largest firm order by any start-up airline in the world.

'So how can people say we didn't want to be successful? We wanted to be successful. We wanted to be outrageously successful,' he says. 'My point was this was something I always wanted to do, believed in and it's starting to see some initial shades of success. There is some satisfaction. I think so.'

Unlike some of the start-ups of today which manage to get a billion-dollar valuation in a few years, IndiGo's birth and rise to be a giant was an idea nursed by Rahul from his early professional years. It has had many ups and downs, and failures. To cross a market cap of Rs 1 lakh crore and have over 60 per cent of India's domestic market share has been a grind that actually started as a thought experiment twenty-five years ago in the late 1990s.

The sixty-three-year-old Rahul (born 1960) had decided to leave the shadows of his father and, therefore, the family business when he was seventeen. Rahul's maternal aunt lived in Canada, and he enrolled at the University of Toronto in the late 1970s to pursue his graduation after leaving the prestigious Modern School in central Delhi.

Canada was a breath of fresh air for Rahul with its superior quality of life and the freedom of living on your own terms, as he puts it. The newfound freedom may have, however, spoilt him because in the second year of his graduation he flunked and failed comprehensively. He then had a choice to repeat the year at the same university or take admission somewhere else.

This also created an embarrassing situation back home and he could not hide this from his parents for very long. He felt extremely sad about this as he thought he was far from home to get a quality education and then he did not make the cut. This put a lot of 'religion' into him. To avoid the shame of living in the same city with a 'flunked' tag, he took a transfer to the University of Waterloo, Ontario. He worked hard to redeem his dignity. Finally, he graduated in electrical engineering with the Dean's honour list in 1984.

Unlike the curriculum at Toronto, which focused more on bookish knowledge, Rahul also seemed to have loved the University of Waterloo's focus on practical work experience.

In 1984, when Rahul returned to India from Canada, he had no intention of entering the airline or travel business as it required too much 'ji huzoori' (hypocritical or pretended concurrence), and 'without that you could not have succeeded,' he says.

This was the time when entrepreneur Sam Pitroda had launched the Centre for Development of Telematics (C-DOT) for promoting indigenous telecommunications technology after he was invited by Prime Minister Indira Gandhi to do so. Pitroda, often seen in the company of Congress leader Rahul Gandhi when he visits the US, felt strongly about telephony in India because he used to have a hard time calling his family in Chicago when he was in India.

Airtel owner Sunil Bharti Mittal had already started making Beetel telephone handsets. So, Rahul formed a joint venture with the Canadian company Nortel (short for Northern Telecom). Nortel produced the 'best telephone exchanges' in the world, called 'digital switches', Bhatia says.

Theirs was cutting-edge technology, and they were keen to set up a plant in India. On his return, Rahul's initial plan was to set up this factory. He obtained a licence for a Nortel unit and set up a five-member team to get all the government permissions and permits. He paid them fancy salaries, but Prime Minister Indira Gandhi then decided that India needed to develop indigenous technology and would only use C-DOT as a vehicle to do so. The start-up failed even before it could take off and Rahul's foray into telecom did not see the light of day.

This left him demotivated and disheartened and he languished for two or three years. He even contemplated a return to Canada, doing a PhD and taking up teaching. In his view, a teacher could live a free life, be his own person, and get time off when he wanted.

But Rahul realized that was not very practical and that he had to return to his father's travel business. He fondly calls his father 'old man' and in return is called 'biba bachcha'—Punjabi for an obedient child, according to people close to the Bhatia family.

He started to help in the travel agency business and founded InterGlobe Enterprises in 1989. The travel agency business had peaked inasmuch as, despite their success and the respect gained in the travel trade, they were still on the periphery. They yearned to be at the core—that is, to have an airline of their own.

Being a GSA of the United Airlines, they were invited to the annual meeting of the GSAs in Chicago in 1991. Rakesh Gangwal was called on to speak that day. Rahul was very impressed with Gangwal. Since he used to visit Chicago often, they both became good friends. Something in his conversations with Gangwal convinced him that whenever he started an airline, Gangwal would be in it. However, Gangwal was a tough nut to crack.

'I have seen what he did in United and Air France, and finally at US Airways. Look at Air France, he was to a great extent responsible for turning that company around, and if you ever were to track the performance of US Airways from the time he took over to the time he left, it speaks for itself. At Air France, he fundamentally changed the structure of the company. It had an enormous bearing on the airline's economics. Rakesh, I always felt, focuses on the fundamentals of an issue, not the stuff around the table. He understands what the core issue is and attacks that. The rest falls into place. I always knew that if I wanted to do this, I would like to bring him into the loop. He was reticent as a person. He didn't want to do it. He also believed that we would lose our money and that will be the end of the game,' Bhatia recalls.

Not just Gangwal, his father Kapil Bhatia was also against the idea of starting an airline as he too thought they would lose all the wealth they had created so far.

'Any sane man will tell you that it's probably insane to get into an airline. And I think without exception, my parents, my family, and some dear friends, and even people like Rakesh, none of them wanted to pursue this. I just felt that there was an opportunity, and we could build something which could be different, that would embrace the growth of India,' Rahul told me.

Not the one to give up easily he kept toying with his airline idea. He even got a consulting firm to make a business plan during the mid-1990s. Despite the many airlines launched around that time including Jet Airways, he was unable to get his own airline up in the air.

In the early 2000s the market was firmly in the control of Indian Airlines, Air Sahara and Jet Airways.

He was a little desperate now. Rahul reached out to oil-major Essar's Ruias to start an airline but that came to nothing. Similarly, he met Gautam Singhania, but his family did not support the idea of investing in an airline, while Nusli Wadia and Jeh Wadia eventually started their own airline, GoAir.

Rahul even held talks with the founder of Virgin Group, Richard Branson. 'IndiGo was very nearly called Virgin. We missed a great opportunity. We should have done a deal with IndiGo. It came close,' Richard Branson confirmed to me during an interview in Scotland when I brought this point up, 'It is one of my biggest regrets.' The talks with Branson may have been dropped because foreign airlines investments in India came with regulatory hurdles then.

By this time, though, Rahul had won one major battle—he had convinced Gangwal and both had started work to get funded by US private equity players. Talks with US-based Indigo Partners had proceeded to the extent of signing a term-sheet (which outlines the terms on which an investor will make investment in the company). Indigo Partners has invested in low-cost airlines around the world including Frontier Airlines, JetSMART, Volaris and Wizz Air.

Gangwal knew the head of the firm, Bill Franke. However, the talks led by him with Indigo Partners turned sour as IndiGo felt Franke was throwing in too many conditions.

Rahul even toyed with the idea of taking over Air Sahara and had gone to meet its chief Subrata Roy with former railways minister Dinesh Trivedi. But for some reason this too did not go anywhere. Plans to be part of ModiLuft too had failed.

Rahul does not regret being able to start the airline with the people he initially spoke to because many of them would not have brought any fundamental understanding of the airline industry since none of them had any.

'I think in 2001, we thought of starting an airline of our own. When this whole Royal Airways thing was going on, we thought we might become their GSA and support them on ground handling. That was in March 2001. Then 9/11 happened and it all collapsed. I think before that also, we had some sort of engagement with Subrata Roy on Air Sahara. I also remember meeting S.K. Modi, when ModiLuft went out of business. So, at a subconscious level, opportunities came, we looked at them, we talked to SKM, we talked to Sahara, and then, of course, we talked to Kansagra. Kansagra was restarting ModiLuft as Royal Airways and we started talking to them as InterGlobe would do the ground handling for the two-class airline—all the sales and services side of the business,' Rahul said.

And how did he ensure the reluctant Gangwal's entry?

'Persistence,' he says, smiling mysteriously. 'I managed to convince Rakesh to invest together without a third partner.'

How did IndiGo get its first round of funding?

Rahul said he put in Rs 30 crore initially and then approached the banks for loans collateralized against the aircraft for making the PDP (pre-delivery payment) or the advance payment obligations to Airbus for the big 100-plane order. IndiGo opted for an Airbus instead of the popular Boeing planes then, because Gangwal found the economics of Airbus superior. The one-off needs that arose were funded by InterGlobe and his 'reluctant' father, who supported him during through thick and thin.

While the primary funding was from the travel agency business, additional funds came from what was a reluctant investment made by Rahul—the technology business.

'One day I got a call from Rahul saying there is a company called Galileo—it's a GDS (global distribution system). At that time, everything (airline ticketing) was on paper. United had a stake in Galileo. And a friend of Rahul, the head of Asia Pacific of Galileo, recommended that Galileo use InterGlobe's services for India. Since I was in Mumbai, Rahul asked me to see someone who was visiting and facilitate the meeting with Air India. Being the national carrier, all the GDSes wanted a relationship with Air India to launch themselves in India. That did not happen. But there was a lot of interest. So, they said—set up a facility in India for training—and asked us to represent them. We did it very reluctantly as if it was a burden that had fallen into our laps. We were doing well selling airlines and also doing some ground handling for them. So, InterGlobe venturing into something related to technology was by accident,' a close aide of Rahul who had worked in InterGlobe for a long time, recalled.

By the mid-1990s, technology was causing a revolutionary change in the travel trade. GDSes were taking over, much like the GSAs had in the 1960s. A GDS is basically a computerized reservation system that helps make real-time air ticketing reservations. Rahul latched on to the Galileo franchise in India, even though he was sceptical about it.

He remembers how he got into the GDS. 'We had a GSA relationship with United Airlines, which owned 40 per cent of Galileo at the time. Someone from their Asia Pacific office in Hong Kong called me one day to say they would like us to assist Galileo to set up a relationship with Air India. So, I talked to Air India, only to discover that they were about to sign up with Sabre. At that time, there was this thing called Sitar. They were down the path to sign an NDC with Sabre. I went back to the Asia Pacific guys and said that things have left town.

Then the Galileo folks turned around and asked me if I would want to do that for them. In the good old days, the GDS vendors liked to think their future was best secured by having a partnership with national carriers around the world. That's why Air India was the natural choice. Once Air India became unavailable, we looked at it and said the system was essentially about servicing travel agents and we had a common customer bank. We decided to give it a try and that's how it came together, and the game began.'

They became exclusive suppliers of the Galileo reservation system in India. Galileo was initially a division of InterGlobe, and then it was spun into a separate subsidiary in 1994.

'We had an acute limitation on capital. If I had to look at the agreement we had with Galileo now, it would be amusing. We had internally said to ourselves that we would be prepared to lose only a certain amount of money and opportunity, and if we lost that money then we would tell Galileo that they could have the franchise back. That's how it was set up,' Rahul said.

But Rahul, like in the case of the 100-plane order, enjoys taking calculated risks. The GDS business fetched them a lot of money. Perhaps more than the GSA business did in the 1980s.

Rahul Bhatia's InterGlobe and Bird Group, then led by late Ankur Bhatia, were also fierce rivals, despite being distant relatives. Bhatia had Galileo, while the other one had Amadeus.

'I still remember, InterGlobe had an annual get-together in Goa and the rivalry (Ankur and Rahul Bhatia) was at its peak. We had taken some of our customers with us. When we landed, there was a band playing holding an Amadeus banner with a cheeky one-liner saying have fun with Galileo but work with Amadeus,' the aide recalls.

IndiGo was not like a GSA or GDS. It sucked up the initial capital quickly as most airlines do. Then as the capital requirements kept climbing, loans got extended by shareholders in 2005, 2006 and 2007. IndiGo made losses in those early years of 2005–06, 2006–07 and 2007–08. From the fourth fiscal year, in 2008-09, IndiGo finally made small profit of Rs 18 crore, followed by Rs 447 crore in 2009–10, and Rs 602 crore in 2010–11.

This must have been a time of relief for Kapil Bhatia as also for Gangwal, both of whom were worried they would lose their shirt in Rahul Bhatia's dream to be at the 'core'. To be sure, the road to profit for IndiGo was not very easy. For starters, the IndiGo brand name was registered by Rahul through SpiceJet, which he was trying to restart along with Bhulo Kansagra. So, he had to buy back the name for Rs 25,000.

Then the Tata Group got upset over the use of the Indigo brand and objected to its use because their Indigo model car was already in the market. The airline replied to the group saying under branding rules, the objection can only be valid if it were used by a group in the same industry. Cars and airlines were two different sectors. The 2002-launched Indigo car was discontinued in 2016.

There was also a perception battle that IndiGo had to fight. Airlines used to order aircraft in tens and twenties. The 100-aircraft order caused a lot of disbelief in the government circles. The then aviation secretary Ajay Prasad even discounted the IndiGo order at a symposium in Mumbai, Rahul said.

IndiGo was the last to take off after Air Deccan, GoAir, Kingfisher Airlines, Paramount Airways, SpiceJet. It had difficulty finding parking bays for its planes. Rahul had to go knock on the doors of aviation minister Praful Patel as the first plane was on its way. The airline finally got two parking bays at Delhi Airport.

This was no surprise. In internal conversations with leadership, Bhatia would often say then, if need be, we will "wipe the floors" also. No work is small, we shall do everything to get the work done, he would tell them. If the people in the department were not getting bays on their own, Rahul in person would land up in the ministry and pursue the matter.

'We used a hotel pool for ditch training, which is done in the US as well, but more often than not, most airlines have their own training facility. At IndiGo, we didn't have a training facility, we had nothing,' Shan Iwanicki, IndiGo's former director of in-flight and crew development recalls. There were also no classrooms. Therefore, initial training took place at the Airports Authority of India's national training centre, NIAMAR, located close to the New Delhi Airport.

'It was an unventilated building and wasn't conducive to the type of training we were doing. I am a hands-on teacher. The class is always away from the seat, doing stuff, simulating how to slide, shouting, jumping up and down, all of those things. I wanted to make sure they were comfortable,' she said. It was difficult to do all that in the heat and when it became impossible to manage, she called Rahul.

'I said the air conditioning is not working. All of us were sweating. Within a few hours he was there, and he had air conditioners installed that day, and delivered tons of water. Whenever he opened his mouth, it was to ask, "What can I do for you, what do you want?"' she says.

While Gangwal was sewing up contracts in the US for IndiGo, Rahul worked to keep everything running locally. 'Rahul is the perfect gentleman, the perfect host. But you know behind all that, the guy knows what he needs to know about everything in the Indian travel and airline business—the total opposite of Rakesh. Rakesh is fast and furious, always cutting and negotiating. Rahul is much more laidback. Rahul is like a swan going across the river—paddling like crazy underneath, but seems absolutely smooth when you watch it. There is nothing smooth about Rakesh. He is more like you can see—all action—and it's in your face. In case of Rahul, it's soft and gentle and beautifully controlled,' says former Airbus executive Kiran Rao.

The reticent Rahul often gets overwhelmed when speaking in public, especially about IndiGo's success. At times people have to give him water because he chokes with emotion. Gangwal on the other hand can make others choke with his cutting questions, which make them feel they don't know what they are talking about.

IndiGo also wanted to avoid being like Gopinath's Air Deccan. Rahul feels the Re 1 fares Gopinath introduced took India's airline industry into a gas chamber. He started a war in the hope that he will come out looking like a hero. However, he ran out of cash and succumbed before anyone else did. No one, Rahul feels, should start such a price war when they do not have enough cash to win the war, because it's a race to extinction.

People must understand that in an airline business the price of the product is one of the smallest factors, Rahul says. The big-ticket item is having visibility of costs. If there are costs that are going to show up at your doorstep that you have not planned for, they can kill you. You, therefore, need to have very tight contracts and be covered for every eventuality, as Kingfisher Airlines realized when it went bankrupt all of a sudden.

In 2010, the airline, initially code-named Project Thunder and reportedly Vijay Mallya's birthday gift to his son Siddharth Mallya, was hit by a major engine problem on its Airbus A320 fleet. Many of its aircraft started getting grounded. IndiGo too faced similar issues but because of better engine contracts that accounted for such situations, it sailed through easily while Kingfisher became history.

'You have to be covered. Look what happened with the engines. Two companies; same engines, but different contracts. We had a sort of fly-by-the-hour agreement on maintenance. You had complete visibility of that cost,' Rahul concedes. 'If the plane had an AOG (aircraft on ground) at Male, you still have to transport spares from Delhi to Male. And you lose production time in the meantime—you have to cancel flights. I have known instances where we would have had a spare engine in Delhi and the plane would be an AOG in another city in India. There is no way to fly that engine from Delhi direct to that city. So, it will be flown on Singapore Airlines to Singapore and then brought to that city. In the West, engines get transported even by road. Here when the engine reaches [on some of our bumpy roads] it would need to be overhauled. Think about it, if we had a world-class highway between Delhi and Mumbai, we would have the engine delivered overnight.'

Actually, Rahul should be thankful to Jet Airways for buying Air Sahara and Kingfisher Airlines for buying Air Deccan as that, in a way, led to their demise. This made way for IndiGo to get hundreds of trained pilots, engineers, airports slots, parking bays, etc., when it needed them the most. IndiGo accelerated its aircraft inductions when Kingfisher Airlines died.

On the rare occasions that Rahul has taken to a podium, like he did while being felicitated by the Indian School of Business, Hyderabad, in 2016, he makes sure to narrate a story about two boys who go out into the jungle and encounter a tiger.

When the tiger starts to walk towards them, the two turn around and start to run for their lives. While they're running one of these guys stops in his tracks and starts to open his duffle bag. The other boy asks, what are you trying to do? He replies: Well, I'm trying to take out my sneakers. The other guy is perplexed: You've got to be kidding me, do you think you can outrun the tiger? No, comes the reply, all I need to do is outrun you.

Although it was the last to launch its operations, IndiGo has by now outrun three of the biggest airline groups in India. There is a scary statistic that I have noticed—every time IndiGo adds or comes close to completing another 100 aircraft to its fleet, one rival airline bites the dust. It is almost like an IndiGo jinx.

In 2014, SpiceJet went nearly bankrupt and had to ground its operations, just months before IndiGo added its 100th plane. In 2018, IndiGo crossed the 200-plane mark and four months later, Naresh Goyal's Jet Airways collapsed. In 2023, IndiGo crossed the 300-plane mark in January and billionaire Nusli Wadia's Go First filed for voluntary insolvency at the National Company Law Appellate Tribunal (NCLT).

'We were a little bit fortunate when Sahara was bought by Jet,' Rahul says, 'It allowed us to employ a lot of pilots. It sort of repeated itself with Kingfisher. One big thing commercially was that it took us a while to assure people that low fare is not low quality. Traditionally, they have been used to low-quality service and products being offered at low costs. It took roughly two-and-a-half years to turn around that perception.' With offers such as free meals, front row seats, and its now legendary on-time performance promise, IndiGo does ensure now that even a lot of corporate traffic fly with it despite it not having a business class.

IndiGo has also mastered the airline processes for Indian environment. Rahul captured this very well when he told the graduating ISB students that one or two big moves never make or break institutions.

'God is in the details. Successful companies tend to break down every process into several small processes and then commit themselves to executing each of these small processes better than the best in the business. Thereby you create collective arbitrage which actually is a very powerful proposition. Systems and procedures that need to be put in place not only have to be good for today but robust enough to withstand the stress of longer-term growth,' he said.

The second key thing to making a company great, he added, is to find people who have a 'fine balance between competence and commitment to service excellence. We think this is a much more daunting task. However, companies that do find people with this unique blend differentiate success from failure and end up winning the game and the mind. You winning is not about being good, it is about being the best in class in the global arena.'

In the early days, Rahul interviewed in person every individual hired for IndiGo. And even now, he gives a lot of weightage to loyalty. His former aide said that sometimes it is not always about whether you are supremely talented that matters to him, but how loyal you are and how comfortable he is with you.

For example, this executive said, Rahul chose J.B. Singh to head his hotels business when Singh's background was of sales in British Airways and tourism and holidays. Similarly, he installed Aditya

Ghosh—a lawyer the law firm J. Sagar had placed to help Rahul with presentations and so on—as the president of the airline later.

'It's not always about them being skilled at the top. The second line of the company is where the skill lies—like the vice presidents etc.,' the aide adds referring to the relatively strong leadership IndiGo has had at the top, which has largely remained loyal as well.

But Rahul realizes that there is no Indian talent that has handled the scale of a 300-plus plane operation. Therefore, to lead India's largest airline, in 2022 he hired a career airline professional Pieter Elbers, fifty-four, who was the President and CEO at KLM but began his career there as a ground staff.

The good thing about Rahul is that, unlike many other Indian promoters, he does not micromanage professionals but keeps a tab on everything. He keeps in touch with some of the leadership officials directly. To figure out if there is any siphoning off happening in vendor contracts, he constantly keeps in touch with suppliers.

'When he meets you, he will play dumb—*mujhe samjhaa de, yeh mujhe samajh mein nahin aaya*—but he knows everything,' says one of his aides. 'In a board meeting, if by the second slide of the presentation he knows where it is going, he will say no, no don't go any further. It's fine.'

If he finds you are hurting the firm, or stealing, you are history for him. A story I heard from multiple sources was how one of his firms sent a watch as a Diwali gift to some people. One of them was Rahul's friend. When Rahul asked him later whether he wears that watch sometimes, the person was puzzled. What watch? The watch was never delivered but billed to the company. The concerned person, an employee of many years, was fired immediately. Rahul had a watch sent directly to this friend.

Rahul also has his quirks. Once, Rahul and Kingfisher Airlines' former CEO Sanjay Aggarwal were sitting at the InterGlobe's IBIS hotel in Gurgaon, and coffee was served. As they sat to talk, Rahul got busy laying the table and putting the regular sugar, brown sugar and sugar-free pouches in three different lines so that there was no confusion.

I noticed this during our meetings too. When I pointed out the habit, he could not think of anything beyond saying that he liked order. Then, as an afterthought, he said this could be an acquired habit from his college days in Canada. His course required him to work in the industry every four months and then return to the campus. So, every four months, he had to go from one place to another and leave the dormitory with all his belongings, put it in a car, and move. The car had limited space and you had to make sure every possible inch was utilized, he said.

Rahul still carries the brick-like Nokia phones whose glory days are long over. He is so obsessed with them that to ensure uninterrupted service, whenever he goes abroad, he tries to find its spare parts and bring them to India. He now often uses a Blackberry smartphone and only cited Nokia's good battery life as the reason for liking them so much. Both Nokia and Blackberry are hard to hack too.

'I have four or five of them,' he says, 'but I keep cannibalizing them—one part to the other, one battery to the other. I do that all the time. It lasts longer than a BlackBerry,' Rahul informs me, dismantling the Nokia and trying to ascertain the names of the manufacturers of the various parts. 'The phone is made in Germany and the battery is made in China,' he reads out aloud.

Although they are old models, he is constantly on them. replying to messages—only those he wants to—even during his meetings.

He has another childlike habit. In the summer of 2022, Y.P. Rajesh, Reuters' political and general news editor, was seated on the emergency-row aisle seat on a Bengaluru–Delhi flight. The adjacent row was empty in which a tall man in a saffron half-sleeve shirt took the window seat. Rajesh knew he had seen the man somewhere. Another passenger who had the appearance of an executive occupied the aisle seat and started to work on some presentation. A peek told Rajesh it had the IndiGo logo on it.

'I then I realized he is the one,' Rajesh said of Rahul Bhatia. Suddenly, the crew dashed about as if their life depended on the quality of that in-flight service. He confirmed from one of them whether he was their big boss and was told he was.

The safety demo was done, to which Rahul listened attentively. Later, Rahul asked for some tea. A member of the crew brought the tea. Rahul asked her—Do you have any biscuits? They apparently only had cookies (the famous Rs 250 Tough Cookie chocolate chip cookie tin boxes which Rahul himself got made). But he didn't want them; he wanted plain biscuits. There was a scramble. Before the tea went cold, the crew should find something. So, a crew member returned and said they were carrying biscuits for the crew, could they give him that? The humble Rs 10 Parle-G was delivered. Rahul tore open the packet, dunked the biscuit in his tea and relished it before the soggy biscuit dropped back into the cup.

'I said this was a photo-op. So, I clicked,' Rajesh said about the photo that went viral. A billionaire airline owner dipping a humble Parle-G biscuit in tea and eating in his own airplane was bound to be noticed. However, even Rajesh didn't expect it to get so much traction.

When they landed, he exchanged pleasantries with Rahul. From the bus he could see Rahul had stayed back. He was surrounded by his staff, explaining to him the new ramp they were testing. IndiGo was then experimenting with a three-way disembarkation from the plane—with two forward ramps and one rear exit ramp—to speed up the turnaround time. It was introduced the month after the picture was clicked.

Are Bhatia junior and senior very different people too?

'The care and concern for people is common to both. Their working styles are very different. Rahul is clinical and dry and has his mood swings. The elder Bhatia is always warm and welcoming,' the aide said.

The care and concern often recounted by people in the trade circles was on view when, after 9/11, United Airlines—one of InterGlobe's biggest principals—stopped their flights overnight. There was nervousness that people would be terminated.

'It was a huge financial setback for the family. They had invested huge amounts in ground handling equipment and one fine day it was all sitting idle. That was the time if they wanted, they could have really downsized, but not a single person was asked to go. There were stories of the family members disposing their personal cars to ensure they don't ask anyone to leave despite all the financial constraints. They take care of employees and they were confident that they will bounce back,' the aide added.

On one occasion, there was some external survey being conducted on best companies to work for. Bhatia senior encouraged employees to vote. Bhatia junior, on the contrary, said we should not canvass and let them do so only if they want to.

Being a stickler for rules sometimes backfires on Rahul himself. In 2006, Rahul stepped out of an IndiGo flight at Delhi Airport and saw the aircraft was parked right next to the exit gate of the terminal. However, buses were to be used to ferry passengers and these buses take a long route to the passenger arrival gates. The airport was not as modernized as it is now. Rahul was in a hurry and thought he could sneak in directly through the gate in front of him.

'I know who you are, but I am sorry, I cannot allow you through,' the employee told Rahul. He clearly disliked the detour but did not mind it as the staff member was not pulled up later for following the rules.

The media-shy Rahul once gave a TV interview on a golf course, but after he reached home, he developed cold feet. He scrambled to ensure that it would not go on air because he may have said some controversial things. After some serious pleading by a senior IndiGo executive who knew the owner of this upmarket south-Delhi English news channel, the interview was not telecast. Thank-you notes were exchanged. But a few years later, when an Air France aircraft crashed, and the same channel asked this IndiGo executive to appear as an expert panellist, Rahul refused, citing company policy. Only the CEO was supposed to interact with the media.

Rahul is, however, very responsive to those whom he values much.

In December 2019, a former Air India board member, Deepak Barara, Rahul's long-time friend and who had joined InterGlobe later, was pronounced dead while on a family vacation in Goa. The death of the very sharp and affable Barara came as a shock to many and to Rahul.

Rahul was awake till late into the night arranging the transportation of the body by an IndiGo aircraft and completing the formalities. Air India was very keen to help but theirs was a late flight.

To avoid the December fog, the family decided to go with IndiGo though they knew that Barara, despite his proximity to Rahul, would have preferred his body to be brought in by Air India. Rahul was present at the aerobridge when the flight landed in Delhi, along with Barara's junior and now Air India Express CEO, Aloke Singh. Rahul attended the funeral with his wife and laid a wreath on the body.

Rahul also attended the funeral with his wife and laid a wreath on the body. If someone he knows well has a medical emergency Rahul goes out of his way to help them. He will recommend the doctors, help with an appointment at AIIMS and even land up at the hospital himself if they are admitted. This includes his own known staff members too.

The Bhatias have largely stayed away from the media limelight. Once, Rahul was featured clad in a kurta-pyjama on Page 3 of a newspaper. This upset him, according to the former aide. He, however, is not antagonistic to the press.

When it is critical for his business, he does not shy away from meeting the press. Both he and Gangwal did a media outreach organized by the airline's PR firm after an uproar over both of them taking away Rs 3,700 crore in dividends when the airline's total profit after tax was only Rs 3,914 crore. This was in 2015, just before the airline was listed.

This left India's most profitable airline with a negative net worth of Rs 140 crore for a brief period. To give confidence to the investment community, Gangwal, who did the talking in such press meets—while Rahul remained preoccupied with his mobile phone—told the media that this was a practice they had followed for many years, and the airline would give out dividends to the shareholders similarly when it would go public. The airline has continued to give dividends thereafter, which no Indian airline has done so far.

In 2005, when the Department of Revenue Intelligence (DRI) seized three BMWs of InterGlobe Enterprises claiming that the firm violated the provision in the five-year, 1997–2002 import-export policy, under which this provision was to help designated travel agents and tour operators to use these cars for their business, Rahul was incensed. The dispute was over whether the firm could use these luxury cars as taxis and earn foreign exchange directly from them.

'Our business partners are top global businessmen, among them, the chairmen of Virgin, Accor and Cendant, the world's biggest travel services company. When they come here, should we get them a yellow-top cab or place one of these cars at their disposal? And when we do the latter, don't the cars work for our business that earn us foreign exchange?' Rahul argued in *The Times of India*.

He did not like the bad press and met Rajdeep Sardesai and various other editors, the former aide recalled. 'And I think that was the first time he met Arun Jaitley (one of the top lawyers and the former finance minister in the BJP government who died in 2019). I had told him don't react to it. And I think Arun Jaitley told him exactly that.'

'He can get vicious [sic] if his name is maligned even if they are false allegations. He wants people to think well of him all the time—which can be quite stressful. He would call whomever he can to put a stop to it. He doesn't like opposition or impolite remarks about him. He is very conscious of his reputation, he is very passionate about his babies and he is quite averse to criticism,' said the aide, adding, 'You will rarely find him admitting that he has made a mistake. He will never admit it. He has made tonnes of them. He will always defend [himself]. Maybe now with age he has changed.'

So, where's the viciousness in this?

'His viciousness is a kind of childlike viciousness. It's not the mean kind of viciousness; it is more obduracy. Like stubborn bacche who are like *hum toh nahin maanenge*, we will not have it that way and we will have it only this way,' the aide said.

An executive herself got a taste of this behaviour when she took a two-year sabbatical around the time IndiGo started because all other InterGlobe projects were suddenly put on hold with a single-minded focus on the airline. But Rahul was worried that she would join competition. She was asked to sign a non-compete agreement barring her from joining any competition for two years.

'So, when I wanted to return to InterGlobe, the conversation with Rahul wasn't very pleasant. The position offered to me was not acceptable so I extended my sabbatical. I had no other financial support; my father was ill. And then in the 2008 stock market crash, I lost a lot of money. It was a learning; a difficult part of my life,' she recalled, but was quick to add. 'It was great working for them, street smart, hard-nosed in some ways—they know their way around and how to get things done. But genuinely nice people. That's why destiny has been kind to them. They have always bounced back.'

Rahul's family—which consists of senior Bhatia, mother Pash, wife Rohini, son Madhav and daughter Sumati—is well liked by the airline professionals who have met or dealt with them. They do not throw their weight around. In an industry where senior officials are often seen helping the promoter's wife with shopping, or getting business class upgrades on other airlines, or carrying their bags or getting their immigration clearance done, etc., the Bhatia family does not expect such fawning nor do they interfere with the airline operations. They are very respectful towards all the staff.

Rohini Bhatia graciously attends the airline's annual general meeting (AGM) when needed, respectfully observing the proceedings. She spearheads the airline's CSR activities. She is also very religious.

'Bhatia parivar is religious-minded. *Sab log pure hawan mein baithte hain aur mantra padhte hain*,' says Acharya Karan Dev Shastri, referring to the Gayatri Mantra that is read at the beginning and the Shanti Paath that happens towards the end at their Chhatarpur home often. '*Bade sahab chutkule sunaa kar anandit kar dete hain*.'

Acharya Shastri, I found out, has been doing these hawans for the family for the past twenty-five years.

Rohini Bhatia organizes the hawan, especially on Madhav's and Sumati's birthdays. All the offices of InterGlobe do hawans during Diwali. The Bhatias follow the Arya Samaj style of religious ceremonies, which relies on oblations to fire and chanting mantras and not the more popular deity worship prevalent in most of India.

When the first A320 plane came, Acharya Karan Dev Shastri recalls that he was ready to do a hawan in front of the brand new Airbus. However, the Delhi Airport officials told them that hawan was not allowed in their premises. A disappointed Acharya Shastri had to console himself by applying a tilak on the aircraft and chanting mantras.

'Cockpit *mein Om likha pehle, baad mein chandan aur haldi se tilak laga diya. Hawan nahin ho sakta hai airport pe*,' he says regretfully. IndiGo's senior vice president for aircraft acquisition, financing and treasury, Krishan Bhargava, distributed ladoos and flowers. Shastri remembers with a lot of excitement the first flight on the new aircraft in the company of Rahul Bhatia and Arun Nehru.

Every new aircraft still goes through a similar ceremony, with a small change though. IndiGo realized that the 'Om' marked on the cockpit was getting erased soon after the puja ceremony. Therefore, the airline started buying and pasting Om stickers in the cockpits.

'*Pehle plane se 100 plane tak toh maine hi kiya. Uske baad bhi kayi karwaye*,' Shastri told me, as perhaps the only priest in the country who would have presided over the induction of one-seventh of all planes inducted in India so far.

Will Rahul's two children follow their father's footsteps and take over the business at some point?

After completing International Baccalaureate (IB) from the British School in Delhi in 2018, Madhav interned with Airbus in Bengaluru, learning about aircraft modelling, simulation and overview of flight management systems. He visited manufacturers of Airbus A320 ancillaries and components. A copy of Madhav's résumé shows that he has an interest in cars and has dabbled in aviation.

In 2017, he interned with IndiGo's engineering department, toning up on the theory of aerodynamics, wings and theory of flight. He also went hands-on with the A320's start-up procedures, engines and repair, including overnight line-maintenance sessions. He skis at Whistler, Canada and Gstaad, Switzerland, and teaches skiing to young children as a part-time instructor during the season there.

He has also written lyrics for over fifty songs; has a passion for automobile engines; has nosed around in a few one-of-a-kind vintage-car garages in Europe; and participated in several prestigious golf tournaments in Delhi. Like Rahul, who took the firm out of the travel agency business to the core, whether the next generation will take it even higher or to another core—manufacturing planes or engines, remains to be seen. In his early twenties, Madhav has in the summer of 2024 been attached to the offices of InterGlobe Enterprises CEO Aditya Pande and is often in the office and in most key meetings. He is also seen taking a keen interest in Archer Aviation's electric planes project under which InterGlobe plans to provide urban air taxi services in India over the coming years.

It has taken nearly thirty years for Rahul Bhatia to turn his dream into a reality. A dream that is now worth over Rs 1.3 lakh crore and over 350-aircraft strong.

'But we have a long way to go,' he says, 'a long way. We are such a small company. In the map of global aviation, we are a tiny, little speck. Airlines fly 600 planes.'

That too may just happen—by the end of this decade—when Bhatia turns seventy years old.

6

The Cabin Crew

Lalu Prasad Yadav and Nitish Kumar—the former an ex-chief minister of Bihar and the latter the incumbent at the time of writing this and often staunch rivals—were travelling together on a Delhi–Patna IndiGo flight sometime in 2010.

While Nitish Kumar had fastened his seatbelt, Yadav, in his trademark white kurta-pyjama, was not willing to fasten the seat belt.

The airline crew told the flight was about to take off shortly but he paid no heed.

Eventually one of them decided to bell the cat.

"'*Sir aap seat belt laga lijiye … aap se chaar bar bol chukke hain hum,*" recalls Manu Rana who was with IndiGo for a decade, first as flight crew and then as a crew auditor who kept standing there looking at him. "*Aap ko strictly bol rahi hun. Aapki safety ke liye bol rahi hun. Please laga lijiye.*"

Lalu Prasad Yadav, a VIP, realized that Rana will not budge now till he fastened the seat belt. One of India's colourful and headstrong politicians had to yield and enable the flight to take off.

A few months later, on a Mumbai-Delhi flight, a person asked for a bottle of water from a young stewardess. After supplying the bottle, she asked for the payment of Rs 40. He claimed his bag was in the overhead bin and assured her that he would pay later. She went to him half-an-hour later and requested for the money. The passenger again asked her to come later.

When the captain announced the landing, she again went to him. Instead of paying up, the passenger got angry and started to vituperate, 'I know what kind of families you girls come from, I know your background.'

The stewardess was humiliated. She started to weep. She realized all eyes were on her. In a low tone she first said thank you for the money and apologized if she had done something wrong.

And then said, 'But Sir, my father is a retired colonel from the Indian Army, my brother is a senior inspector in UP Police and I have done law. So, I hope you know my background.'

The passengers around her started to applaud her.

While alighting from the aircraft, the same passenger walked up to her and apologized.

The life of the airline crew is not as easy or glamorous as it appears to those looking in, especially in a LCC as IndiGo where efficiency is critical for profits. One has to handle not only VIPs but will encounter passengers with prejudices and pre-conceived notions and many first-time travellers.

It begins when you click on IndiGo's career page to apply for the position of a cabin crew and, effectively, the face of the airline.

Over the years, IndiGo has become India's cabin-crew training assembly line. The airline has around 10,000 crew members for its fleet of over 350 planes. It hires around 500 cabin crew every month to sustain its every expanding operation. The requirement also covers attrition—around 150 crew, mostly the crème de la crème, leave the airline every month. They are absorbed by not only local airlines but Qatar Airways, Etihad Airways, Emirates Airlines etc., as they offer better pay, perks and lifestyle. Since 2022, Air India, now privatized and under the Tata Group, has become the latest magnet for many of these crew members.

Attrition at such nightmarish levels has led IndiGo to start a new training facility called iFly in Gurugram, which is now being expanded even further. It churns out trained cabin crew by the hundreds; a far cry from the era when cabin crew were selected by Bollywood superstars such as Sharmila Tagore and Jaya Bachchan for Air India.

IndiGo's selection process is a hard grind. It has three rounds and the focus of the airline is to ensure it selects candidates who can be moulded to its needs and not necessarily someone who looks pretty. Once selected, the airline provides them with free fifteen-day stay in Gurugram after which they need to take up their own accommodation for the three-month long training. Free pick-up and drop-off are provided all through.

The three months are nothing less than a military boot camp for many of the candidates. 'It is so intense I almost thought of quitting it,' said Antara (name changed on request), one of the cabin crew who passed out in late 2023.

Why did she think of quitting?

Among the many reasons, the main one was the modules that had to do with customer handling. In this module, the airline trainers can get really rough with crew presenting themselves as angry customers (why is my pre-booked meal not here?) and test how the crew react and their patience levels.

'Girls did not cry, but they panicked, really panicked,' Antara said.

In early 2023, a video went viral in which a passenger could be heard shouting at an IndiGo stewardess and was heard saying that she was a servant to which the crew retorted with 'I am an employee, but I am not your servant.'

Undoubtedly, the passenger was obnoxious. Many supported the crew and hailed her on social media. But a few others said that the crew is trained to handle, precisely, such situations and should not become 'hysterical' the way the stewardess in the video had done, as one crew Tina (name changed) put it.

'Even if the passenger was nasty, there are so many policies that support you. IndiGo has such open and supportive policies that they would have supported her and filed a FIR the moment they landed,' Tina said. 'How hysterical had she become; she could have slapped that passenger if the other crew had not taken her away.'

It was possible, said Tina, who has handled such situations herself at IndiGo, that the passenger was having a bad day. The stewardess perhaps should have tried to explain to him the problem. If the passenger was still not amenable, then the next step was to apologize and give him something close to his expectations. If he would not still calm down, she should have given him the feedback form and the IndiGo customer complaints email address to send it to.

I did check with people at IndiGo on what happened after the I-am-not-your-servant episode. I was told that the crew member was extended the required support. However, she was also sent for an anger management module later because, while the airline would defend her and itself publicly, it did not want a repetition of the episode and make it an example that other crew members follow. An IndiGo spokesperson confirmed, 'the concerned crew member was provided professional support and counselling' and 'rostered back on active duty a few days thereafter'.

The drill to instil discipline in the young crew members—who maybe fresh out of high school or college—starts from the time they join iFly. Some perhaps find it extreme.

'There they are treated like school kids. You know like in an army school?' says Natasha (name changed on request) a senior in-flight executive who worked at IndiGo and now flies with another Indian airline, 'I have seen the hiring process—nothing matters to them as long as they can make them learn to talk. They don't need very headstrong people. And smart enough people who can challenge things logically—they won't hire them'.

The trainee crew have to reach on time for the training sessions and greet every person in the room. One hundred per cent attendance is compulsory. If anyone is 15 minutes late—they will mock, start a banter on her. Anyone coming habitually late will be asked to write an email explaining their tardiness. The underlying message is—if you can be late for your training, you can be late for a flight which is not acceptable.

'There is a very fine line,' Natasha says, 'if you deviate even a little bit, you have to write a lot of mails, you get relegated to the next batches. It's not a very nice environment for training. Most of them are freshers and they get shaken as they have not seen anything like this. So, they just give in altogether.'

There are multiple modules they need to get through. Those who fail to clear even one are often sent back to a fresh batch till they get it right. One of the reasons is that the crew has to clear not only IndiGo internal exams but also the aviation regulator DGCA's exams.

Grooming also forms an integral part of this training. During the training, IndiGo insists that not one even a hair should be out of place when they are on-board. Not even a single strand should fall over their face. Many cabin crew are compelled to buy hair spray at their own cost and spray liberally to keep their hair intact, held with the help of hair pins placed in designated places. Only two hair pins can be visible. This precision is important because the hair has to stay smooth for almost 8 hours. The grooming in-charge would even come and touch the hair to ensure it's perfect. Crew have a choice of four-five hair styles or a hair bun. They can use a wig which saves them time. Recently, the airline has discontinued use of wigs since they were very high-maintenance. Now nearly 90 per cent of its crew sport hair buns and the rest keep their hair short.

'The current look needs to change. This generation wants trendy uniform and dress code. This 60s look needs to go,' said an IndiGo official who prefers to remain anonymous.

Daily use of hair spray and gels, both full of harmful chemicals, are known to damage hair. This is a major grouse that the crew voice. 'I see a lot of crew, when they remove their wigs, are bald or have bald patches,' Natasha recalls. 'The trainers know all these things, but nothing is done. I have had people, who have flown for six to seven years, tell me that their hair partition has now become permanent.'

Rana said while this is true, she herself has applied gels for 18 years. Using water-based gels reduces the damage. 'Some crew even go for lip pigmentation, permanent hair colouring, Botox injections, nail extensions too. Are they not harmful?' she asks.

IndiGo has a signature eye make-up style called winged eyeliner. This is meant to 'create a geometric, bold and defined flick around the outer corner of the eye' so as to make it stand out. It is mandatory for all the girls; during the training the grooming head makes them line their eyes fifty times if needed till they get it right. This overwhelms some of the trainees.

The training then shifts to 'suggested verbiage'. The crew is required to cram everything that need to be spoken with the passengers during the entire flight cycle. The airline has listed every conceivable question that can be asked by the passenger and has prepared scripted answers for each. The girls have to cram all these answers and regurgitate them to pass their tests to graduate.

If a passenger asks for a newspaper, there is a standard four-line paragraph the crew has to say. If the person sitting next to this person also asks for a newspaper you must repeat this paragraph again.

'If there is a question,' Natasha says, 'which needs an answer as simple as "No sir, we don't carry newspapers", they can't often say so because they have to say the entire paragraph. Sometimes the person will stare back at you as if wondering "Why such a long answer?"'

I went through IndiGo's extensive training modules and found several examples of suggested verbiage. If a passenger asks, why don't you provide newspaper, the crew should say, 'It is one of our efforts to maintain on-time performance. We do not provide newspaper as the winding up of the newspaper circulation post flight will affect our quick turnaround time,' or 'As we do not have newspapers, allow me to check if some other passenger has a spare newspaper or has finished reading one, I will get it for you.'

If a passenger is complaining and the crew sees in the manifest that he is a VIP (very important person)/CIP (commercially important person)/FF (frequent flyer), they are required to make special efforts for service recovery using phrases like, 'Sir, Madam/Mr. Last name, you are very special to us and we value your feedback.' Service recovery is a term used for offering something extra—say a hot beverage and a cookie—to the passenger if he or she is upset. Sometimes the crew is generous enough to give their own meal to passengers.

In a 2012 flight, a lady, travelling with a four-year-old child, asked Rana the price of a sandwich. She said it was Rs 250. The lady hesitated; perhaps it was too expensive for her. Her child was adamant. Rana was then called by a passenger sitting on the first row. It was the former Maharashtra chief minister, Sharad Pawar. He had overheard the conversation and requested that his meal be given to the kid. The child was elated.

During the training the trainee crew get a monthly stipend of around Rs 15,000. There is a graduation ceremony after the three months following which they are deemed ready to go on the flight under the watch of the lead cabin crew. The salary is Rs 35,000 and based on 'claps' received from their colleagues on an app used internally and other performance yardsticks this goes up to around Rs 70,000 after a year or two, when they have a chance to become the lead crew.

Antara, however, plans to be with IndiGo only for a year and, after soaking in all the experience, will join some international airline by her own admission.

'The training and grooming really changes you. It is very tough but you see the change between how you looked and behaved when you joined versus what you are now,' she adds.

However, even the one year would be not a bed of roses. Flying duties are not easy. The reporting times keep changing from dawn to dusk, upsetting the biological clock and taking a toll on a crew's body. Besides, the attendance process for a flight at IndiGo is narrowly choreographed with very little wiggle room and tolerance for errors. The process has six-stages starting with pre-flight preparation, boarding, door-close, take-off, descent, and landing.

At the pre-flight stage, the crew members receive their cab details one day in advance. If the flight is after 7 p.m. or early in the morning, a security guard accompanies them in the car. All the cars are GPS-enabled. The crew should be fully ready when they enter the cabs. They should not apply any make-up inside for fear of staining the cars. IndiGo insists on strict cleanliness and pilots, also transported in similar cabs, are asked to often audit these cabs.

Their bank accounts are credited with Rs 2,000 before every flight. To save time during the on-board sales to passengers, the crew themselves should arrange small denomination currency notes—50 notes of Rs 10, and the rest in denominations of rupees 50s, 100s and 200s.

Reporting time at the airport is 80 minutes and at the plane 40 minutes before the flight departure. On every flight, all the cabin crew must carry an extra pair of stockings because they may get ruined by getting caught on the seats or meal trolleys; an extra wristwatch; and a calculator in their bags. The watch is for timing any safety or medical emergency, and the calculator is to ensure not a penny to be taken from the passenger is missed. It lends accuracy and speed while calculating in-flight sales.

The airline is very strict when it comes to leaves. If a cabin crew member requests for leave beyond two days, a fitness certificate from a doctor should be produced. They should come to the airport to be examined, or a doctor is despatched to their home. A similar check is mandatory for Diwali, New Year's Eve etc., when leaves are not allowed because of spike in travel demand. All hands must be on the deck.

Once on the plane, they have to ensure that the *Hello 6E* in-flight magazine is well-placed and replenished if missing; window shades are open in winters and closed in summers; tray tables are clean and closed; and food carts have been uplifted and tallied. Any discrepancy in food and beverage counts should be notified immediately.

They also have to ensure that the toilet seats are clean and dry; the sinks are clean and dry; the hot water in running; soap bottle is minimum 60 per cent full; waste-bin flap is spring loaded; flush is operational; toilet floor is clean and dry; mirror is wiped; mop is available and stored discreetly; hand tissues and toilet paper are present in sufficient quantity; and toilet-roll ends are folded in a triangular shape. Trays of water in cups should be kept ready in the galleys, in case customers request for it after boarding.

The second stage, boarding, starts 35 minutes before the scheduled departure. The drill is a four-point greeting that includes standing in poise, making eye contact, greeting with a smile, directing passengers to their seats and assisting them with their luggage. They have to profile the passengers identifying special-needs customers such as differently abled, unaccompanied minors, elderly people, expectant mothers, passengers carrying infants or anyone with a medical condition.

This is not easy. Accosting a lady who appears to be pregnant has to be done very carefully. They should be on their haunches, if the passenger is on the aisle seat. They should first seek their permission with, 'May I please ask you a personal question?' and only then, 'Are you pregnant?' They have to avoid saying 'Pregnant by any chance', 'Are you in the family way?', 'Are you carrying?' and similar lines.

If the passenger affirms, they have to congratulate and continue with the special briefing for pregnant women. If she denies, then apologize, 'I am extremely sorry for the confusion. Thank you for your time. Have a nice flight.'

If an obese lady is mistaken for a pregnant woman, the crew member has to immediately apologize. If the person is upset, they have to say, 'There is some confusion as I was informed that a pregnant lady would be seated here, and I have to brief the lady on some safety aspects. Maybe she is seated somewhere else. I once again apologize.'

Similarly, if they see a baby sitting on the tray table, they have to politely build rapport and request 'Kindly hold your baby' as 'the tray table is designed for food and beverage and if it breaks, the baby may get hurt.'

Before take-off, they have to also ensure everyone has fastened their seat belts; the window shades are open; and all overhead bins are closed. After arming the doors, they have to remove their hats and their high-heeled shoes in the toilets and not in the galley and wear cabin shoes for faster cabin service and for swift action in case of any safety issues such as emergency evacuations.

During the safety briefing, the crew is taught to look four times to the left and five times to the right while making safety announcements and to synchronize with other crew members. This process too came about as many stewardesses were not making eye contact with passengers and instead were looking at the floor or at the ceiling.

The third stage starts after take-off when they have to switch on the cabin lights, take refreshment requests from the pilots, play the pre-recorded announcement, prepare food carts and switch on the boilers for coffee and tea.

The carts are then to be rolled out from the forward galley five minutes and from the back galley three minutes after the crew members are released for services. The entire service is timed and has to be completed in approximately 45–50 minutes for a passenger load of 180 for a two-hour Delhi-Mumbai or similar flights. This is expanded or compressed for longer or shorter duration flights. During service, they have to inform customers when pouring hot water and hold the glasses and cans from the bottom and not at the rim.

The crew is also required to be aware of the food options available on that day's flight and have to suggest, using the passenger's last name only, new choices or personal recommendations while ensuring IndiGo logo always faces the customer. They are also trained for sales. Even if you decline something first, they will say, 'If not poha, how about a cookie sir, it's very popular ... and some coconut water to go with it?'

The crew members receive incentives too for these sales and this is jointly divided between all of them later.

During the flight they also have to keep an eye out for unruly passengers. Typically, they are trained to follow a five-step process—first give a verbal warning; if the person does not stop, give him a stern, second warning and ask him to stop or he may be offloaded. If the disruptive behaviour continues, a red warning card has to be given, and five passengers should be requested to sign as witnesses. While handing over the warning card, if the passenger does not read it, it be read aloud to him. An uncontrolled, unruly passenger is handed over to the security as the flight lands.

Immediately after the food and beverage service, they have to commence trash clearance with the help of a small plastic bag. They also have to ensure that toilet is clean after every 2-3 customers and every time before a lady goes in. They have to return or take any cash that is due and carry water bottles for sale after every ten minutes.

This is followed by a round of customer interaction where each cabin crew—there are typically four of them—have to interact with a minimum of five passengers in their respective areas of the plane. During this session, the stewardesses ask if the passenger had a comfortable flight and she may talk about the destination he or she is travelling to, whether he or she is a frequent visitor, or about the book the person is reading.

During the fifth stage, the cabin crew prepare for landing which starts 20 minutes before touchdown—the usual pilot announcement that every flyer is familiar with. Now the crew has to move quickly to make sure carts are stowed, braked and latched; boilers are switched off; water and hot water flasks are empty; and there are no loose items on the galley top. They have to again take another round to ensure that the windows are open, mobiles are switched off, seat belts fastened and trays latched.

During a transit stop, to minimize the turnaround time, the cabin crew also has to do what is called pit-stop duties that include placing seat belts in place; putting down the window shades for 1–7 and 24–30 rows; leaving trays open that are dirty for cleaners to clean; ensuring no trash is in seat pockets and replacing any dirty headrest.

Once the aircraft lands, they have to wear their hats and open the door. They have to allow cleaners to enter the plane first to clean both the washrooms. The cabin crew have to control and hold back the passengers to allow the cleaner's entry. This saves time and ensures faster turnaround of the plane. They have to then wish goodbye to the passengers as they leave.

During the post-flight stage, at the airport office, every crew member has to report their sales in the IndiGo sales portal and submit a flight report on passenger handling, safety, first-aid, and any on-board incident or unruly passengers.

They then get ready for another flight or head to the hotel for rest. The crew typically does around four domestic flights a day. At the airport while waiting for the cab the stewardesses should not be seen putting their hands in their pockets or sitting on their bags.

Crew Auditors

In 2007, the airline started a team of crew auditors called e-force, chosen from senior long-service crew members. They were put on flights as normal passengers to watch how the crew performed through the entire flight.

Rahul himself is an excellent auditor and this was his idea. At the time of the launch flights in 2006, he often sent in his own observations to the top management. On one such flight, according to a copy of an email trail that I reviewed, he observed that the in-flight service started thirty-five minutes after the aircraft was airborne, because apparently the crew chose to eat first.

'Wonder who the real customer is?' Rahul wrote in an email to the top IndiGo leadership.

He also noted that due to regular visits by the cockpit crew, the front galley curtains were drawn for more than half of the duration of the flight at the cost of inconveniencing customers; the lead attendant was not at the base of the aircraft checking on passenger boardings; and a crew member was too plump. He also gave technical inputs—the engines were at full-throttle far too long after take-off; the landing gear was let down too early prior to touch-down; and 'the captain never came out to bid customers good-bye during the disembarking process.'

The message was clear: everything was being monitored minutely at the highest level and departmental heads could not just relax in their corporate offices. Even a cursory look of the IndiGo checklist makes you realize that the moment the crew lands at the airport their every move is being monitored.

The nearly 100-point checklist includes everything from grooming as per 'IndiGo standards' including make-up, eyebrows, waxing unwanted hair, hair length and wig condition etc., to the uniform—which cannot be too tight; belt should not be hanging down; tunic buttons should not be discoloured; the uniform should be well ironed and there should be no stains. The crew is also advised to use only a mild deodorant or perfume.

The crew has to disciplined, courteous and respectful not merely to peers, but also to base staff and subordinates. The crew should also not be seen holding loud conversations amongst themselves or use colloquialisms such as Hi/Hello, Ya/Sure, Veg/Non-Veg during the entire flight. Among other things, they are also marked for following the eight-point lavatory cleanliness, on the gentle closing of doors, on the response to passenger calls, and on the use of suggestive and link-selling sales techniques.

At the end of the flight, the auditor gives 'developmental feedback' to the crew with the lead in attendance. If there is a safety related issue, such as a crew member sleeping on the jump seat, the briefing will be done in front of the base manager.

It is possible that out of, say, 10 points raised by the auditor, the crew member had explanations for five. In that case she is only marked for those five in the submitted report. Nevertheless, these briefings can be intimidating and sometimes demotivating; the crew does not look forward to them; the auditors create a dread in them. IndiGo also issues caution letters for repeated deviations. If a cabin crew member gets a certain number of warnings, she is asked to leave the company.

The Culture

According to several staffers, in IndiGo people often complain against one another and carry the tale to the seniors. 'That's the culture,' says Natasha. 'I once got late for my flight and I called the airport staff to ask if they could help me check-in, but didn't get any help and was later only questioned "Why were you late?"'

The airline, says Antara, has created this as a robust feedback mechanism to know what is happening across the network. However, Rana says while IndiGo may push one towards excellence it should not be to such an extent that one has a breakdown. To take care of the crew's mental health, the airline has professional counsellors with whom they can talk privately.

Natasha says she also did not like the 'Hail IndiGo' culture at the airline. 'People actually start "bleeding blue" because they have been filled with this excessive spirit of IndiGo all the time—oh we are the best, we make so much money, we are growing so fast, etc. There are seminars and town halls, and they get together, and they praise IndiGo there. Every month or so, they will get together and sing praises of the airline. And IndiGo hands out recognition awards with such pomp that they look like some Nobel Prize.'

At the same time, people complain that while "Hail IndiGo" gets talked up, they are often unable to speak their minds. The only time they listen to the possibility of bringing in any change is if someone comes up with a cost-saving idea, Natasha feels.

The airline, for example, rewarded a manager who made an elaborate presentation on how if the on-board 3 kg steel equipment box is replaced with a simple bag, it would lead to a certain amount of fuel savings annually. Another nominated crew member, who had saved someone's life while returning from a flight, did not receive an award, but in another instance, when a corpse with blood everywhere was found in the luggage hold of a plane that landed in a North-East airport, the staff who cleaned it in 25 minutes and enabled the flight to take off quickly was handed an award.

Pilferage

Food is an area where major pilferage happens with many airlines. Some cabin crew members take the money from the sales and do not credit the proceeds to the airline. There are a few modus operandi for this.

Many corporate customers get complimentary meals but they often refuse the pre-paid meal because they have already had dinner or lunch, or it is a short flight. A few dislike eating on early morning flights. The crew member can tick such meals as eaten by the passenger it is intended for and sell it to another customer and keep the money. Some cabin crew members sell a sachet of coffee or green tea from the crew quota and collect Rs 100 for it.

A few cabin crew members buy at the open market prices the same brand of cup noodles, coconut water, etc., that are sold on-board and sell them to passengers at the airline's inflated prices. The Rs 50 Maggi Cuppa Noodles in the market costs around Rs 250 on the flight. The airline's stocks are then shown unsold. For passengers, the only way to check if the noodles or similar products are that of the airline is if it reads, 'Specially packaged for' followed by the name of the airline.

Apart from such individual pilferages, there are organized mafias that operate in collusion with some caterers. On a Delhi–Mumbai–Kolkata flight, for example, there will be some pre-booked meals. On the first sector, Delhi–Mumbai, some passengers may not eat their pre-booked meal, and some of the for-sale meals will remain unsold. The crew saves these unclaimed pre-booked and unsold meals. When fresh meals are loaded at Mumbai for those boarding to Kolkata, the unclaimed pre-booked and unsold meals from the previous sector will be sold first, before selling the new ones. Even if ten old meals are sold this way, on a flight with around 180 people, the cabin crew member can earn an average of Rs 3,000 per flight.

'I have seen people not withdrawing salaries because of this. Sometimes they make Rs 20,000 a month from such sales,' said Sarah (name changed), a seasoned cabin crew member.

Airlines have tried to crackdown on such revenue loss by doing surprise checks when they land after their flight but because the amounts involved in food-sales are substantial, the mafia in some airlines has even developed moles within the airline. The moles alert the crew on which flight they will see a pat down. So, one among the cabin crew quickly gets off the flight and heads to a washroom or to some eatery at the airport, deposits this extra cash with them, and then goes to dispatch where they are checked. Nothing is found. Then another cabin crew member goes and collects this deposited cash and gives it to the team concerned.

One of the reasons why some cabin crew indulge in such malfeasance is because their standard of living changes very swiftly once inside an airline. They also have pilots as flying companions who, having had to spend a high amount on their licence and aircraft type rating, are paid Rs 3–9lakh a month. Pilots and cabin crew members are often called 'EMI Kings' because they splurge on the latest iPhones that cost Rs1 lakh, high-priced cars, spa treatments, etc. While pilots can afford such luxuries, most cabin crew members cannot match up and some are tempted to find additional sources of money to maintain their lifestyles.

Cold Behaviour

Given that flying is not an easy profession and can take a toll on the youngsters especially because of the odd hours, some passengers of IndiGo complain that the airline's crew comes across as robotic.

Was this intentionally built in? And if so, what was the genesis of this? In 2005, IndiGo brought in expats to set up the airline and included Shan Iwanicki who had worked as a cabin crew with PanAmerican Airways (Pan Am) and is now with the US aviation regulator FAA as a Cabin Safety Inspector (CSI). Pan Am gave its cabin crew new recruits six weeks of training back in 1989, and this formed the bedrock of IndiGo's training in many ways. While Iwanicki tried to mellow some of the tough training given by that airline, the legacy remains.

'I was scared to death during the training,' says Iwanicki, referring to her training at Pan Am. 'You couldn't breathe wrong. I brought a lot of that to the IndiGo training, albeit softened. I wasn't mean to my girls. I thought we could have fun and keep the personal and the professional separate.'

Iwanicki's priority was to pick girls ready to work hard. Rahul himself would meet every candidate who was being hired then. 'If the candidates came from another carrier, we spent more time with them because when you hire experienced people, they bring a lot to the table, but they also bring bad habits. When we knew a flight attendant was coming in from SpiceJet, Air India, or Air Sahara, we would zero in on them,' Iwanicki says.

These girls could expect to face questions, such as the following: 'This is a new airline, we are trying to create a new image and low cost too means being professional. How are you going to do that? Have there been situations when you have lost your temper? How would you define good and bad customer service in the airline sector? Can you give examples of both? What would you do in a situation where everyone's life is in danger due to some technical fault and the pilot asks you to inform the passengers what are the necessary actions to be taken when the danger is confirmed?'

IndiGo was aware that as a LCC it needed a crew that could deal with people from all strata of the society unlike Kingfisher Airlines which was very choosy in its early days. 'So basic indoctrination had modules for handling all kinds of passengers—first-time traveller, frequent flyer, business traveller, grandmother, children, etc.,' says Iwanicki. 'I designed the course to give access to everyone the same kind of customer service. Additional ways to identify the first-time traveller were also put into the modules. The cabin crew knew that it was vital to be in the aisles continuously, speaking to the passengers, understanding their needs so that they could offer verbal assurances about the aircraft, how safe it is, speak about IndiGo, the destinations we have lined up, and its future.'

In some cases, IndiGo came up with slogans on the crew's posture in the aircraft which flight attendants could easily recall. 'During the Pan Am training, we spent two weeks on service, on how to stand when facing the passenger—never reach across with your arm in front of their face, use your opposite arm, so that you are not right in front of their face, serving the women first, etc. I made sure I didn't bring bad service practices from other carriers,' Iwanicki said.

Keeping everything in sync was a top priority. 'Everything was standardized, not that I wanted them to look like robots, but I wanted the information to be built into them from day one. This helped us in accomplishing our vision—ensuring that people wanted to fly IndiGo even though they had to pay for things on-board the aircraft. It was all in the delivery. How do I sell these cookies? And despite that, how do we get people to say it was a great flight, not that I just took the worst flight in the world. We asked them to smile a lot. They won't remember they had to pay for the cookies if they remember smiling faces and a clean aircraft.'

A clean aircraft was always an obsession with Rahul who would send emails when he would see sloppiness. 'So,' said Iwanicki, 'I had incorporated a process that every time a passenger used the lavatory, a flight attendant needed to go in, clean it, and make sure there was no tissue on the floor, or water splashed on the mirror, and it was all tidy.' Rahul was particular that no liquid should spill on a passenger while being poured by an attendant. IndiGo also introduced voice training for pilots because Rahul found all of them were making announcements in different accents.

How did the use of so much verbiage really began? An awkward situation led them to instituting it. 'The need arose when we started to sell water on board. In India, even to an enemy you give free water. We had to sell the concept and so Bruce (Ashby, first CEO of IndiGo) said let's come up with a term, some sort of a campaign or acronym to sell it. That triggered the need for verbiage,' said an IndiGo official who asked not to be named.

After Iwanicki left in 2008, IndiGo took this practice to a whole new level under the new President Aditya Ghosh who focussed immensely on iFly. Soon just about everything was included in the syllabus and crammed.

'The regimented system came in late. We told them it's not a production floor and one can't have FAQs for every situation,' recalls another executive from the early years, 'but they went ahead anyway.'

Antara says that the regimented system works to some extent for IndiGo because the airline is getting crew from different states of India with different thought processes and accents.

'To cut down the errors, to avoid them going blank in front of customers, they have put in verbiage. Now it is in their blood. If there is something out of the course, they might just smile or just leave because they are so used to it now,' she adds.

Another person said it was time to let the crew think on their own feet. 'What if a passenger asks a follow up question after you have said your lines about fetching the newspaper from another passenger? Training needs to be redefined.'

Another area that needs improvement is how rostering treats the crew members. For example, the crew is asked to go out of their way for sake of the company. However, if they do not want to accept certain flights, they are often told to report sick and that there is no 'flexibility'.

The airline did accept some suggestions in 2019 after a lot of feedback. It has tried to cover this 'robotic behaviour' by introducing new modules. Thanking the customer in the last round is part of that initiative.

During Covid-19, as part of the cost-cutting move, the airline discontinued its e-force team of auditors and asked 8-9 people to leave. Many feel that this has made the crew bolder. Some of the recent passenger related incidents could be a result of this freedom with no fear of surprise checks. 'Earlier, the cabin crew used to behave and stay within limits, as they used to think every second person could be an auditor,' in Antara's view.

Without any freshness being introduced, the crew culture has stagnated and has brought in complacency. 'Unlike Jet Airways and Kingfisher Airlines, there is no emotional bonding with IndiGo but only practical bonding,' Antara notes. The work life though tough is simplified as everything is processes-oriented and there are apps for everything from travel to cabs to leaves.

This practical bonding became visible when hundreds reported sick in the peak summer travel time in June 2022 because they all had decided to take a crack at the Tata-owned Air India crew interviews. Nearly 55 per cent of the IndiGo flights were delayed because of this. Industry-wide this was seen as a brave move, given that the airline has no unions and the pilots—who are typically a much stronger group and capable of such industrial action—had not succeeded in doing something similar, despite both the groups being on Covid-19-induced pay cuts then.

All this perhaps explains the high attrition rate which has often soared to as much as 30 per cent at IndiGo. It could aggravate further with the Air India-Vistara consolidation, more international flights and the famous Tata legacy for benevolence towards their staff.

As for Lalu Prasad Yadav, the real reason why he was not fastening his seat belt was because of another kind of fear.

'*Ab hamara kurta kharab hua ... utarte hi humko Rabri ji* (wife of Yadav) *puchengi ... hum unko apka number denge aur bolenge kya kiya aapne,*' Yadav told Rana. She smiled and replied, '*Main unko jawab de dungi sir, magar abhi aap apni safety ke liye belt laga lijiye.*'

7

Brand IndiGo

In 2006, when the airline had just taken off, Rahul found himself seated next to one of his pilots who was flying on a staff ticket. As the seat belts signs went off and meal carts rolled in, the pilot choose a sandwich. After eating it, he wiped his hands with a tissue and dropped it on the floor.

At some point the pilot started a conversation with his co-passenger and asked him what he did for a living?

'I am the owner of this airline,' said Rahul, according to a senior InterGlobe executive who has worked closely with him but chooses to be anonymous. 'The guy bent and picked up the tissue.'

Rahul, who moves around in a Jaquar Land Rover, is a stickler for cleanliness. He is also a foodie who enjoys his Raj Kachori as much as Rocket Salad. Which is why, while Gangwal was weaving his magic by making rock-solid aircraft contracts for IndiGo, Rahul focussed on the brand identity of India's largest airline, including its food menu. The menus evolved overtime, an indication of not only how IndiGo has changed but also how India's tastes have changed.

When LCCs started in the US in 1970s, they caused various apprehensions among travellers. Passengers would call up and ask, 'Do your pilots have licences? Do you land at the airport? Do we have to bring our own chairs?' Some passengers actually showed up at the airport with chairs.

In India, when the concept of LCC arrived with Capt. Gopinath's Air Deccan, it again drew a lot of attention. The airline offered dirt-cheap tickets to wean first-time travellers from Indian Railways which dominated long-distance travel. Air Deccan had decided to adopt free seating. This meant in smaller airports people would even run to the aircraft to get a good seat. This urgency ensured that the aircraft flew more; the more you sweat the asset, higher is the revenue. However, this also meant that there were fewer Air Deccan executives to remind passengers that their flight was leaving. Free seating created lot of commotion at airports as people ran to take seats like kids placing their bags in the school bus.

When IndiGo was launched, it did not want to be known for such chaos. It wanted to position itself between Air Deccan and the more luxurious Kingfisher Airlines which called its passengers guests. IndiGo wanted to be a LCC but without yelling out it was one. It wanted to be home to both the aspirational, but cost-conscious, middle-class traveller and also a darling of the high-paying corporate travellers. Getting tagged with the word poor or cheap, like Tatas realized with their small car Nano much later, was never a good idea.

This had to reflect in the brand. IndiGo had sought creative pitches in 2005, a year before it started, with a relatively small budget of around Rs 8 crore. Most big names, including Mudra, Lowe, Grey, O&M, McCann-Erickson, JWT, Percept H, Leo Burnett and Everest, showed interest though none of them made the final cut. Perhaps they were not impressive enough or were too expensive for a start-up LCC.

A small agency called 'A' however had no such hang-ups. 'We were out on holiday in separate places when somebody called up saying a new airline was being launched, it had an exciting team, and we had to go and see them. I think we missed a lot of the initial pitch. We came back from our holidays and popped in to see Rahul [Bhatia] with almost no advertisements in hand,' says Mohit Jayal who ran 'A' with creative head Sunil Vysyaprath and had just a handful accounts with them including Incredible India and Royal Enfield.

Jayal and Sunil entered the IndiGo conference room in Gurugram's DLF Corporate Park to pitch for the airline. The room had the entire top leadership of IndiGo, who had spent half their lives chasing planes, or chasing companies that flew planes.

The presentation was simple. The duo told the audience that they imagined themselves as passengers who had just landed from a train ride from Dehradun to Delhi.

'We took with us a customer experience cycle chart—from the time the customer is at the railway station where they first see the airline's poster, to when they log on to the website, to when they arrive at the airport, when they get X-rayed, when they get tagged, to when they board the plane, to when they see the merchandise on-board the flight,' says Jayal. 'They are all very receptive and it was an unusual pitch because we were talking to people who had been there, done that.'

A lot of the understanding of how to pitch for an airline's account came from Jayal and Sunil's experience of flying across the world.

'I think we had a massive lead over everyone else because we are obsessed with civil and military aviation. We also fly a lot for work—US, Brazil and what have you. And we try and take as many different flights as we can. What for all the other people is commute, for us it's a time to keep eyes open, ears open. It's an audit all the time as a passenger,' Jayal says, 'They really liked it. They were like, if passenger experience turns you on, it turns us on as well. From there on, we became their creative thinking-arm.'

Being a 'creative thinking-arm' meant they not only put up hoardings for IndiGo, and made television commercials and animated movies, but also came up with innovative biscuit tins on-board their flights.

'It's a different approach. It was a big collaborative effort. We were so close to them that proactivity is guaranteed. If someone calls me and says I hate IndiGo, I can't stand it. I won't sleep at night because it's our baby too. So, it was a good relationship, and it got the best out of us,' Jayal says.

IndiGo started by creating a new catchy brand language to cut through the clutter of other airlines. Instead of saying, 'Fly to Goa', the airline said, 'IndiGo to Goa'.

IndiGo management would often complain, 'Why are we not using an aircraft picture in the advertisement, aren't we an airline? Why are we not using the word "fly", when we are an airline?' The agency would then show them case studies and references of how jetBlue, Southwest Airlines and Virgin America created their brand.

The focus was not to be like the legacy carriers—Lufthansa and British Airways—but to be 'cool'. 'It's like Blackberry and iPhone. A Blackberry was like Jet Airways—stable and business-like, while iPhone is also a smartphone, but cooler, and people moved on to it,' Jayal said.

However, cool can sometimes border on being too casual. If you are landing in Delhi from London, most airlines would say it is 44 degrees Celsius outside. On the other hand, some Virgin Atlantic pilots would say, 'Well, the temperature—it's bloody hot outside.'

Similarly, during safety announcements, pilots in some LCC in the West would say, 'All our aircraft are non-smoking. If you still want to smoke, you can open the over-the-wing exit door and head for the wing, where we're doing a special screening of *Gone with the Wind*.'

Several such attempts by the duo to tempt the airline into accepting radical, fun stuff were shot down without a second hearing.

There was also a clear dislike for Air Deccan. Perhaps that ensured that IndiGo did not borrow much from it. 'I have great respect for Capt. Gopinath, but if you were flying Air Deccan, they made you feel like you were making you pay for the cheap ticket,' Sunil says, 'It's difficult to understand how buying an aircraft is not like buying a car—how do you buy such an expensive machine and make that whole experience really cheap? I never flew that airline. Whether you look at the staff, the aircraft, the samosas—everything felt unwholesome. On top of that, they went and used R.K. Laxman's The Common Man. I know many people like it. But why? Why do you have to be reminded that you are a common man?'

While the Kannur-native Sunil feels the Air Deccan brand was cheap, it created a strong pull and still remains memorable. The touch of the human element and some excellent advertising rooted in aspiration to fly gave it immense recall value. One of its advertisements, The Old Man & The Sky, was perhaps the longest TV commercial ever in India. Instead of the usual thirty seconds it was almost two minutes long and showed a Hemingwayesque story of a father-son relationship and describing how an ordinary Indian embarks on his first-ever flight. It was directed by Manoj Pillai together with cinematographer P.S. Vinod and starred actor Murali.

The advertisement starts with a village carpenter making a plane out of a wooden log for his young son. The son leaves home in a few years. The next scene shows a postman in his bicycle delivering a letter from the son. When the father opens that letter, he also finds air tickets in it. An overwhelmed father goes around the village showing those tickets. The villagers, in the next shot, gift him a small bag to travel by air, and he reluctantly reaches the airport. The last shot shows the airport staff gazing suspiciously at his bulky bag in the X-ray machine. When opened, it shows the same wooden plane he had made for his son, and he insists on taking it along. The carpenter is then shown taking his first flight. The Air Deccan tag line follows: Simplifly.

But IndiGo did not want all of that rural-to-urban play. 'People don't just want to fly, they want to fly and reach somewhere. It's not good enough to say you can fly now. That's old news. So, when we started, we said, the only thing cheap should be the ticket. Every other experience, with a little bit of thinking, can be made better. So, all of us put our personalities into the airline,' Jayal and Sunil recall telling each other.

'Rahul's personality is all over IndiGo—clean, crisp, subtle, no-nonsense, nobody knows who runs it,' Sunil says, likening IndiGo to Andhra Bhawan—a popular state-managed cafeteria in the capital, that provides sought-after food at low rate (unlike Andhra Bhawan though, many do not find IndiGo's tickets 'cheap' and sometimes they are even more expensive than the full-service airline, Air India).

'Deccan had already set precedents, but by and large, we were still talking about taking train customers to the plane, and how to overcome that barrier. So, we started work on customer touch points. We said, I am coming from Dehradun, I have gotten off the train, I am not a frequent flier, I am someone who thinks of aviation as inaccessible. I get off the train, pull out my bags, and go to a relative's place. As I step out, I see an advertisement, and it says something to me. I go home, use their computer, and see what is going on,' Jayal says, remembering how they planned customer touch points.

This was the most important stage because the customer now has to book and pay. 'How many steps till I get my ticket—five, or three, or two? Obviously, it should have the least number of steps and should be as quick as possible. Also, what did that one poster tell me that got me excited—how did it feel different from the ones before? Then, I land up at the airport with the print-out of the ticket, what does it look like? I stand in the queue, what does the tape-divider look like, what is it telling me? Ours says "no red tape" because it is blue and theirs is red. I go to the counter—what do people look like, how do they sound? I get on-board, the sick bag or the flight instruction bag—what is it saying to me? Is it winking at me, saying, "Hey man, we know you are there and here's a joke for you, get well soon",' Jayal added.

When the team came back and said something is really dull—say the flight instruction card, Rahul would say let it be clean, precise and functional first, and then feel free to add some jovial stuff to it.

There was a problem though. The 'boring' flight instruction card for passengers that is placed in the seat pouch became one of the most stolen item from IndiGo planes, because it had been redesigned to have cartoons on it. And for a low-cost airline everything is a cost.

The agency was not just involved in branding but also the cabin of the aircraft. They used to find themselves sitting in Toulouse, France with Rahul and his old-time friend, Anisha Archary, the ex-vice president of customer service, South African Airways.

'We spent time in both Toulouse and Hamburg,' says Sunil, 'understanding the whole mechanism. Since one can only buy from certified vendors, it's a question of figuring out things like what kind of skin should be on the wall of the aircraft, what kind of curtains, carpet colours, and so on. We had experts like Anisha, who helped us with the whole customer experience part. Now, when you walk into our aircraft, it feels spacious because of the use of colours and lights. We could have done beige [instead of blue] and red [for the seats], but our cabin looks calming because it is designed like that.'

Instead of the usual yellow lights in the cabin, for example IndiGo, used white lights, which Sunil feels, makes the aircraft look bigger and more spacious. LCCs with 180–186 all economy seats configuration in their Airbus A320 can look very cramped when you enter their cabin, compared with say Air India's A320 which have around 150 seats including business class and often more leg room and better cushioned seats.

At airports, IndiGo painted all its equipment, from tow-truck to ramps, in the IndiGo blue colour. Its tow-trucks and follow-me jeeps were labelled 'ground force'. The airline also decided to custom-build flat ramps in place of the stairs-like ramps to get on the aircraft. This helped more passengers get into the aircraft at the same time and turn-around the aircraft for next flight faster. However, many in IndiGo were apprehensive that the ramp was heavy and needed care to avoid dashing against the plane.

Some branding ideas also did not work. Buses that ferry passengers to the aircraft had a decal pasted around the driver's seat, to make it look like a pilot's seat from outside. The daily wear and tear made the decal peel off, making it look like a beheaded bus pilot. These were removed from the buses later.

IndiGo also tried to keep the messaging about pricing subtle. 'We do not want to say "Fly on Rs 999 airfares", which everyone was doing then. Instead, we said let's first give them a reason to fly,' Sunil continues, 'Hence our messages were, "In-laws in town? IndiGo to Mummy."' The airline's then-CEO Bruce Ashby had made it clear that pricing should be left alone; it should not scream; the focus should be to let people get a feel of what IndiGo is first.

Therefore, the first pre-launch copy read: 'Announcing the arrival of IndiGo—India's newest low fare airline. No frills. No fuss. No red tape. No silly excuses. No unnecessary delays. No long queues. No sulky faces. No pain.'

The first creative outdoor, when the airline launched, was also a simple teaser—the IndiGo's dotted plane icon in the sky which said— 'Ready for take-off'.

As new stations got added the lines kept changing—'IndiGo to the City of Joy', 'IndiGo to Garden City', 'IndiGo to Bollywood', 'IndiGo to Capital', 'IndiGo to Anjuna'.

There were also some tweaks. When launching short-haul flights between Delhi and Jaipur, a route that had an efficient highway, IndiGo erected a hoarding on the highway that said: 'Don't Drive. Fly. Daily flights to Delhi.'

The next set of advertisements encouraged discretionary travel: 'Stale fish in Delhi? IndiGo to Kolkata'; 'Sweating in Delhi? IndiGo to Bangalore'; 'Girlfriend in Delhi? IndiGo this weekend'; 'Life getting you down? IndiGo to 35,000 feet'.

Once, IndiGo also placed a billboard outside Gurugram's upmarket Golf Course road. It read 'Sleep with your wife—same day return flights'. The airline wanted to test how the Golf Club-frequenting CEOs would react to it. 'These are the guys who go to cocktail parties and start talking about it. How do you gauge it is working? Because people would call up and react,' says Jayal.

But it backfired elsewhere. Consumer complaints reached the Advertising Standards Council of India. The council ticked off the airline: 'This will give a wrong message to the younger generation in particular, and public at large. This slogan is highly objectionable when read separately and can mean otherwise.' It was pulled down.

Similarly, the airline placed another big hoarding at ITO in Delhi that showed a girl on a beach in a bikini, which read, 'IndiGo to happiness. Daily flights to Goa. Book now.' Apparently, it caused a traffic jam. But some people must have been offended. Letters started pouring in from women's groups demanding removal of the hoarding stating, 'You are promoting infidelity!'

In its early days, IndiGo never placed full-page advertisements in newspapers, although it was fashionable then to launch airlines with big front-page advertisements. Instead, IndiGo ran smaller advertisement on page three, or in the business section, because it felt marketing, sales, consulting and IT people fly the most.

IndiGo then rolled out some quirky recruitment advertisements. 'Every supermodel's favourite airline'. It showed only the model's legs. The airline's intention was to generate chatter in the market without spending too much. It tweaked its cabin crew hiring to look like matrimonial advertisements. So, instead of saying, 'Let your career take off', it said, 'Wanted tall slim girls for a young cool airline' or even, 'Call for Miss IndiGo'. Much like some of the best brands in the world, like Apple and Nike, where every single piece of communication passes through the top leadership, at IndiGo too, Rahul used to (and often still does) clear all the brand communications.

'Rahul is very brand conscious,' says Jayal. 'He is a creative director in himself. He owns restaurants like China Club. He has a creative impulse. We would get a call at eight in the night saying he didn't like the biscuit tin—'mazaa nahin aaya', and he and Sunil would be off in the morning looking at food items and designing tins.'

This drew some amount of ridicule. 'Rahul sat with us on every little thing in the first couple of years of IndiGo. Other agencies told us we were spending time on stuff that people didn't care about. We told them maybe you guys are right. Maybe we are wrong. But we just have to do it. And if Rahul and his team think it's the right thing to do, it can't be that crazy, they are not children,' Jayal says, recalling conversations with his peers in advertising.

Airline promoters, often love being in the limelight and hobnobbing with celebrities. There are pictures of SpiceJet promoter Ajay Singh lying on the tarmac in front of a Boeing wearing his full business attire for a photo shoot. Vijay Mallya was a Kingfisher brand ambassador himself, with Bollywood stars like Yana Gupta, Deepika Padukone and Katrina Kaif to help. Naresh Goyal was happy inviting and partying with the likes of Sridevi, Boney Kapoor, Shabana Azmi, Javed Akhtar, Shah Rukh Khan etc. at his home.

Rahul and Gangwal did not want any Bollywood in IndiGo. They themselves didn't even want to be photographed—not then, not now. 'We never pushed for an airline which is personality-based once we walked into a room with him,' Jayal said, 'Here the point is we can engineer something which works beautifully—tick-tock-tick-tock. It's not about the man, it's about what the man can produce. It's the philosophy. It removes you from the product and that gives you the pride.'

While the brand was being built, Rahul was also pushing for a mascot for the airline. A blue box had IndiGo written on it, a special typeface, but Rahul wanted something as an identifier for the airline. Sunil was doodling something on a paper napkin while in discussions with Rahul. He drew this small plane and he looked at Jayal, and Rahul said, 'Go for it.' That simple dotted plane became to IndiGo what 'Swoosh' is to Nike.

When I asked Rahul about the dotted plane, he said it matched the airline's philosophy because it connects the dots—it's simple, almost childlike. The dotted plane was used to convey many meanings. In one of the early campaigns, an advertisement showed kids running on the beach, one faster than the others, and soon after the last kid came the dotted plane to convey the message of 'Individuals on the go'.

The name IndiGo itself was coined by Rahul because he loved that colour. The G was capitalized because it also signifies 'India on the Go' and 'Individuals on the Go.' The dotted plane now appears on the belly of all IndiGo planes making it easily identifiable even when it is in air.

IndiGo also refrained from television advertising. Its first big TV campaign came many years after the launch and even this was inspired by the airline's operations. Its tagline was, 'On-Time is a wonderful thing', and it was produced by Bang and written by Keshav Naidu. IndiGo chose to present its on-time performance in a retro-inspired commercial with the following script:

'When our chefs wake up on time, our kitchen works on time. When our kitchen works on time, the food leaves for the plane on time. When the hostesses wake up on time, they do their make-up on time. They look oh-so-pretty, on time. When our ground forces do their work on time, our pilots take off on time. People get to meetings on time. We get our work done, on time. And when we get our work done, we become the world's most powerful economy on time. On time is a wonderful thing.'

'Then IndiGo went international, and we said time to do one more dhamaka type thing. So, we went and did a musical,' said

Jayal. The lyrics for this 'We are going international' commercial also kept the focus on performance:

'We're here to be the model of a modern global airline, an ambitious mission we remind ourselves of all the time; flying more than ever with a flock of new planes in our fleet, you'll be greeted once you're seated by many captains just like me; Called the ground force for a reason, we're machine-like in the way we work, queue-less check in, engineering, traffic handling, baggage clerks, passengers with preferences, their fragile items itemized—they're an operations army that keeps every aspect synchronized.'

To be sure, while it seemed like a peppy original number, some research showed it appeared to be heavily inspired by a Broadway hit song from Gilbert and Sullivan, which also sounded the same 'I Am the Very Model of a Modern Major-General'. Its lyrics went:

I am the very model of a modern Major-General
I've information vegetable, animal, and mineral
I know the kings of England, and I quote the fights
Historical
From Marathon to Waterloo, in order categorical
I'm very well acquainted, too, with matters
Mathematical

Jayal and Sunil's IndiGo branding also sometimes mimicked their Incredible India account. IndiGo's sandwich packaging, for example, was called 'IndiGo Tiffin' while the Indian ministry of tourism, which runs the Incredible India campaign, too had an 'Incredible Tiffin'.

Airline advertising can get very nasty because there is a lot of ego involved in this public-facing business. In April 2007, when Jet Airways went for an image makeover keeping its international push in mind, it released an outdoor campaign that stated, 'We have changed'. The Jet billboard in Mumbai, where outdoor advertising is big and unmissable, soon had company. Mallya's Kingfisher Airlines placed a hoarding over Jet's, which read, 'We made them change'. It is the kind of low-cost Zomato vs Swiggy virtual wars that we see today—except that those billboards existed much before the era of hyper social media addiction. Jet was forced to withdraw that campaign and started a new one with a 'Take Off to New York Daily' tagline. Not to be out-manoeuvred, Mallya told Kingfisher to add its own hoarding which read, 'They've flown from here to New York', implying it was because of Kingfisher's launch.

Similarly, a year later, Jet Airways put up outdoor hoardings for its LCC JetLite that read, 'Our smile lights up 502 flights to over 50 cities every day' together with pictures of cheerful staff. Soon, Mallya's LCC Kingfisher Red (the rechristened Air Deccan) put up its own hoarding right next to JetLite's and it read, 'We'd rather you smile' with pictures of their smiling customers.

IndiGo initially stayed away from such tactics during those early days possibly because it was a small fry compared to Goyal and Mallya. But in 2008, IndiGo ambushed Kingfisher which used to sport the tagline 'Fly the good times' and was struggling with newly bought Air Deccan. IndiGo came up with an advertisement that read, 'Let the bad times roll. The airline business is in a flux. But one airline has been going about its business efficiently and quietly. Thanks to IndiGo, you have a choice. With the industry's leading on-time performance, unmatched service, quality and affordable fares, IndiGo's brand-new aircrafts make 124 flights daily across 17 cities. Fly IndiGo in good times and bad times.'

Kingfisher responded swiftly—'Why fly low-cost carriers?' in an advertisement that was painted half blue and red. On the blue halve it wrote 'Indifferent', while the red said 'Different'. Another read 'Go hide' in blue and 'Fly with pride' in red. Yet another went: 'Go Degraded/Fly Upgraded'.

In 2016, Air India and IndiGo wrestled in public too. Air India had put a cheeky advertisement next to IndiGo's airport counter in Mumbai: 'Wish you a comfortable flight. Next time, fly with Air India and feel the difference. IndiGo hit back with its own which said: 'Yes Air India, there is a difference. Says the Government.' Below it was a small chart that showed IndiGo was the 'best' in on-time performance, while Air India was the 'worst' as per the DGCA data.

Air India was livid and shot off a letter to Mumbai airport saying the airline had never disparaged any other airline in its advertising. It had only said how its own product was better, but 'to our shock we found that IndiGo airlines has kept placards on their check-in counters at Terminal 1B displaying Air India in a very negative way, which is not acceptable to us and we at Air India do not believe in such type of negative advertisement for our competitor airlines. You are requested to kindly advise IndiGo Airlines for removal of these placards on urgent basis.'

It is quite possible that the aviation ministry was also dragged into it and 'counselled' IndiGo against such tactics at the airport which was then run by GVK. The placards were quickly removed.

Anxiety also flooded IndiGo leadership in the same year as Delhi Metro which passes right outside the gates of IndiGo's Gurugram headquarters was giving out semi-naming rights for its metro stations for 10 years. The one outside IndiGo headquarters was called Guru Dronacharya station, a prominent figure in the Hindu epic, Mahabharata.

The airline feared that its arch rival of many years and located few kilometres away, SpiceJet would bid for the station and paint it all red to embarrass it. 'We did not want them to take it. A SpiceJet station right outside the IndiGo office would have looked like a daily joke on us,' one of the airline officials said.

So, IndiGo pulled no punches and went ahead to secure rights over this station. Although it came for a hefty price—Rs 20–25 lakh a month plus Rs 30–40 lakh for painting it blue with the IndiGo signage—it gave the airline a lot of visibility. All of the Gurugram's traffic to Delhi and the upmarket Golf Course road passes over it or under it. No wonder, in Gurugram, it has now become known as 'IndiGo-wala station'.

Enthused by the attention it got, IndiGo decided to take over Delhi Airport's metro station too. It managed to win the rights, painted it blue and called it IndiGo Terminal 1 metro station. However, this time SpiceJet got upset; it lobbied and protested that 'its passengers were getting confused where to take SpiceJet flights from'. The IndiGo Terminal 1 station name lasted only for around two months. SpiceJet prevailed.

In 2017, IndiGo, SpiceJet (and also Vistara) were at war with each other repeatedly giving newspaper advertisements laying claims to the title of the best on-time airline. A year later, Vistara launched a TV commercial that showed a cabin similar to IndiGo in its advertisements. The crew in the commercial were shown offering cold and unappetising food to passengers and then the next shot showed Vistara crew inviting people to 'fly higher' and offering warm food and different cuisines. Ironically, Vistara had made a faux pas by comparing IndiGo's economy class with its own business class. They were roundly trolled on social media.

IndiGo did not respond this time. When asked about it, IndiGo a much bigger beast now, responded by saying that it carried 200,000 people daily and profitably, while Tata and Singapore Airlines' Vistara was rolling in losses since its inception in 2013. 'We did get angry,' said Sunil. They had readied campaigns to lash out at the competition, but those were killed by the IndiGo team in the end.

Full-service airlines typically spend about 2–3 per cent of their revenues on advertising. LCCs spend much less. IndiGo spends around 0.20 per cent. In 2010, when it had around 30 planes, the airline's marketing budget was around Rs 25 crore a year. Before Covid-19 struck, when the fleet was 150 planes, this grew to Rs 40–50 crore. Currently this stands at approximately Rs 60 crore when it has over 350 planes, according to an IndiGo executive who did not want to be named.

The spending pattern has also changed over the years with digital taking a much bigger pie of the spends now. While earlier 70 per cent of this budget used to be spent on print media, 20 per cent on outdoor advertising and the rest on other media, events etc., this has now shifted to 40 per cent on print, 20 per cent on outdoor, and 40 per cent on digital and events.

A significant portion of this also used to go to its ad agency whose mandate was to do everything from 'pin to plane'. Initially as 'A' and then later—when 'A' was acquired by Widen+Kennedy—as W+K, the agency dedicated 4–5 people to the IndiGo brand and some shared resources with other teams and got around Rs 3–4 lakh a month which later shot up to around Rs 20-25 lakh. In 2023, the account moved again to the erstwhile J. Walter Thomson now (after its merger with WPP) known as Wunderson Thomson (WT) because of a lot of leadership changes at W+K. The new agency has since been focussing on ramping up and understanding the IndiGo brand.

One of W+K's handicaps were their weakness in the digital space. In 2018, IndiGo, therefore, brought in Nitin Sethi to head its digital foray. Under Sethi, IndiGo created a 50-people team and pushed for #6EDigital. Sethi then hired an external agency, 22feet Tribal Worldwide, for around Rs 5 lakh a month to help him further. When the pandemic-hit, the airline decided to let go of 22feet to cut costs and to consolidate its digital operations in-house with the help of some freelance video and other agencies when needed.

Starting 2018, IndiGo had a hard time in its brand projection. Sometimes, the brand language used in digital media was not in sync with what W+K was putting out in other mediums. At other times, some of its ad campaigns seemed way too over the top. One campaign dealt too much in double entendres. In a 2019 campaign—IndiGoAbroad: Happy to be your first—meant to stimulate first-time travellers to its new destinations in Turkey, China, Vietnam and Myanmar, the airline used rather cheesy lines.

One ad showed an apparently honeymooning couple standing in a Thai location and the copy read: 'Our first time involved very ripe papayas.' Another had a girl with a mountainous background with the copy, 'My first time was on an island'; another said, 'I will never forget my first time.'

This chaos led Rahul to bring the old guard back. Sunil who had quit W+K in 2016 and had started his own firm called Motherland Ventures with Rahul and Jayal now oversees the IndiGo account from Rahul's InterGlobe offices as a 'mentor', as one IndiGo official puts it. Jayal had also joined one of the other accounts the duo had—Royal Enfield.

The way it works now is that when the airline has to launch a new campaign, WT does a lot of the grunt work, then Sunil gives his thoughts and picks and chooses what works best in conjunction with associate vice-president (digital and marketing) Nikhil Dhar and Rahul.

So, when IndiGo launched Nashik recently, WT and Sunil would create a wisecrack, say Grape Escape to represent India's wine capital. This will then be used in city hoardings, especially at airport sites including the departure and published as small ads in top three to four papers. A radio and digital campaign will also be unleashed. This would go on for around a month and half, and would also include travel agent get-togethers, after which the flight would be left to survive by word of mouth.

Another addition to IndiGo's branding in recent years is influencer marketing where the airline has cultivated some travel influencers who promote its flights to a new city. The airline has used them many times in its 'India by IndiGo' campaign. For the longest time, IndiGo only had a two-person team of Nitin Arora and Ankit Ratra working with the agency when it came to branding. Since they left in 2019, the in-house team of IndiGo, now led by Dhar, has grown bigger with over half-a-dozen people in it.

Food

IndiGo's in-flight food menu was a very big challenge to start with. The airline had decided not to give any free meals unlike Jet Airways, Air Sahara and Indian Airlines. Its policy of no ovens on board meant that the food was to be served cold.

The first few flights were bad. The airline had only cookies and cold drinks to offer. Angry passengers would often tell its staff that the airline did not understand the Indian palette and would shut down soon. 'It was a very bad time for us,' said one of the IndiGo officials who did not want to be named, 'In the US some airlines gave peanuts only, but Indians cannot relate to a flight journey without food.' The passengers were also very upset because the airline had decided to reduce the load by serving water in paper cups instead of 200 ml plastic bottles. 'We received a lot of flak because many wanted to carry the bottle with them,' this same official said, 'and there was no bottle to take.'

Having no bottles and no ovens reduced weight of the plane too and therefore costs. But those were not the only ways IndiGo has gone after shaving off load with a vengeance and continues to do so.

But do such small things really matter? An oven weighs 60 kg; four of them installed in the plane would lead to Rs 6000 extra fuel per flight on average. On the nearly seven lakh flights per year, this meant a pretty packet. A back-of-the-envelope calculation suggests the savings from oven-less flights itself could be around Rs 400 crore annually.

In 2015, IndiGo also lobbied hard with the Indian aviation regulator to become the first airline in the region to launch Electronic Flight Bag (EFB) reducing 25 kg of paper on its Airbus fleet by replacing paper charts and manuals with iPads. This, the airline claimed, reduced carbon footprint annually to the tune of 2,500 tons approximately. In 2023, it received DGCA's permission to remove technical paper manuals weighing around 40 kg each from the cockpit of its Airbus fleet.

Inside the cabin too, IndiGo keeps a female-only four-member crew to serve 180 passengers whereas Jet Airways used to have both male (who often weigh heavier) and female crew of five or six. IndiGo also asks its pilots to use only one engine of the aircraft while taxing on the runway instead of both the engines, saving precious fuel that makes up around 40 per cent of an airline's operational cost in India.

IndiGo also tries to cut air conditioning costs. On ground, the airline used to pull down all the window shades so the aircraft remains a little cooler. It also used to shut down the Auxiliary Power Unit (APU) used in cooling the cabin when on ground. It not only extended the life of the expensive APU but also enabled the use of the much cheaper diesel-operated Ground Power Unit (GPU) to keep the plane cool.

IndiGo's aircraft livery was never meant to be so bland. In the early days, the airline was particularly obsessed with a rather bright livery that was to have special iconography covering the entire plane with basic primary colours, almost like hieroglyphics that resembled a design language.

But Rahul and Gangwal freaked out at the proposal claiming it was too busy and too loud. The real reasons possibly were to cut out the extra cost of $30,000–40,000 and additional time in production; reduce running costs because the darker the livery, the more is the fuel burn.

Perhaps the quirkiest experiment to save costs was with the plane's washroom. A few years back, IndiGo launched a project to study the volume of water used on its flights. They found that in winters, less water was being used. So, they started to half-fill the tanks meant for the toilets; instead of 200 litres it started carrying only 100 litres of water. The fuel saved was considerable. This is now implemented in all its sectors.

The airline also realized that only serving cookies and soft drinks will not get it loyal passengers. Therefore, it started to develop food items that could work without ovens. The result was big loaf sandwiches including the Cheese-Tomato, Chicken Junglee and Spinach Corn ones.

Next came flavoured cashew nuts, samosas, juices, etc. IndiGo's challenge was not only to render cold food tasty but also get the consumer to buy it. Therefore, the airline decided to spice up the packaging with colours, fun stories and puzzles that made its tin boxes for cookies famous. When they landed on someone's dressing table they also became hairpin holder or pen holders when on a desk and therefore the airline's brand souvenirs.

Sometimes the airline's experiments fell flat as in case of the Gujarati burger. Gujaratis have a reputation of being finicky travellers with a rigid preference for their own food—often vegetarian. The Gujju burger was the result of a contest at the airline's advertising agency A, because the airline felt most of the airline burgers were bad. An art director from Gujarat won and that recipe was presented to Rahul who approved its taste. The sales never took off. The recipe was revised. It failed again and was finally canned. Similarly, IndiGo's Stick Man potato sticks did not work as customers did not like its taste. It had to be replaced with the more popular Pringles.

IndiGo then ran into another problem. Sandwiches were aplenty, but so many were wasted as few buy meals on board. Nearly 5–10 per cent of the food was ending up as waste. One official estimated that less than 50 per cent passengers pre-book their meals, including corporates travellers, and around 25 per cent buy on board.

This forced IndiGo to introduce ready-to-eat meals, including biryani, dal chawal, rajma chawal, upma, and cup noodles. The crew only had to pour hot water into them and they were ready to eat in a few minutes. 'Dal chawal worked well initially but I think it didn't taste fresh like homemade tadka-fresh dal chawal,' said an IndiGo official. 'Similarly, neither did rajma chawal because rajma needed much more time to soften. Rajma was not good to eat.' These have come in for a lot of criticism in recent times as a food blogger's video went viral in 2024 reiterating how ready-to-eat meals like Magic Upma have 50 per cent more sodium than Maggi, which is already considered to have large amount of sodium. High sodium is bad for health and its continuous intake is said to lead to a higher blood pressure in the long term.

Interestingly, a stuffed croissant was also brought in but it worked well on some flights but did not on flights to Patna. Similarly, nobody ate health bars; they only enjoyed buying the cookie tins. Rolls worked very well, but salads did not. Buying patterns differed from region to region. 'In the North East there is a lot of demand for non-veg food compared with say Varanasi flights,' this person said.

There is also another new trend that this official has noticed. 'The young generation takes coke and noodles at the most; they don't prefer sandwiches. They prefer muffin, or a chocolate shake at the airport's Starbucks before boarding,' he said, 'People buy most on leisure flights to Goa and the like; when, I think, they are in a mood to spend.'

In the past few years Rahul has also personally landed up in the crew training rooms which had demo carts and pushed the trainees towards better sales techniques. He would set the cart in person and inform that was how he wanted it. He wanted the items on sale to be so arranged that everything was visible to the passenger when the cart was being taken down the aisle, recalled a crew member who was present during these sessions.

Ironically, while on-board food looks very expensive –a sandwich plus a beverage come for Rs 500—the reality is that it is not the biggest profit centre for the airline when it comes to ancillary services. Of around Rs 70,000 crore IndiGo makes in annual revenue, it gets about 15 per cent of this from ancillary revenue. Of this, the biggest source of ancillary revenue comes from ticket cancellation fees and name/date change fees which gives around 7 per cent or Rs 4900 crore. An astonishing 15-20 per cent of customers cancel their tickets or change their bookings and these fees are steep at around Rs 3500. The next big item is cargo which at 5 per cent brings in around Rs 3500 crore. The next big revenue source is excess baggage which comes to around 1-2 per cent or Rs 700-1400 crore. The rest of the items are less than 1 per cent and include things like inflight food, seat selection etc. The revenue from inflight food is around Rs 100 crore of which around 40% is profit. In recent years caterers have hiked prices, lowering profit margins for airlines.

However the airline is also facing some challenges. For one, the airline feels, its menu has expanded way too much, which is harming operational efficiency and causing unwanted stress. Under the current SOP, the IndiGo crew has to go to everyone and announce the menu. This is followed by a small conversation and by the time they are done with serving all the 180 or more passengers, they are readying for the descent. Often, the ready-to-eat meals that take 4–8 minutes to become consumable add to stress to wind up the service. Therefore, the airline is now pushing to streamline its menu and forcing customers to pre-book if they want things like sandwiches. The airline has also stopped giving corporate passengers meal choices and instead just hands them a packed box which many refuse to eat now. The airline will also try to see if it can simply make a single broadcast of its menu instead of having a conversation about it on every seat.

On the wide-body aircraft, wet-leased from Turkish Airlines, IndiGo has reinvented itself in one way. On these flights, the Turkish Airlines crew serve the business class passengers with hot food, while IndiGo crew serve the economy passengers. Sometimes the passenger is coming to Istanbul from the US and continuing to India. He is entitled to a free meal because he has booked it through Turkish Airlines. This had created confusion on whom to serve the meals free and whom to sell them to. Therefore, IndiGo has now decided that on these flights it will offer free meals to all its economy passengers too, a first for the airline that has remained resolute on not giving any freebies.

IndiGo's in-flight magazine is an interesting story in itself. A small part of its ancillary revenue is from Hello 6E that has gone through multiple avatars. In order to avoid additional load, it avoided thick magazines published by other airlines. It started with a catalogue selling products. This led to inquiries for advertising on the catalogue. To start with, 8–10 advertisements were added. To get more brands in reading material was added to it later.

The airline then outsourced the magazine based on a minimum guarantee of advertisements. When advertising went beyond a certain threshold it also got a share of the rest of the revenue as well. The front and back covers of this magazine now sell for Rs 4–10 lakh each and inside pages for about Rs 2 lakh. The magazine, therefore, fetches around Rs 1–1.5 crore revenue per month for the airline.

IndiGo's fetish with weight, however, continues here too. The airline does not place this 100 gm magazine in every seat but only in some of them.

The attempt to reduce the weight further, however, had to be shelved. IndiGo tried to reduce the quality of pages from 170 gsm to 90 gsm; the pages became transparent and advertisers fumed. The idea was dropped quietly and quality restored.

Social Media

IndiGo was a reluctant social media entrant. It debuted much after most of the other airlines were tweeting and creating Facebook pages. Insiders attribute this to the airline's focus on making the experience more "productive." 'Kingfisher had a Twitter account,' Jayal recalls, 'They kept saying our Goa flight has just landed. Why? A lot of people are there just to be there. You should be on social media for a reason. If you have nothing to say, don't say anything. Twitter can become a channel to drive business and keep in touch with people. Managing it is a problem. Heathrow does a great job of it. They would come on in the morning and say, "Good morning from Heathrow, let us know if we can be of any help". They don't say something like, "a BA flight just took off".

IndiGo started its Twitter (now X) account in 2012. This too, in its usual way, happened after many studies and training and took a considerable time to implement. The airline hired a social media team which was sent to Amsterdam-based KLM for training to learn KLM's safety protocol, emergency response systems in case of a safety crisis, and to understand enterprise risk management etc. It also decided to create a detailed playbook with all possible replies for the various tweets about the airline. This playbook has evolved over time. It also identified politicians, journalists, lifestyle influencers etc., and when they tweeted something positive or negative these were immediately highlighted to the senior most level.

Depending on the contents of the tweet, the response time was kept between 1–12 minutes. The airline did not want to post trite comments on Twitter/X. Therefore, it made it a listening post and integrated it to its operations control room (OCC) which has all the details of flight movements—which flight is delayed and for what reason? Is there a weather issue? Is there a strike at some airport? Is there a VIP movement planned?

IndiGo also deployed Salesforce's social media listening tool which monitors everything on Twitter/X, including when the post is not tagged with its handle @IndiGo6e or a hashtag is created with its name. The tool also segregates and pigeonholes all the information the way the airline needs it.

This came in handy in September 2014 during the record floods in Kashmir valley after the Jhelum River had overflowed. Over 300 people died and property worth millions of dollars was damaged. In the resultant chaos, some IndiGo employees were untraceable.

Senior managers from IndiGo had to reach there and mount a search and rescue operation using boats. Most of Srinagar was water-logged; passengers were unable to reach airport and those arriving were stranded at the airport. DGCA was forced to cap the airfares on Srinagar-Delhi flights to Rs 3,000 and asked airlines to fly them free and take the money in Delhi if so required.

As chaos mounted, so did the volume of conversations on Twitter asking for help. IndiGo made a war room next to the OCC to respond to snowballing information flow during this crisis and direct people to the right person. Twitter became the most critical tool to get out the right flight information to the passengers.

Similarly, in 2017, when a video that showed an IndiGo staffer manhandling and dragging an elderly passenger on the Delhi Airport tarmac became viral on Twitter, the airline's social media team was groaning under the weight of a deluge of comments. This time though the team could not handle the crisis well.

The airline had a defined process as per which, the moment this incident erupted on Twitter, the team reached out IndiGo's customer services head, recalled a person aware of what had transpired then. However, by that time, the issue had gained immense traction. The mainstream media picked it up with television stations playing the clip-on loop. All the team could do was to give a 'holding statement' that the airline was looking into the matter. Clearly this was too little for an outrage of such magnitude.

The matter was escalated to the leadership team including then president Aditya Ghosh. It was also sent to the legal team. When the government and regulator stepped in, the airline had to figure out a way to deal with it more professionally. It offered an apology, finally.

Social media outburst also ends up forcing airlines to tweak their planned outreach. When the 'I am not your servant' video of its crew went viral, for example, IndiGo was working on an extensive 'IndiGoa' campaign for the launch of flights to the new north Goa Manohar International Airport named after former Goa chief minister Manohar Parrikar. The airline had planned to showcase their own crew as models and do a photo shoot at the beaches in Goa. 'This was called off because people may have said that IndiGo's crew have now stopped doing their duties also and are into modelling,' one of the persons in the know of things told me.

Twitter/X is now fully integrated at the airline to respond to IndiGo customer's needs. The team of 10 people that handles it has also grown to over 20-strong and operates in shifts. 'It's a tool for reputation management,' one of the person who works on it said.

IndiGo also has a reputation of largely keeping its planes spick and span. I was curious to know how this was ensured. Don't all airlines clean their aircraft as soon as the passengers leave and before it turns around for the next flight? Even the chemical agents, it turns out, that can be used for cleaning planes are approved by Boeing and Airbus, and therefore that could not be one of the reasons.

The secret sauce has another source. The chefs are the airline's engineering team who have a specific mandate. Every time an IndiGo plane goes for a major maintenance check, a significant part of the outlay is on restoring the cabin experience up to the mark. When the aircraft is in the hangar typically for four days, it not only gets an engineering reset, but is also given a coat of paint wherever needed—the doors, overhead bins, etc. In the cabin, even for a minor scratch, the mandate is to completely change the lamination.

Over the years, the airline has also come to the conclusion that the aircraft carpet is good enough only for 18 months. Airline carpets, not available off the shelf, are expensive. They are imported especially from Airbus-approved manufacturers such as the Netherlands-based Desso. The aisle portion which bears the brunt, needs to be replaced every six months.

An aircraft undergoes a C1 or a heavy check after 7,500 flight hours. This costs US$100,000–150,000. A C2 check is done after 15,000 flight hours and costs around US$140,000–170,000. When the cabin refurbishment is included, the expense could go up to US$300,000–400,000 depending on the condition of the interiors of the aircraft.

Most airlines avoid such expenditures on their aircraft. The carpet would be persisted with till it starts to become threadbare; if they can overlook a paint peel or a broken armrest, they will. But at IndiGo this a no-go zone. The airline is so particular about cleanliness that a special squad does random night checks and escalates any gaps found on the aircraft's upkeep to the relevant department head (even though in recent months some pictures of broken IndiGo seats have gone viral on social media). Or else Rahul himself will intervene in person.

This was succinctly captured in an internal email from the former CEO Bruce Ashby to his top management team that I happened to review. 'Every time Rahul flies,' it read, 'I get a list of ten people I should fire.' Perhaps that pilot who dropped the tissue on the floor as Rahul watched could have been one of them, had he not been quick enough to pick it up.

8
Lobbying

In 2012, Rahul Bhatia was giving an interview to Shereen Bhan, the current Managing Director of CNBC-TV18, in his China Club restaurant.

'You like to be a low-profile entrepreneur,' she asked in her disarming style, 'how do you deal with the fact you are in a business which is dependent on government regulation, which sees hectic political lobbying?'

Rahul assented and replied promptly, 'You deal with it with a great amount of difficulty.'

'Is it imperative to learn to manage the system?' she probed further.

Caught in a bind, Rahul took a pause, looked up dramatically at the ceiling, and then replied, 'To an extent, yes.'

The aviation business thrived on and has been a hotbed of lobbying. From Jet Airways' Naresh Goyal who, for a long time, stymied the entry of the deep-pocketed Tata Group into airline business, to Kingfisher Airlines' Vijay Mallya, who flush with liquor funds, had for a short while displaced Goyal as the most powerful voice in aviation, this space has always been the playground of those who can juggle airline economics with the hard lobbying and power play.

Realizing that there were powers that could scuttle its ambitions, IndiGo kept a rather low profile to begin with. 'IndiGo really flew under the radar for the first few years,' says the former aviation secretary, Ashok Chawla. For its maiden flight, it prudently avoided Mumbai, where it could have attracted more eyeballs and received more column inches and flew to north-east instead.

Goyal's presumption that IndiGo would shut shop soon enough helped, since, in his mind, there was nothing like a low-cost model when the airports fees were the same, fuel prices were the same and so were the staff salaries.

What worked in favour of IndiGo those days was that Mallya's only target was Goyal and that kept them both busy for many years. The third major player, Air India, was in a mess because the then aviation minister Praful Patel had bought planes for the airline worth Rs 50,000 crore on an equity base of only Rs 145 crore and merged Indian Airlines and Air India into one. This led to severe financial crunch, losses, total chaos internally—seniors were sometimes reporting to juniors—and a near-paralysis at the airline. Two major players at daggers drawn and a third undergoing a botched merger left only SpiceJet and GoAir as rivals who themselves were finding their feet during those days.

However, to assume that IndiGo did not know its way around the business would be foolhardy. Rahul had known his way around the aviation ministry for years and he used it to good measure when possible. At times he did not get his way and sometimes he did.

Aviation ministry officials of that era recall that IndiGo had applied for its licence in early 2005. The accompanying business plan said it was going to order 100 aircraft. This was the first-time ministry officials had heard of such a number; it looked ludicrous to them. One of the joint secretaries in the ministry, Sanjay Narayen, went to town on this application and raised multiple queries– one such was, where is the space to park these planes? This dragged on for weeks. The file remained stuck.

But then suddenly, it was sent to an empowered committee which used to approve scheduled airlines take-off.

What about the objections? One of the aviation ministry officials recalled the then Airports Authority of India (AAI) chairman, K. Ramalingam, spoke at that meeting out of the blue and said he would be able to provide parking space and other necessary infrastructure to IndiGo. AAI works under aviation ministry and the joint secretaries often have strong hold on the AAI chairman. Sometimes the joint secretaries themselves have gone on to become AAI's chairman.

The committee cleared the proposal and granted a no objection certificate to IndiGo to fly.

Rahul can charm anyone when he wants. 'Rahul has a knack of managing relationships very well. He is very good at networking and knowing and meeting the right people,' the former InterGlobe aide recalled.

Narayen, who presided over the privatization of Delhi and Mumbai airports, also ran into a controversy himself. Soon after quitting the IAS in 2006 over a delay in promotion, he joined GVK Power and Infrastructure Ltd., the group that had won the Mumbai airport rights. This became very controversial as he would have helped draft the privatization agreement while in the government and knew all the loopholes in it. And then chose to join the other side.

What is relatively unknown though is that Narayen, who opposed IndiGo application initially, may have also consulted with Rahul's InterGlobe soon after, IndiGo's ex-vice-president of operations, Shakti Lumba, recalls. One day, Lumba got a call from Narayen advising him not to walk in to Rahul's room whenever it pleased him. Lumba was flabbergasted. 'As he is your employer and not your friend,' said Narayen. Lumba says he realized then that Narayen may have been working with Rahul for a few months after he quit the aviation ministry. Lumba, 'not one to suffer fools', told his St Stephens' college mate to 'take a walk'.

Another powerful joint secretary in the aviation ministry then was R.K. Singh who quit from the civil service after he was not seconded to the International Civil Aviation Organization (ICAO) as India's representative. And voilà, almost instantly he turned up at IndiGo's parent firm, InterGlobe.

'R.K. is credited with successfully leading the Indian side for bilateral negotiations with more than thirty countries, including multilateral negotiations with the European Union and ASEAN. InterGlobe's rapid-fire growth requires us to not only reinforce our current skills, but build new ones to steer the enterprise to the next level. R.K.'s appointment is a step in that direction. Please join me in welcoming him to Team InterGlobe,' Rahul wrote in an mail to his leadership in 2009, which I happened to have reviewed.

Singh was so upset, another top aviation ministry official close to him recalls, that he did not even take the pension benefits from the government. 'I told him just sign here and I will do the rest, he just wouldn't listen,' this person said.

Singh hailed from a political family with a well-to-do background. His father, Shankar Dayal Singh, belonged to Congress Party and was a member of Parliament from Chatra constituency in Jharkhand. His brother Ranjan Kumar Singh is a journalist and his sister Rashmi Singh an IAS officer. In 2023 she was the Commissioner Taxes & Administrative Secretary, Mining Department, Jammu and Kashmir. R.K. Singh had been Mulayam Singh Yadav's close aide when Yadav was the Defence Minister. In essence, he had the right credentials and the network to yield desired results for IndiGo in Delhi's 'House of Cards' type of environment.

He was also very sharp and had excellent grip on the subjects under his purview. Aware that his next many years would be spent in aviation, he obtained a LLM degree in Aviation Law from Leiden University. However soon enough he was embroiled in a controversy, after being called out by the office of the Comptroller and Auditor General (CAG) in a bruising report on Air India. It became the nouvelle du jour and the subject of prime-time discussions on TV channels.

In its 2011 report, the CAG said that the aviation ministry under Patel and R.K. Singh gave 'one-sided … benefits to Emirates/Dubai' by increasing rights for flights to India—from six cities and 10,400 seats a week in 2003-04 to 14 cities and 54,200 seats a week by 2008-09.

While the airline regulator, DGCA, commented that 'there was no justification for permitting Emirates's request (for more seats and bigger aircraft)', Air India too disapproved of it. The auditor's report said that the then aviation ministry's joint secretary (R.K. Singh) 'indicated the minister of civil aviation had discussed this case with him and in view of the winter rush and the problem of getting seats on the flights, it was felt that we may agree to the upgradation request. This was approved by the minister.' 'The sequence of events clearly demonstrates the one-sided nature of benefits to Emirates/Dubai,' the CAG said. It added that while Dubai's aviation authority protected the interests of its airlines, India's did not.

This led to claims of one more scam, kickbacks, and corruption. Nevertheless, only the lobbyist Deepak Talwar, a close friend of Praful Patel, ended up being in jail for an extended term. He was charged by the CBI with lobbying politicians, ministers, other public servants and officials of ministry of civil aviation for airlines such as Emirates, Air Arabia and Qatar Airways and securing undue benefits for them.

The investigation agencies alleged that Talwar had created a web of entities owned by him and his family members in India and offshore havens, to launder Rs 272 crores received from the foreign airlines through Asia Field Limited registered in the British Virgin Islands. This money was used to construct Holiday Inn in Aerocity, New Delhi.

The agencies alleged that Talwar's firm, Advantage India, 'received a total Rs 174.40 crores as donation and CSR (corporate social responsibility)' contribution mainly from Airbus which it said was nothing but payment to Deepak Talwar in lieu of deals struck by Airbus with Air India.

'Praful Patel is a dear friend of Deepak Talwar … Talwar used to finalize the communication to be sent to Patel on behalf of entities such as Emirates, Dubai Aerospace Enterprises etc.,' the Enforcement Directorate told the court adding, 'It has been alleged that the officials of the ministry of civil aviation and Air India, by abusing their official positions as public servants and receiving illegal gratification, in conspiracy with other public servants, private domestic and foreign airlines, made the national carrier give up profit-making routes and profit-making timings of Air India in favour of national and international domestic and foreign private airlines.'

Interestingly, eight months after NCP leader Praful Patel, along with Ajit Pawar and other party leaders, joined the BJP-led NDA, the CBI has on 19 March 2024 filed a closure report in the Air India-Indian Airlines merger case.

Through these years the very well-read and soft-spoken R.K. Singh continued to work behind the scenes for IndiGo. He would, said a top DGCA official, invite government officials to the Air Force Club in the proximity of the aviation ministry and talk shop. That changed around the time Rakesh Gangwal exited the airline's functioning in 2018. Singh was brought into IndiGo up front as a special director and is now the number three official after CEO and COO on IndiGo's leadership page. He also remains the point-person for IndiGo for handling government policy, aviation ministry and the DGCA.

In its nearly two decades of existence, IndiGo has dealt with multiple IAS officers and aviation ministers.

During the launch party of IndiGo, there were only two key politicians present—the then aviation minister Praful Patel and the minister of commerce and industry, Kamal Nath. It was a two-day bash—one day was reserved for employees and one day for the guests. The entire venue was set up as an airport; at the check-in counter the guests were handed entry passes that resembled an airline boarding card.

The flamboyant Vijay Mallya landed up at the check-in counter only to be asked, 'Your name please, sir.' The young girl did not know who he was, leaving the King of Good Times embarrassed. A proud Rahul Bhatia was on the stage flanked by Praful Patel and Kamal Nath where Patel quipped that it did not look like a party organized by an LCC. To which Rahul replied: 'This will be the first and the last.' For the most part, it has indeed been like that.

While in many ways having the aviation minister launch the new airline was sound political optics, Kamal Nath's presence set tongues wagging furiously. Since the public knew that launching and sustaining an airline requires deep pockets, the knowing smiles and chatter went up over the next few years. And for good reasons as Kamal Nath's son Nakul Nath (richest candidate in 2024 Lok Sabha elections with a net worth of Rs 716 crore) joined the board of another InterGlobe group company called InterGlobe Established Private Limited or ESTD. The second son Bakul Nath followed suit a few years after IndiGo's launch. This company was founded to sell Koenigsegg, Ariel and Gumpert super cars and several other luxury products, including Arcadia and Messerschmitt yachts. It did not do well and was eventually shut down.

There was another common connection between Bhatia and Kamal Nath—Anil Chanana, who runs an agro-trading firm called Amira Group. Anil was also given shares in IndiGo during its inception possibly because he had invested in the airline. In 2004, Rahul and Chanana started a business named Ara Hospitality that operated restaurants such as Sola Topee.

However, Chanana was a controversial figure too. At least two of those controversies are publicly known. First, in 2004, he was intercepted by customs officials at Delhi airport and was found to have smuggled in two pairs of diamond earrings worth Rs 1.16 crore. He was arrested, as he had not mentioned the earrings in his declaration form and had aggravated the crime by walking through the Green Channel. Four days after his arrest, he voluntarily deposited the customs duty of around Rs 48 lakh. He was later released on bail.

'Those were three really bad phases that I have seen Rahul go through—when United Airways pulled out of India; when his friend Chanana got arrested; and when his cars were impounded,' the former InterGlobe aide recalled, 'I could see personal distress then.'

Three years later, Chanana's name cropped up again in a basmati rice scam. Kamal Nath was the commerce minister. The Centre had, vide a government notification in October 2007, banned the export of non-basmati and 25 per cent broken rice, ostensibly to strengthen the nation's food security in times of high inflation and to ensure there was enough stock in the public distribution system to provide subsidized grain to those below the poverty line, according to an article in the *Outlook* magazine.

However, there was a twist. Since India was a major exporter, the ban immediately triggered a steep increase in the price of rice in international markets. Then followed a chain of events in which guidelines were flouted and rules bypassed by state-owned trading companies, to allow select private rice-exporting companies to export 1 million metric tonnes of rice despite the ban.

Ghana, for example, wrote to the Indian government seeking several thousand metric tonnes of rice but wanted it only through Amira Foods. This was cleared without inviting any tender. There were allegations that Kamal Nath-led commerce ministry facilitated this export arrangement for a few chosen private companies. The Congress-led government later admitted in the Parliament that public sector units did not follow a transparent procedure for non-basmati rice exports during the UPA's first term.

Although Chanana and Rahul were close friends, their relationship appears to have soured when the IndiGo IPO was in the offing. Chanana reached out to Lumba in distress one day. Chanana had been allotted preferential shares instead of equity shares. Chanana wanted the latter while Rahul refused to budge. Equity shares represent the ownership of a company while preference shareholders have a preferential right or claim over the company's profits and assets.

Lumba informed Chanana that he was helpless in this matter and he should reach out to Rakesh Gangwal. It worked. Gangwal eventually set it right, an indication of how influential he was till 2018. When I reached out to Chanana, including on his WhatsApp requesting a comment on his 'contribution' to IndiGo, he read the message and blocked me on his Dubai number – where he is said to spend most of his time now.

Meanwhile around 2010, the airline was soaring under Patel's tenure. It was now ready to fly abroad having closed in on the mandatory five-year experience mark. IndiGo executives met officials of the civil aviation ministry in November 2010, to convince them that they be given permission to start international operations and fly to as many 15 international sectors including Dubai, Bangkok, Singapore, Kathmandu, Jeddah, Maldives, Abu Dhabi, and Sharjah. They argued that as an LCC they will not eat into the market of full-service carriers such as Air India, Jet Airways, and Kingfisher, as the 'passenger class is different'.

After the massive uproar over the CAG reports and how Air India was short-changed by it, the aviation ministry was reluctant to give bilateral rights. However, on 19 January 2011, IndiGo announced that it had received permissions, seven months ahead of it completing five years in domestic aviation. Patel had cleared the file perhaps as a last-minute parting gift to IndiGo. His last day in the ministry as aviation minister was 18 January 2011 as he was moved out because of the same CAG reports. An old Congress hand from Kerala with strong trade union roots, Vayalar Ravi, was brought in to head aviation.

Ravi turned out to be a tough cookie for IndiGo. Once, while he was waiting for his flight in Kerala, an IndiGo station manager went up to him to say hello out of courtesy. According to a ministry official who was with the minister, Ravi snubbed the manager without any provocation saying something to the effect, 'Because of you, my Air India is in such a state, you have taken away our passengers.' The embarrassed station manager left quietly. That was not all. The aviation ministry withdrew the overseas flying rights granted to IndiGo on the Muscat sector. Air India, which had earlier operated those services, wanted to restart those flights.

IndiGo was lobbying for more international routes but Ravi had decided it would not happen on his watch. Once Patel was moved out, IndiGo had fallen out of the good books of the ministry. Its international expansion was stuck. According to a bureaucrat present at the time of the meeting, Rahul even paid Ravi a visit at Rajiv Gandhi Bhawan in Delhi, requesting for more international rights as his expansion trajectory was steep. At some point during the meeting, things turned sour between the two. In what was seen as aggressive behaviour, Rahul got up abruptly and left. 'Ravi felt intimidated, he didn't like it at all,' this bureaucrat recalled. The minister was rather upset.

Ravi was the minister from January to December of 2011. He was succeeded by Ajit Singh who stayed in power till 2014. IndiGo's fortunes took a turn for the worse now. As Singh took charge, the loss-making Kingfisher Airlines and Jet Airways were lobbying hard to allow more foreign airline investments into India.

Rahul felt helpless and upset with the government. 'We spoke of overseas flying rights. I need to know why the government can't open these up. These are sovereign rights. People who want to fly should have unfettered access for this to happen. Allow companies to have opportunities to blossom. In the process, of course, some will make it and some won't, but that's life. Don't constrain and constrict the industry. When you try to constrict the industry, you also constrict the supporting industry—airports, and therefore employment. The fact that you don't allow Indian carriers to grow, you consciously hand out revenues that actually belong to Indian carriers to carriers outside of this country and that cannot be right. I'd love to know which country in the world has a policy of capping an airline's operations to domestic flights for five years?' Rahul went public.

He also targeted Jet and Kingfisher asking them why were they in such a loss-making state. 'Some constituents of the industry need to ask themselves why are they in the shape they are. Have they treated the business differently than they should have? These are fundamental questions. Whether we like it or not, the problem with the airline business is that it is so fast moving that if you don't set it up right structurally, it can be very painful. And the recovery can be equally painful,' he said adding the government should not change foreign direct investment policy suddenly just because Kingfisher is in trouble.

He also brought up global examples. 'Globally, the aviation business is not something that you make a great return on but you have success stories. You have Ryanair, easyJet, jetBlue, and Southwest. They have been profitable for years. It is not unknown that in certain geographies of the world, certain carriers deliver profitability all the time and some don't. Does that warrant change of government policy? Does that invite change of government policy? So why does it here?'

Logic and rationality did not matter. Rubbing the aviation ministry the wrong way only invites more pain. Rahul, who had started lobbying in Rajiv Gandhi Bhawan much before IndiGo was started, should have known better. In September 2012, Ajit Singh, who was very powerful then, had the Union Cabinet approve 49 per cent investment by foreign airlines. He also floated a proposal making it mandatory for airlines to operate flights to smaller cities to 'improve regional connectivity'. IndiGo was the only major airline then that did not have small aircraft.

This was the backlash after Rahul's public comments. He, however, did not back down; instead he chose to become more critical of the ministry. In a function at Kolkata, Rahul spoke up, 'Our principle issue is, why is the government tinkering with policies for a select few in the industry? If you look at any mature aviation market, such as the US, in terms of safety, they are the finest in the world … In the US, the Federal Aviation Administration is equivalent to the DGCA. If they were confronted with a situation where the crew was not paid for months, be it pilots or technical staff, I guarantee that they would shut the airline down on safety grounds.' He was referring to cash-strapped Indian rivals who were delaying salary payments while IndiGo paid on time.

Four days after his comments, when India was hosting a major aviation conference in New Delhi, journalists (including me) covering the event received a statement on their mobile phones from the aviation ministry: 'Clarification: Government Not Discriminating Against IndiGo or Favouring any Specific Airlines'. The aviation ministry gave a point-by-point rebuttal to Rahul and said, 'The government strongly refutes the allegations made by Shri Rahul Bhatia, Promoter, IndiGo Airlines … that it is tinkering with the aviation policies for [the benefit] a select few.'

The uncharacteristic government clarification was an embarrassment for IndiGo. As I understand, Singh stopped giving appointments to IndiGo officials. All bets were off; communication lines had completely broken down.

At the same conference, in sharp contrast to IndiGo's accusatory tone, Naresh Goyal was all praise for the 'good work' done by minister Singh. Goyal and Singh were seen giggling, seated on the dais. 'We would like to highlight in particular the ministry's decision to focus on infrastructure development, open more international routes for private carriers and their ongoing efforts to reduce the taxation on ATF (aviation turbine fuel) through discussions with the finance ministry,' Goyal said in his speech adding that he appreciated the 'strenuous efforts' of Ajit Singh 'in taking several significant measures to aid the industry'.

Singh was a Jat leader from western UP and the son of former prime minister Chaudhary Charan Singh. He was vain, headstrong and triggering him was a rather bad idea. IndiGo found that out a few weeks later.

Import of aircraft into India was cleared by an empowered committee of the aviation ministry's bureaucrats, airport officials, and the DGCA.

IndiGo was known to add one aircraft a month to its fleet. It had sought approval to import sixteen Airbus A320 aircraft during Ajit Singh's tenure.

But Singh did not grant permissions for long. Manmohan Singh's Prime Minister's Office (PMO) intervened too but the then powerful Singh overruled PMO. The sixteen Airbus A320 jets, many of which were ready at Toulouse, had to be inducted starting January 2013. IndiGo had a rough time and received the clearance after considerable delay and only for 5 planes around February. Singh said the ministry was framing guidelines for regional connectivity and the import of the rest of the planes (which were not meant for regional flights) will need to be looked into accordingly. Interestingly, during the same year Singh swiftly released hundreds of controversial flying rights to Etihad Airways, which had agreed to invest $600 million in Goyal's cash-strapped Jet Airways.

Similarly, IndiGo had run into regulatory headwinds in 2010 when Syed Nasim Ahmad Zaidi took charge as the DGCA. Zaidi decided to tweak an existing DGCA rule that allowed an aircraft to take off as per its manufacturer's specifications at a particular level of visibility. Airbus A320 could take off if the runway visibility was around 125 metres, while Boeing 737 could do only at 150 metres. During winters, when the fog descended on north Indian airports, especially in Delhi, this small advantage meant a big difference – the air-traffic control (ATC) permitted Airbus operators such as IndiGo, Air India, GoAir, and Kingfisher to clear their backlog of flights first. This left Boeing 737 users Jet Airways and SpiceJet with irate passengers yelling at their staff.

At the peak of the 2010 winter, Zaidi decided to normalize the take-off visibility from 125 metres to 150 metres. He defended his decision stating, 'Nowhere in the world' is take off allowed below 150 metres. The biggest beneficiary of this move was Jet Airways.

After his retirement, Zaidi was appointed as the Election Commissioner of India. In July 2017, while demitting that office, he told a reporter that he was gratified with his career. There was some speculation that he would be nominated to the post of the vice president of India when Mohammad Hamid Ansari would retire in 2017. Zaidi was seen as close to the Congress government which did not win a five-year term in 2014. However, the Narendra Modi-led BJP government anointed Venkaiah Naidu the new vice president.

In the July 2017 interview, Zaidi also said he planned to spend more time with his Persian cats Burfi and Laila and write a book on aviation and that his son was a lawyer who lived in the US, and daughter Fayrouz, a baker, lived in Hyderabad. This was taken with a pinch of salt because people in the aviation ministry knew that his son worked for Jet Airways. Middle East press reports of June 2017 shows that his son was the general manager of Jet Airways for Oman. According to his LinkedIn résumé, he joined Jet Airways in 2009 as assistant legal manager. He was a student at Delhi Public School; did his law degree from McGill University in Montreal in

2007-2008; and an internship at ICAO from May to June 2008. Zaidi was India's representative to ICAO during that period.

When Zaidi came back to India as the DG of DGCA from 2008-2010, his son joined Jet Airways. After he retired as the EC, to the surprise of many journalists present, he showed up at the Jet Airways AGM in Mumbai. He was now a board member of Jet Airways. Pictures of Naresh Goyal whispering in his ears on the AGM dais got talked about everywhere.

When I confronted Zaidi with allegations of bias, he tried to play it down. On tweaking the policy that helped Jet, he said, 'I don't remember it but if it was, it must be part of my professional work.' On being close to Goyal, he said, 'There can be such a perception, I can't dispute that. I really don't know.'

While Zaidi was leaving the ministry in 2012, Tatas were toying with the idea of re-entering aviation. To test the waters, Ratan Tata sent an aide to an aviation ministry officer. It is possible that he had already received a green signal from the higher-ups in the government. 'Ratan thought that with Kingfisher dead, that spot was open to be taken up by someone,' this official told me, 'I said go ahead.'

Vistara was born soon in collaboration with Singapore Airlines. At the same time, Ratan Tata could not say 'No' to Malaysia's AirAsia whose founder Tony Fernandes loved planes and sports cars as much as Tata. Therefore AirAsia India was born too. However, this riled IndiGo. Rahul was upset with Tatas entry. 'We need to take them down with all our might,' he told another airline promoter who mentioned this to me during a conversation in 2023. 'He was very unhappy.'

Both Vistara and AirAsia wanted the government to relax rules for international flying in order to connect to their hubs in Singapore and Malaysia and create a huge network feed. The minimum five-year rule seemed to be going under. Rahul could have also been upset because the ministry was not willing to tweak this rule when IndiGo wanted to go international before completing these five mandatory years. When it came to Tatas that was no more the case.

The airline lobbying body, Federation of Indian Airlines (FIA), of which IndiGo was the biggest funder, charged that the ministry was being 'biased against the entire existing industry.' One can clearly make out the tone of these lines resonate closely with Rahul's public outcry in the past. 'The new proposed policy is totally unfair and unjust because it proposes to not only alienate the rights already earned by the existing airlines in order to exclusively benefit the two new latest entrants both of which are partnered by one industrial house but also because it frees the new entrants from socio-economic requirements of serving the domestic market,' wrote the FIA in its 22 January 2015 letter which was addressed to Asok Kumar, the joint secretary in the aviation ministry.

Seeing IndiGo's intense lobbying, AirAsia's outspoken founder and CEO, Tony Fernandes, minced no words. 'IndiGo and the Federation of Indian Airlines have been trying to squeeze us out. I have never seen competitors like these. They pushed me the wrong way. I have been shocked only by the ridiculous reaction (to AirAsia India's operations) from IndiGo. This is a small market. You know the leaders. I think the leader (in lobbying against new airlines) is IndiGo. The rest are just followers,' Fernandes told me in an interview.

While the FIA lawsuit was eventually unable to achieve what it wanted—stopping both from flying abroad before five years—it helped because the matter dragged on for a long time allowing IndiGo to continue to expand fast and increase its market share. AirAsia India also got implicated in a corruption controversy and could not fly international. A case has been registered against Fernandes too because of which he cannot enter India. Vistara was better off because, in 2016, Tatas seemed to have succeeded in getting norms for international operations relaxed under the garb of a National Aviation Policy.

Eventually, in 2022, an embarrassed Tatas announced they would buy the AirAsia stake and merge the airline with Air India Express. Getting into bed with Fernandes turned out to be a nightmare for Tatas. Ratan Tata's former executive assistant, Ramachandran Venkataramanan alias Venkat, was named in a CBI FIR in 2018 for alleged corruption. It also included Fernandes, Rajinder Dubey (director of HNR Pvt. Ltd, Singapore), Sunil Kapur (chairman of Total Food Services, Mumbai) and lobbyist and middleman Deepak Talwar.

Rahul's grip on things in this sector can be gauged from the fact that he was aware of all these men, especially Sunil Kapur, aiding AirAsia much before the CBI FIR was filed. I have this on the authority of someone who has worked closely with Rahul.

With Vistara and Tatas in for the long haul, after Kingfisher and Jet Airways went under in 2012 and 2019, respectively, IndiGo was pitted against SpiceJet's Ajay Singh. While Singh has been called out for various issues including SpiceJet's near-bankruptcy in 2022, delayed salaries, delayed taxes, multiple lawsuits etc., he has turned out to be a hardnosed operator when it came to his interests. Singh is a former aide of BJP leader Pramod Mahajan and is operating under a BJP-led government since he took over the airline in 2015 from Sun TV's Kalanithi Maran.

You would often see his black Maybach parked in the lush green aviation ministry. Unlike Rahul who now does most of the frontline lobbying through R.K. Singh, Ajay Singh does it himself for SpiceJet. When it comes to the minister, the secretary, or the DG, he will be in Safdarjung Road in minutes. From my conversations with them it appears that for the senior government officials this amounts to him paying his respects to them and it means the world to them. Rahul, sometimes, fails on this count.

Singh also knows how to press the right buttons that may be appreciated all the way to the top. In 2021, SpiceJet painted Narendra Modi's face on one of its aircraft to celebrate 100 crore Covid vaccinations. Every time the plane flew across India and abroad it carried that message with it and the PM's picture.

Sometimes the speed at which SpiceJet, with little funding and no corporate backing, gets its work done is phenomenal as well. On 11 April 2019, SpiceJet wrote to DGCA seeking an in-principle approval for taking over 16 of Jet Airways' Boeing 737 aircraft. The very next day, the reply, with a copy marked to the aviation ministry arrived from Ved Prakash, director of operations (air transport) of DGCA, 'Please refer to your four applications … dated 11 April 2019 … based on the approval granted by the competent authority, the in-principle approval is hereby granted for import/local acquisition of 16 Boeing 737 type of aircraft.'

The same year, Singh pushed for a new airports slots policy targeting the cash-rich IndiGo which dominated the slots allocation at all major airports of India. IndiGo already had 150 and 97 daily slots in airports at Delhi and Mumbai, respectively; Air India held 169 and 111. At Bengaluru airport, IndiGo had 140 daily slots while Air India had 36. As Jet went bust, IndiGo took over dozens of lucrative slots at the congested Mumbai airport. Jayant Sinha, the civil aviation minister from July 2016, too appeared keen on the new slots policy.

He took over the process and asked all the airlines to submit details of the aircraft they were importing or leasing and the workforce to operate those planes. He declared that the ministry will distribute slots on priority to newly inducted aircraft. The second priority was to be given to those who were rerouting flights from their existing network to Mumbai.

IndiGo was furious. If IndiGo flies a plane for 12 hours, it said, and extends its use by two hours daily, it will be as good as adding 30 new planes. It also told the ministry to first ask SpiceJet to use up the slots of its 13 grounded Boeing 737 Max planes. Two Boeing Max planes had crashed and in early 2019 globally the Max fleet was grounded, handicapping SpiceJet's planned expansion.

Since the formula is designed to recognize the 'investment and efforts'—including serving remote and unprofitable routes—that each airline had undertaken to build its network across the country, IndiGo also wanted that as an overarching principle, the last five years of domestic capacity deployed should be considered while allocating such slots.

The draft minutes of an all-airline and airport-operators' meeting at that time read, 'COO IndiGo (Wolfgang Prock-Schauer) mentioned that the incremental capacity/capacity addition should be considered on net basis, i.e., after taking into account any shortfall on account of on-ground/utilized aircraft. Additionally, airlines in India should be free to restructure their network in order to utilize such slots as long as they adhere to RDG (route-dispersal guidelines that mandate airlines to connect far-flung places) of the MOCA (minister of civil aviation).' Remarkably, this point made by IndiGo was absent when the final minutes were circulated, inviting another protest letter from IndiGo.

The ministry even proposed that an upper cap may be set for the percentage of landing or take-off slots an individual airline can hold in congested airports—this too aimed to benefit newer airlines.

Eventually though the slot policy did not make headway as the national elections were imminent and Hardeep Puri was brought in to replace Sinha in the summer of 2019. Sinha who had already been demoted from the finance ministry to the aviation ministry was not given any portfolio in the second term of the PM Modi's government.

The biggest lobbying push of this decade however came when the pandemic hit in early 2020 and airlines had to ground their planes across the country, lockdowns were announced to keep people at home and avoid getting sick with the merciless virus that was out to take your breath away.

When the pandemic struck in 2020 grounding aircraft and cancelling flights, many airlines repurposed their passenger seats and flew cargo to generate some revenue. Getting masks and ventilators from China instead of launching flights to Dubai was suddenly more profitable.

Eventually, when the airlines were allowed to restart passenger flights, albeit with many restrictions, India's major aviation players split into two camps—the cash-rich IndiGo and Tata-backed Vistara on the one side; Singh's SpiceJet and Wadia's Go First were on the other side of the fence. If airlines offered cheaper fares, the cash-rich ones will survive and the financially strained ones will die; this would allow the former to reap the benefits later and make up the losses incurred in the interim.

Singh could not take this lying down. He, therefore, pushed and succeeded in getting the aviation ministry to intervene in something that it avoided meddling with—airfare management. Even at the peak of political and public outcry during Diwali or Durga Puja or New Year's Eve, when fares have skyrocketed beyond a common man's or even a middle-class family's reach, the ministry had avoided regulating fares.

This time though, it agreed to bring fare bands and introduced minimum and maximum fares that the airlines could charge.

IndiGo was dead against it, as was Vistara. Their protests were ignored. While Singh's lobbying may have worked to some extent, conversations with ministry officials indicate that government did not want another airline to go down making IndiGo even become more dominant.

Unfortunately, as the pandemic tailed off, while SpiceJet limped on, Go First declared bankruptcy indicating that the fare caps only delayed the inevitable.

For IndiGo, the time was ripe to go aggressive on international operations because it wanted to secure its footing in the market before a rejuvenated Air India, now owned by Tatas, became too strong. However, it was unsure how to go about it. Immediate purchase and deployment of wide-body aircraft which may be unviable could bleed it as Kingfisher realized with its international operations. So, it came up with another innovative plan—largely Rahul's idea who had strong ties with Turkish Airlines leadership.

It requested the DGCA for permission to wet lease (aircraft with operating crew and engineers) wide-body Boeing 777 aircraft from Turkish Airlines for two years—one year initially, extendable for the same period. This was not allowed. India had been rejecting Turkey's request for additional flight rights out of India for years now. Under president Recep Tayyip Erdoğan, Turkey had also become vocally anti-India, forcing India's hand. Over the last one and a half decades, one would often see the Turkish ambassador visit the aviation ministry with boxes of Turkish Delight only to leave pretty much empty-handed.

At first DGCA rejected the IndiGo request. The plan was perceived as a way to bypass the bilateral agreements. IndiGo will lease the wide-body aircraft with Turkish crew and fly Indians till Istanbul. From there, Turkish Airlines will take them to US, European destinations on its massive network much like Emirates,

Etihad and Qatar do via their Middle Eastern hubs. Thus, Turkish Airlines would get more passengers from India using its own bilateral rights with India but also by using IndiGo's rights The director-general, Arun Kumar, made a detailed presentation to the ministry officials stating that wet leasing aircraft is a big handicap for DGCA because the regulator's job is ensuring safety and this cannot be done entirely as wet-leased aircraft do not remain under its full jurisdiction. This apprehension had led to wet-leases being allowed only for six months till then.

IndiGo argued that it was only helping aviation ministry in its stated policy of connecting India to international markets with wide-body planes and helping feeding Indian hubs like Delhi and Mumbai. Kumar rejected these too saying they were taking passengers to feed Istanbul and not feeding Indian hubs.

The DGCA even submitted its objections in writing. However, this was eventually overruled by the Jyotiraditya Scindia-led ministry, reasons for which were never made public. The aviation secretary R.K. Bansal wrote on the file that this should be allowed.

A former DG said that one reason was quite clear. IndiGo is the only stable airline with aircraft that can connect smaller towns. A financially-weak Alliance Air and SpiceJet with their often grounded turboprop planes cannot provide the required connectivity to smaller cities—which is crucial for politics and optics. While earlier, one could see minister Scindia virtually flagging off many SpiceJet flights from his desk, such flagging off have become more pronounced with IndiGo flights in recent times.

"That has given them (IndiGo) the leverage," a recently exited former Director General of DGCA said asking not to be named.

IndiGo's named also popped up in the controversial electoral bonds scheme in 2024.

In a landmark judgement in mid-February of 2024, a five-member bench of the Supreme Court struck down the electoral bonds scheme, terming it 'unconstitutional', and directed the Election Commission of India (EC) to reveal the names of entities that made the political donations and their recipients. Noting that political funding through electoral bonds promoted corruption, the chief justice of India DY Chandrachud said in the ruling that it also resulted in a culture of 'quid pro quo' and brings 'unrestrained influence of corporates in the electoral process'.

While IndiGo's co-founder Rahul Bhatia and his companies including IndiGo donated around INR56 crore to political parties between 2019 and 2023 including Rs 29 crore to BJP (at the peak of his fight with co-founder Rakesh Gangwal and the biggest corporate battle of his life), Mamata Banerjee's All India Trinamool Congress (TMC) also got around Rs 16 crore, former aviation minister Praful Patel's Nationalist Congress Party (NCP) got around Rs 4 crore and Indian National Congress (INC) got Rs 5 crore.

Ajay Singh's cash-strapped SpiceJet paid INR65 lakh during the same period to Aam Aadmi Party (AAP) in 2021 when one of its sister concerns, Spice Health, was trying hard to tap into an opportunity created by the pandemic.

But beyond this, and lower down, the world of airline lobbying is even more murky.

To figure out how lobbyists went about their business, I met one who is considered a pro in Delhi circles. Why has IIC become a hub for lobbyists, I asked. That's because, he said, bureaucrats in the Modi-led government are not comfortable meeting people at five-star hotels. 'They are more comfortable in an IIC-type setting. Or at parties at common friends' home,' he told me. Influential bureaucrats are invited to common friends' house where the airline promoters will also be guests and push their agenda.

Some government and regulatory officials are made amenable by offering free airline tickets, free upgrades, special handling at airports, family vacations or even sending cars so that their wards can play tennis at the Gymkhana Club. Pilot schools are happy to give free pilot training. There are other idiosyncratic ways of illegal gratification. One regulatory official is famous for demanding gold coins for getting work done. Others are given corporate credit cards with generous limits; and the bills are paid by the airline. There is also other kind of non-monetary sleaze but that is not worthy of being mentioned here.

Dinesh Trivedi, the former railways minister from BJP and a pilot himself, openly says on Twitter that the DGCA is "unprofessional and ill equipped, not independent in the real sense, run by babus (IAS officers) not having domain knowledge". The DGCA is also often openly accused of corruption on social media; letters accusing specific top officials have been sent to ministers. There are RTI requests filed. But the DGCA remains unfazed, and does not contest these charges.

'As far as corruption is concerned, in any organization 5–7 per cent people are corrupt;10–15 per cent are very good; and the rest 80 per cent are fence sitters and they turn to honesty if the boss is good and to corruption if boss is corrupt,' said A.K. Chopra the former joint director general of the DGCA and one of India's top plane crash investigators. 'DGCA is no different.' He said another problem with DGCA is that, more often than not, an IAS officer is placed at the helm of affairs. He does not know the technicals and is therefore taken for a ride by his subordinates.

The DGCA also has a lot of discretionary powers which is the nub of the problem. Wherever there is discretion, money can be made. The DGCA, for example, can give a dispensation that, in emergency situations, an aircraft part can be used 5 per cent longer than its permitted life. This 5 per cent can mean a lot of money for the operator and this discretion could, therefore, drive corrupt practices.

One of the best ways to make the organization transparent is to ensure any discretion applied or dispensation given is immediately placed on the regulator's website. This way, an operator can question if a discretion is being given to someone but is being denied to itself.

The airlines are heavily connected and are good at obliging people, Chopra said. 'The DGCA comes under the pressure of the operator and that's why you see all these pilots agitating about FDTL (flight duty time limitations) now,' he said, 'Two things an operator can do: oblige you in many ways and they have got direct links to the politicians.'

In 2009, Chopra said, he cancelled the licence of Ligare Aviation, the charter airline business of former Ranbaxy promoters Malvinder and Shivinder Singh, because the company's plane had an accident and it still flew to Singapore without informing DGCA anything about the whole episode. Chopra said he was given hell; he started to get calls from the PMO; aviation minister's office called and asked him to not suspend the operator's licence. He did not budge, but finally conceded and placed them under a one-year suspension instead. Ligare was not even an airline operator, which have much higher stakes in the business.

Similarly, he recalled how the nephew of a top Planning Commission's official pressed him through a minister's office to make a navigation component mandatory for airlines. Such a contract would have won him Rs 500 crore in business. But he refused. When the pressure became unbearable, he wrote on the file that it should be examined by the ICAO first, effectively sending the proposal down a rabbit hole. 'We already had ACARS, why should we want another component to find the position of the plane?' he said.

Such rectitude comes at a cost, says Chopra who used to drive a Maruti 800 when he was in the DGCA and continued till the emission rule made it ineligible. 'If you look at my career, I got all my promotions through the court only,' Chopra says and laughs.

Most people end up taking another way. Not to bend and follow, but join the club. Dozens of DGCA officials have had their family members working in the same airlines they are supposed to regulate and monitor for safety. While in itself it may not seem as a big issue there have often been allegations of quid pro quo.

Multiple requests by me under RTI seeking names of DGCA officials whose immediate family members and relatives were in aviation firms were denied by the regulator.

One director general of DGCA even quipped to me, 'You should stop filing RTIs, I can give the names but eventually I have to get work done from these officers only.'

Some of the names I could figure were powerful enough though. The daughter-in-law of the former joint director general, Ravi Krishna, considered the most powerful after the DG, Vikram Dev Dutt himself, worked for Go First. One of Ravi's close friend, often found sitting in his office, too was a Go First employee. Ravi's friend has now moved to IndiGo.

The deputy director general (DDG), Tuhinanshu Sharma's husband works for Air India; sons and daughter-in-law are with IndiGo. The former DDG Pawan Kumar's son works for IndiGo. Now a consultant for the DGCA, Pawan Kumar looks after eGCA, a project to take DGCA online for most of its application and clearance processes. Incidentally, IndiGo is pursuing this project very closely. The joint director general DC Sharma's son, who, a few years back, was declared medically unfit for taking flying lessons, has now been found medically fit now and flies with Vistara. Some of them may have moved jobs too.

These officials declined to comment.

Is this conflict of interest? The officials will likely say that they do not handle the concerned files. However, possibly their junior or fellow colleagues do? 'If the joint director general of DGCA has its son in IndiGo, do you think those below him will take any action against the airline? The juniors will not make things worse for their bosses,' said another person who deals with DGCA often.

Chopra agrees with this. 'If a joint DG calls up and says take him as a pilot, no airline in India can refuse, because they know a lot of work, that is entirely discretionary, will need to be cleared by the DGCA.'

Another officer explains how this process works and lays bare the level to which operators have infested DGCA. He recalled how an operator, who employed his junior's son, behaved like a spy for the operator. The father always passed on this particular operator's file to be cleared by the senior officer to "avoid" conflict of interest. So, technically he did not work on that file. However, when the senior delayed the decision on that operator's file the same officer immediately alerted the operator about the delay who would start making calls to the senior then or even to the senior's bosses.

Speedy clearances and therefore cooperation is critical for an airline's revenue. IndiGo, for example, was successful in usually getting its aircraft registered in one day after they landed in India. These aircraft were good to go and earn revenue from day two and were not on the ground for many days like that of many other airlines who were slow in getting the clearances. IndiGo also encouraged more pilot get-togethers with ATCs so that there is better 'communication' and 'understanding' and hopefully IndiGo gets quicker landing clearance for its flights, as one official put it.

Then there are slots. A good slot makes a lot of difference to the flight's commercials. An 8 a.m. slot that attracts a lot of corporate traffic is more desirable than a 11 a.m. slot. 'Right from the aircraft to right slots, everything has to be fought for to ensure that you win over others,' the lobbyist quoted earlier said. 'And everyone has to be taken care of down the line –nothing will work otherwise. You have to find who wants what. It has become difficult to give things openly now. So, we give it at their homes. Earlier, it was top down; now it is from bottom up, as people below can create lot of problems for you.'

Those below have become smarter too. 'They know how much something is worth; so they ask accordingly what they want.'

The selection of a lobbyist is, therefore, done carefully. So, it could be the wife of a top military officer or the son of a former principal of a top Delhi school. 'It is all about access. Once you say you are the wife of a senior military official, you will be accorded some respect and given access and therefore a hearing,' said a top former aviation ministry official.

Similarly, the son of a famous Delhi school principal—who would have helped a good number of students into getting admitted and in the process created substantial goodwill—becomes worthy of getting fat salary as a lobbyist. Nobody forgets a favour like getting your son into a school or getting a top doctor's appointment in times of emergency. Favours are often loans and have to be returned.

The lobbyist for ministry also differs from the one for DGCA. The one for the ministry will be a polished operator like Niira Radia, with a modulated accent, breezing through the low-ceiling Rajiv Gandhi Bhawan trailing a heady perfume. The one for DGCA would be more obsequious; may drive an Audi, yet will wait outside the officers' doors for hours; does not flinch when given a dressing down, replete with local swear words; is willing to carry his airline's file to another building for approval; and will wait outside the DGCA official's room after office hours to take him out for drinks at the Delhi Flying Club, right across the street.

For IndiGo, DGCA is so important that it has even opened a big office right behind the regulator's office in Delhi from where some of its lobbyists work. Notwithstanding IndiGo's penchant for highlighting its branding and its dotted plane everywhere, curiously this office is only painted navy blue but otherwise remains unmarked.

IndiGo has learnt how to drive the system to work for it most of the time. For me, nothing captured its persuasive lobbying prowess more than one of the meetings I had with the DG, B.S. Bhullar, in 2018 at the peak of IndiGo's Pratt and Whitney engine crisis. In 2016, IndiGo's new A320neo aircrafts' engines started to malfunction, leading to dozens of emergency landings. DGCA kept mum for a long time. Then in early 2018, when news channels went to town focusing on these emergency landings and a public-interest case was filed in the courts, the DGCA grounded the planes just before the court verdict could be pronounced.

Bhullar's replies to my questions sounded so much like what IndiGo had been briefing us that he could have been an IndiGo spokesperson rather than the DG of civil aviation in India. 'They are the most successful airline. *Is liye, woh* highlight *bhi zyada hojate hai na? Taang keechne wale bhi bahut hote hain na,*' Bhullar said, as if advising me that I too should play down the story. 'It's a machine. Machine *mein kuch na kuch toh hota rahega. Baki* news *nahin aati kabhi.* Air India *ke bhi* A320 *hain. Auron ke bhi* A320 *hain. Baki ka* highlight *nahin hota magar inka toh* each one will be in focus. IndiGo manage *bhi karte thhe pehle.*'

While I will never be able to figure how IndiGo used to 'manage' news, what was incorrect in Bhullar's argument was that Air India was never in the news. By virtue of being unionised and under government, Air India always provided easy stories to journalists almost on a daily basis—from a rat jumping in a flight, to leaky toilets or to snag-hit delays. Bhullar even seemed to be apologetic about his own role. 'There are two things we are trying—one is regulation, literally inspector *raaj hai na* (in DGCA). Then there is the commercial part. They are investing money. If aircraft is grounded, why will they be happy with it?'

Every time IndiGo engines shut down mid-air, the aircraft would shudder and passengers would hear loud bursts that sounded like gun-fire. When I asked him why had he taken such a long time to act, whether he had not seen the pictures of highly burnt engines circulating on the TV channels and on WhatsApp, his reply was, 'If you take a close-up, you can highlight anything. Every engine has stringent checks. Even as we speak, any engine may be having a problem. This is a normal process—it's never *ki machine main koi problem hi nahin ayegi*. Read ICAO, even it says safety is not absolute. I think we are focusing a lot more than what is required.'

Listening to him, my mind went back to the question Shereen Bhan had posed, 'Is it imperative to learn to manage the system?'

9

Headwinds

By 2011, IndiGo's fleet had 50 aircraft; it held nearly 20 per cent domestic market share; and was the only profitable airline. Air India had fallen behind in domestic market share. The loss-making Jet Airways and Kingfisher Airlines had a very high-cost structure and were constantly under strain, seeking capital.

But over the past few years as IndiGo scaled up rapidly it also started to face many headwinds. These included conflict of interests, accusations of data theft, union woes, leadership insensitivity and arrogance, passenger abuse, and then the unthinkable exit of its architect Rakesh Gangwal himself.

The evolution of the airline over the years and its true character emerged gradually. During the 2008 crash, when oil touched US$145 a barrel, the big guys –Jet **Airways, Kingfisher and Air India—and then IndiGo, GoAir and SpiceJet agreed to come together and join hands in public to bring some sort of parity in fares with the LCCs.**

As the pain grew, the big boys lured other LCCs to join them in announcing a strike to pressurize the government to reduce taxes on fuel. On 31July 2008, all the airline chiefs gathered in Mumbai. Jet Airways' chairman, Naresh Goyal, Kingfisher Airlines' chairman, Vijay Mallya, GoAir's promoter, Jeh Wadia, and IndiGo's Rahul Bhatia came together to deliberate on how to ensure that their airlines remained afloat with fuel prices at an unprecedented high and with no sign of any relief from the government.

Barring the state-owned Air India, all the other airlines decided to suspend operations from 18 August. Praful Patel—considered close to the owners of private airlines, many of whom were his friends—was in Maldives at the time. He denied that the strike was happening with his tacit support. He flew back to Delhi when the PMO swung into action, even as TV news channels led with this story playing up the imminent passenger chaos ahead.

Thereon, Patel was under tremendous pressure to break the strike. He made statements on how he had asked Air India to increase the number of flights to reduce inconvenience to passengers and fly the jumbo Boeing 747s on domestic routes to help passengers. The ministry even held talks with airlines to drop the agitation. Soon enough, IndiGo broke ranks and decided to walk out of the agitation, stating that the airlines should engage in dialogue with government to resolve matters.

'IndiGo appreciates the sentiments expressed by the Ministry of Civil Aviation that it understands the problems faced by the Indian aviation industry and that we should all engage in a dialogue with the ministry,' IndiGo's president, Aditya Ghosh, said in a statement then.

IndiGo would operate flights as usual, he said. SpiceJet followed suit. The strike was called off. In one masterstroke, Rahul had done two things—he had got Patel and the government on his side, and also won passenger sympathy. And because he was not as affected by fuel prices as much as the Goyals and Mallyas were because of lower cost structure, he could afford to not join the strike and roast the already overbaked full-service airlines.

Rahul smiles when I asked him about this. 'When we backed out, these guys got mad. Very mad,' he says. But Rahul reasoned that the question IndiGo faced at the time was, 'Why are we fighting their battle? We internalized it. These guys are hurting and they want to do this thing. Why are we getting sucked into it? We decided to pull out. Of course, the industry was not pleased with us at all. And I think from that day onwards, there has always been a lack of trust.' Rahul acknowledges the lack of goodwill towards his airline. 'I think we called the rest of the industry and said we want to extricate ourselves from this position. And I think SpiceJet followed,' he reminisces.

Rahul then got embroiled in another battle when Air Deccan founder GR Gopinath's book Simply Fly: A Deccan Odyssey hit the stands months later. Gopinath accused Rahul as one of the perpetrators who killed his airline. Air Deccan, which had started two years before IndiGo, had outsourced its reservations systems to Rahul's InterGlobe Technologies (IGT). Gopinath wrote in the book:

'I had begun hearing rumours that Bhatia was going about the business of setting up his own airline. I called Bhatia and said that if what I had heard was true, then there was conflict of interest. I pointed out that he would become my competitor and he would have access to all my data. He denied the rumour, but when I asked him to commit his denial in writing, he dithered.'

Later when IndiGo became a reality Gopinath was shocked. And while the basic reservation system made by ITQ was perfect for a start-up airline, it was not good enough when Air Deccan scaled up. The reservations system would collapse, and frustrated passengers would go to other airline websites such as IndiGo and buy their tickets. It was a commercial disaster to have booking systems down.

Ideally, why did he not have a non-compete clause in the reservation system agreement of ITQ, I asked him later? 'I never imagined I would need one at that time,' Gopinath recalled. 'When I signed it, I never imagined that the guy who was giving me the software would start his own airline. Later, when I heard the rumours, I told him to put it in writing that he was not starting an airline. He said he couldn't. Then why claim that you aren't starting an airline? Everyone was talking about it. It was leaked out to me, some of the investors who were talking to him at that time told me. It was a lesson. When an airline's reservation system collapses, it is over. The airline is over. Aditya Ghosh was the lawyer representing him in the deal for the reservation system. I had a big fight with him. I told him God will punish you.'

Rahul Bhatia never publicly reacted to the book. In an interview he laughed it off and said the accusations were not worth replying to. However, it turns out that both Gopinath and Rahul did lose their cool when they met in person after the book had come out. 'In Hyderabad, we were at a dinner for the airport inauguration or something, and I was at the bar,' recalls Gopinath, 'Rahul had read the book and was very upset. Moreover, my office had sent him an invitation to the book launch, so he was livid. He said, "Captain, you first bugger me in the book and then you invite me to the book launch. You should have the decency to at least not invite me." I said, no, I don't think you should take offence. I just wrote what actually had happened. You can always write your story. You know the story; you know what happened. He said, "No, no, you did not know how to run the airline." I said I knew how to run an airline, but I didn't know how to cheat like him and stab in the back. And I used a bad word and walked off.'

I asked Gopinath if he thought Rahul had intentionally cheated him. 'I think he had a definite plan to start an airline. I don't think the bid was submitted to sabotage (Deccan). But he gave a bid and we gave the contract to him. And it just happened that when he started his own airline, the system that he gave us would not work. It was beneficial for him if the system did not work, because every time the system collapsed, people would buy his ticket. Anyway, I thought all is fair in love and war, and so, all is fair in war and business,' Gopinath said.

The episode also reasserted Rahul's secretive style of working which you often hear of at InterGlobe. I put this incident to Rahul and he smiled saying he was indeed furious as to how he could write all this in a book and then have the audacity to call his secretary to invite him to the book launch.

On data theft, Rahul mocked Air Deccan and said if he had looked at Gopinath's airline data, he would have been scared to even contemplate starting IndiGo. Rahul was clearly very angry about this episode and one could see it in the way he replied to the charges.

But this was not the only data theft charge that he had faced. InterGlobe had an altercation with Air India too. InterGlobe Technologies had bagged the tender for the national carrier's call centre despite the fact that IndiGo was already operational and was competing for almost the same set of passengers.

All of Air India's critical data—its frequent fliers, their names, addresses, travelling patterns, choices of seats, frequency of travel, modes of booking (whether from travel agency or online) and many others—was now available to InterGlobe.

This meant that InterGlobe would know strategic details –such as when Air India changed pricing on a particular flight sector- almost as soon as the data was punched in. The group even knew the number of seats vacant on a particular Air India flight, the routes which worked well, and which did not. This blew up when Air India slipped to its lowest in the domestic passenger market share, and a vigilance report found irregularities in outsourcing. Curiously, the InterGlobe contract was not terminated.

But then in 2012, the matter escalated to a different level. Air India found its frequent flier data had been compromised through the creation of fake accounts, and asked travel technology provider, InterGlobe Technologies, to investigate the matter. The airline suspected that passengers had been sold tickets by the call centre through the use of fake frequent flier accounts.

Air India also filed a first information report (FIR) with the cybercrime branch of the Delhi Police to initiate an investigation. 'Some people have created false accounts. We have asked IGT to investigate the matter,' said Rohit Nandan, Air India's then chairman and managing director. Air India had 1.5 million frequent flier accounts and this data was very valuable. For context, Jet Airways loyalty programme Jet Privilege was itself valued at around US$300 million by Etihad Airways in 2014.

Only then did Air India finally scrap the InterGlobe Technologies contract.

IndiGo, meanwhile, was seeing a change of guard. Many of the airline's founding expat team had exited. Rahul and Gangwal had decided to make Aditya Ghosh the President of the airline. In early 2000s, Ghosh had been assigned to Rahul as a lawyer by the law firm J. Sagar & Associates (JSA) run by Jyoti Sagar, according to another of Rahul's close aide.

Jyoti Sagar's wife, Prema Sagar, runs the public relations firm Genesis BCW. It has been IndiGo's publicist arm since the beginning. 'Sagar was a very costly firm so we had asked them to give someone cheaper. So, they said, take this new kid—he is smart, good with computers, can make presentations etc. He became our legal aide. Then later, when aircraft deals were being negotiated, we said can we please take him because we wanted someone loyal and good in typing and who can read lengthy documents and give legal advice. Aditya and Gangwal had started talking in Bengali already. So, he moved to InterGlobe. Sagar did not like it when we said we want to absorb him. Rahul also was not keen at that time to have a new employee. But he came in. Then, as the expats were to leave, he saw an opportunity and created his own space,' recalled Rahul's aide.

Although he was designated as the President, the CEO designation was kept in abeyance.

After taking charge, Ghosh started to introduce changes in IndiGo. He brought in a new head of operations, Saleem Zaheer to replace Shakti Lumba with whom he did not get along at all.

Zaheer, a former Indian Air Force officer, would communicate in polished English instead of having informal chats with pilots like Lumba did. Memos to pilots became a norm. As the airline grew precipitously, it had to wring out the most out of its pilots. Together this became a recipe for disaster.

On 29 September 2011 a long anonymous email hit dozens of IndiGo mail boxes complaining of a suffocating work culture with no redressal mechanism and called for the formation of a union.

This was IndiGo's first brush with unionization, a prospect it fears like no other. Ghosh knew it was not a fanciful email but a widely felt resentment, caused largely by himself. In his two years as the president, he had pushed pilots too hard. Ghosh may have also missed the simmering discontent focused as he was on the cabin crew training academy iFly. On completion of every batch's training, they had a party where parents were invited, Ghosh cut the cake and gave a speech. The youngsters were elated as they would fly soon; their parents were delighted to see their wards in the uniform and groomed for the sky. Many came from small towns.

Ghosh had invited me to one of the ceremonies too. He clearly revelled in these events and relished how the cabin crew trainees and their parents looked up to him as the 'architect of the airline'. The passing out crew too thought much about it since the president himself was present for what was a routine event.

To understand Ghosh's leaning towards iFly, we need to consider where Ghosh came from. Ghosh had no airline experience. Nevertheless, Gangwal made him the President because he needed someone like Ghosh, whom he had once referred to as 'Chief People's Officer'. Gangwal had structured the airline in a way that the heads of verticals were strong and they drove the business under Gangwal's guidance.

Dubai-based Riyaz, then the chief financial officer, led aircraft orders and leasing under Gangwal's direction with help from Gurugram-based vice-president Krishan Bhargava. Former chief commercial officer Sanjay Kumar built a massive airline network while head of engineering SC Gupta has kept that key part of the airline working smoothly. Ashim Mittra, too, has largely ensured there are no pilot strikes at IndiGo or union formations despite a lot of discontent in the rank and file. The human resource department, branding and in-flight food were Rahul's turf. Some say that Ghosh was left with only crew training, presiding over HR events, presenting the airline to the media and meeting the government and regulatory officials. The latter was only for routine matters and if anything got out of hand, R.K. Singh and eventually Rahul had to step in to meet the ministers and bureaucrats.

A few days after the 29 September email, a worried Ghosh finally wrote back to his pilots saying he is going to take steps to address their problems.

IndiGo was compelled to hand out fat bonuses to retain pilots. After the crisis blew over, the airline management did some brainstorming. The conclusion was that the airline did not listen. Why did they need a union? Because nobody was listening. What if we start listening to them regularly? Weekly meetings were mooted and Ghosh started to meet batches of pilots who came in from various stations and spoke of their life at the airline and how to improve things for them.

The complaints could be about poor cockpit food, layovers, laundry trouble or noisy hotels. Every demand was listened to and the one that could be met were met. After this imbroglio, Ghosh mellowed towards the pilots. He realized that while the promoters may have a different perspective on the importance of pilots in an airline, it was he who had to deal with the pilots on a day-to-day basis. Therefore, it was best to buy peace, respect their work ethic and empathize with the erratic work hours that impacted their mental and physical health and do what was practically possible.

He decided to avoid more escalations that may blight their operations. He started periodical visits to various stations to meet the staff there. Not just for a pilots' birthday but even for wedding anniversaries and other happy occasions, personalized cakes were sent directly by Ghosh. He memorized names of his staff members; asked after the welfare of themselves and their children. Over the years, pilots and crew members became his buddies in many ways. For the pilots, cabin crew and other staff members, who never knew the promoters, Ghosh was now truly the airline's 'architect'.

Now Ghosh started to pander to all the crew demands, ignoring even senior management protests. In a way, in the crew he had found his echo chamber. Gradually Ghosh's comfort level with his position in IndiGo grew; he started to work on projecting his own persona. He had an image makeover; went into extreme bodybuilding; moved from Nissan Teana to Audi 6; wrote emails that overflowed with his personality cult.

In one email to the employees, for example, he wrote of his personal involvement with Prema and Jyoti Sagar's Genesis Foundation, set up to help critically ill orphan and abandoned children. That was a good thing. The next paragraph, however, made one wonder what he was really trying to say. He went on about how Genesis had organized a fund-raiser named 'CEO Chefs Share-a-Smile Lunch', where ten CEOs cooked lunch for those who bought a seat at the table. Ghosh said he was one of the chefs and he manned the dessert section.

'I prepared crêpes flambéed with Grey Goose and served with a range of sauces—Cointreau infused orange, chocolate, mango, kiwi, and mixed berries, topped with whipped cream and chocolate flakes.' He then listed the other chefs present: Manu Anand, Chairman & CEO, PepsiCo India Holdings; Martin Jones, CEO, Marks and Spencer India; Vineesh Kochhar, CFO of DuPont India; Sashi Mukandan, Country Head of British Petroleum India etc. He seemed to be more at pains to prove that he had moved up and into the big league of corporate heavyweights.

The promoters felt no need to be in the limelight. However, Ghosh loved the visibility. However they pulled him up now and then. In 2013, there was a half-page story on him in the *Business Standard*. The story was seen as projecting Ghosh way beyond what he was and this time Gangwal made his unhappiness explicitly clear about this at IndiGo.

However, these were temporary blips; he carried on merrily. He started to organize town hall meetings where musical bands played; 'leadership meets' on the banks of Ganga at Rishikesh; invited TV stars, gave pep talks, sang with them on stage in halls jam packed with his employees. He booked stadiums for cricket matches and flew down staff from various stations to play. He came up with idea of building gyms for police officials in various cities as a part of 'CSR activities' mandated by the government. Gangwal did not like much of this. Instead of building gyms in the name of CSR activity, 'shouldn't we have mobile eye hospitals for those with cataract in rural areas?' Gangwal asked someone.

IndiGo's fleet touched a 100 plane mark in 2015. In the IPO that followed, the company had a valuation of around Rs 25,000 crore. Ghosh met Rakesh Jhunjhunwala around this time seeking his support for the listing (this meeting also ended up making Ghosh his eyes and ears in Akasa Air in 2022, an airline where Jhunjhunwala later invested).

Most of the senior IndiGo officials who had been with the airline for long were given bumper bonuses and shares unheard of in the Indian aviation industry. Ghosh got around Rs 150 crore worth of shares and bonus; former CEO Ashby's shares were worth Rs 450 crore; chief aircraft acquisition and financing officer Riyaz Peer Mohamed made over Rs 350 crore; former chief operating officer Steve Harfst clinched Rs 100 crore; chief commercial officer Sanjay Kumar received Rs 25 crore worth shares; and former operations head Shakti Lumba's shares were worth around Rs 6 crore.

A little later, on an average, 80,000 shares worth Rs 2 crore (at that time per person and now worth Rs 12 crore) were given to key senior management people over a period of four years. This list included CFO Pankaj Madan; head of operations Ashim Mittra; in-flight head Suman Chopra; head of human resources Sukhjit Pasricha; head of training Summi Sharma; corporate affairs head Vikram Chona; head of customer service Sanjeev Ramdas; head of legal Priya Mehra; vice-president of finance Vineet Mittal; and senior vice president for aircraft acquisition Krishan Bhargav. A total of 14 people received this largesse. This was repeated in 2019 and the same set of people (or those in that role) plus another 10 senior vice presidents were given shares. This time the number of shares on average was around 50,000 per person, locking in their loyalty and making them partners in taking IndiGo and its stock price higher.

IndiGo's new CEO Pieter Elbers has also been given around six lakh shares and keeping in mind that some have been given at Rs 10 while others at around Rs 1800 a share and the current share price is around Rs 4000, these alone will be valued at over Rs 150 crore. Some of these are linked to the performance of the company and are staggered over four years.

This is over and above his salary and bonus which the airline has not disclosed as of early May 2024. His predecessor Ronojoy (Rono) Dutta, 71, got around Rs 17 crore a year. With shares, he would have exited 2023-24 with around Rs 30 crore, had he not been asked to leave.

Assuming Elbers gets the same salary as Dutta, together with stocks his yearly pay therefore could be around Rs 50 crore. He is the highest-paid Indian airline CEO ever. Jet Airways' last CEO Vinay Dube made around Rs 10 crore a year. One of India's most valuable companies Tata Consultancy Services (TCS) CEO Rajesh Gopinathan made Rs 25 crore in 2022-23, in a year when the company made profits of around Rs 40,000 crore.

IndiGo is therefore quite an upgrade for Elbers who was making around Rs 10 crore in 2019 while he was the KLM CEO and the pandemic-related salary cuts had not been announced. Following global airlines that are posting record profits in post-pandemic travel boom, IndiGo too is estimated to post a record profit of around Rs 8000 crore or $1 billion in 2023-24.

To step back a little, soon after the 2015 IPO party was over, IndiGo bumped into a major trouble. In the winter that year, the airline's on-time performance, its key selling point, dropped to 75 per cent from the usual over 90 per cent. Flights were getting cancelled all over and there was chaos at airports.

Why did this happen? The airline was trying to extract more out of its network by reducing the time between two flights. Let us say a flight reaches Delhi at 12 in the noon and the next departure is 12.55 p.m. with 55 minutes ground time. IndiGo said it does not need the 55 minutes so it reduced it by 20 minutes and slotted the next departure for 12.40 p.m. The more a plane flies, the more money it makes for you. IndiGo could not handle this schedule. The winter of 2015 was among the worst on-time performance it has had.

Gangwal lost his cool. The airline had to rejig its entire network. For the next winter it ensured that its CAT-IIIB compliant pilots—those who are rated to fly in low visibility—were always available in adequate numbers at the airport so that they could fly the planes the moment visibility improved. They also kept extra crew ready at the airport. Departures were also staggered. Since fog sets in around 7 a.m., they advanced their departures. Flights to Lucknow, Patna, which are subject to heavy fog, were postponed by two hours; those to Chandigarh were suspended altogether for the winter. All this added pressure on its staff.

IndiGo also had to do large-scale terminations—mostly those in airport operations. Many who lost their jobs were close to Ghosh. Gangwal thought that Ghosh's patronage and proximity had made them complacent enough to refuse to step out of their rooms in the terminal to control the chaos caused by the fog-impacted cancellations. They were lulled into thinking that being someone's blue-eyed boys/girls meant that not only were their jobs safe but they were vouchsafed frequent promotions.

Gangwal got even deeper into the problem. When pilots could do 75 hours of flying a month, Gangwal asked, why were they sticking to 50-55 hours? Pilot salaries had gone through the roof. IndiGo appointed ABC Consultants, a placement consultant, to benchmark the staff salaries. It was uncharacteristic of IndiGo to appoint a consultant; this was possibly indicative of a lack of trust of their own internal audit capabilities. The new audit found that salaries were 25 per cent higher than industry standards. The salary hikes had also not been merit-based.

The drop in on-time performance made everyone sit up and take notice. To me, this was beginning of the end of Ghosh's run at the airline. Gangwal could see that the airline's operations were messed up. Making things worse it had stopped offering competitive fares and were losing a lot of business.

What was happening internally at the top was different from what was dished out for public consumption. Ghosh's social media posts projecting himself as the IndiGo 'architect' continued to flow uninterrupted. 'Employees would ask if the president is spending so much time on Twitter and Facebook who is making decisions in the company? You have to run the company also. Which other person running such a large company would have this kind of time?' Gangwal asked someone.

IndiGo even got a publicist at a fancy salary during this time. The over-the-top publicity planned using the new hand was not agreed to by the promoters. Plans to "plant stories" to bump up the share prices were canned. This made the publicist frustrated; he started to gripe to other IndiGo employees about not being allowed to execute his 'strategy'. Eventually, after an internal investigation into the circumstances of hiring this person, he was fired.

'He was a chalu aadmi, pump up the stock? What the hell is he doing? He is not a smart communicator; he changes the message cleverly I don't believe in it ... *Jo hai seedha-seedha bolo*. I don't like to mislead people. If you don't want to answer all the questions don't, but don't mislead' was Gangwal's view according to a person close to him.

He feels, once you manipulate something, then you will continue to do this all across the airline. 'Safety is the most important thing in our culture,' recalling Gangwal's words, this person said, 'The airline industry is very safe because of this culture of ethics, honesty, full disclosure and sharing information. If one part of the company starts spinning facts—it doesn't happen instantly –but in five or ten years—suddenly the marketing guy will think *thoda toh spin kar hi dete hain,* mistake *hogaya*, but I can spin it. Then one day pilots and mechanics will start spinning; then we don't know what the truth is. It's very dangerous. If this becomes a culture, you will have huge problems later.'

If this internal combustion was not enough, IndiGo got into a fight with the powerful GMR-led Delhi Airport. The airline refused Delhi airport's request to shift its operations partially to a new terminal. Shifting operations from Terminal 1 to Terminal 2 would not only cause 'grave inconvenience and confusion' among the passengers, it would also reduce flight options for passengers connecting through Delhi, argued IndiGo. Because IndiGo was unwilling, SpiceJet did not budge. If both did not move, the old terminal could not be expanded.

At the highest levels of the family-run GMR Group, IndiGo's stance was seen to be in bad taste. Ghosh, who many found very affable in early years at IndiGo, led the parleys with the airport operator. In one specific instance, during the stand-off that lasted for months, tense emails were exchanged between the airline and the airport for two-three days in which aviation-ministry officials were copied. 'There have been many tiffs with IndiGo but this was different,' said a GMR official who saw events from close quarters. 'Their body language in recent times had changed. There was a feeling within the community, whether right or wrong, that they were getting too big for their boots.'

IndiGo decided to approach the courts and lost the plea. However, by approaching the court, IndiGo bought time and did not have to shift flights during winters and have to countenance fogs and resultant flight disruptions.

IndiGo also felt different in public offices. IndiGo's lobbyist Vikram Chona, for example, would reach ahead of time for key meetings and even hold the lift for Ghosh on the second floor and not allow anyone to get in. I myself was stopped from entering the lift by him. Ghosh would then emerge and the lift would then become free for me and others waiting there to use.

IndiGo was changing rapidly and this was becoming more apparent post 2017 when it got caught in multiple episodes that brought bad press. IndiGo was seen as gaming the system in a number of episodes. In Feb 2017, securities regulator of Bureau of Civil Aviation Security (BCAS) suspended the licence of IndiGo's training facility for violating norms. BCAS alleged lapses in the examination system. The same set of question papers were repeated for many months. The rapidly growing airline had moved away from computer-based system to pen and paper tests. BCAS discovered that, for as many as eight batches of 35-40 students, all the candidates had scored over 95 per cent marks.

Then, in 2018, aviation minister Jayant Sinha informed the Parliament about an alarming fact—that airlines in India had reported 24,791 snags in 2017. With a fleet of 151 aircraft, IndiGo had reported a mere 340 snags—lower than the much smaller GoAir, Vistara and AirAsia with fleet sizes of 32, 17 and 14, respectively. Jet Airways had 9,689 snags (110-aircraft); SpiceJet

4,903 (57 aircraft); Air India 4,563 (164 aircraft); GoAir 1,888 (32 aircraft); AirAsia 1,367 (14 aircraft); and Vistara 1225 (17 aircraft).

It baffled everyone. According to a former top DGCA official, who did not want to be named, later it turned out that IndiGo did not qualify or report anything as a snag if the plane returned to the tarmac after taxiing out because of a glitch.

Two bigger embarrassments were on way. A Parliamentary Standing Committee on Transport, Tourism and Culture summoned IndiGo for a hearing after reports of its poor service standards were tabled. Ghosh appeared and apparently justified the airline's actions.

'We have lot of young people with so many degrees but the talent we require is not there,' Ghosh told the committee headed by All India Trinamool Congress MP, Derek O'Brien. 'IndiGo is hiring people from tier-II and tier-III cities and creating jobs there. Those who studied in government schools or mohalla-village areas cannot be trained to speak fluent English within a span of four to five weeks.'

This was deemed as a classist statement. The committee slammed the airline stating it 'totally disagrees' with Ghosh. It pointed out that government schools and colleges produce some of the best students in the country. While that may be arguable in the matter of spoken English, Ghosh's claims remained controversial.

'If a particular airline has grown exponentially, they should deploy a proportionate amount to the training of their staff instead of misbehaving and manhandling the passengers or blaming the youngsters from tier II and III cities and government schools,' the committee wrote in its report. If this scathing report was not enough, an IndiGo employee thrashed a passenger at Delhi airport soon enough.

After the video that showed an IndiGo ground staff member manhandling a passenger in his early fifties went viral on social media, Ghosh's face was all over the television channels. On prime time and live, TV anchors were calling Ghosh on his mobile phone—it was either busy or unavailable. For the staff in a service industry—while on duty and in uniform—to beat up their passenger, even if the passenger was pushy, without any fear of repercussions was beyond the pale and unthinkable. This was also different for the aviation industry because so far there had been episodes of Air India staff been manhandled by passengers sometimes, not that it was any less of a crime.

The 'IndiGo Beating Passenger' video had become biggest public-relations disaster for the airline since its inception. #IndiGoonstrended on Twitter/X with memes and cartoons flying around. Even Amul joined in. The legendary Amul Girl cartoon showed two airline staff holding a bespectacled man who his holding a buttered bread and trying to wriggle out. The copy read 'Have OnDeGo', followed by a cheeky one-liner below: Can be pan handled.

All the top IndiGo executives I spoke to recalled how the whole episode had shaken Rahul and Gangwal. IndiGo continued to request their PR agency Genesis BCW to get the mauling that was happening on the TV channels to stop somehow. However, nothing worked. They failed to stem the bleeding and was nearly booted out after the fiasco. However, they managed to survive.

As one executive of IndiGo said, 'The media had gone completely against us.' The episode 'led masses to believe that we are a very arrogant and insensitive airline. It created havoc internally. For the first time in IndiGo it led us to think—could we have handled this better? It will take us years to get out of this damage.'

In another case soon after, Saurabh Rai, a doctor with Narayana Hrudayalaya in Bengaluru accused the staff of IndiGo of manhandling and forcibly offloading him from an aircraft at Lucknow airport after he complained about mosquitoes in the plane. 'The staff termed me as a terrorist. They threatened me with dire consequences and pressurized me to write an apology letter, which I refused as I had done no wrong. They mistreated me. I had to arrange my next ticket for Bengaluru after a lot of hardship,' alleged Rai. IndiGo claimed that Rai had been offloaded due to his 'unruly behaviour' and for instigating other passengers.

By now, even government agencies were openly refuting claims made by IndiGo. When Urvashi Parikh Viren was injured after she fell from a wheelchair while being ferried by IndiGo staff at the Lucknow airport, IndiGo tried to pass on the blame to Airports Authority of India (AAI) citing a crack on the path and low lighting. State-owned AAI, usually slow to react, hit back swiftly and said IndiGo was lying and the lady fell due to the 'gross negligence of IndiGo staff' as he had chosen the 'wrong path on the tarmac and mishandled the passenger'. The area was sufficiently lit, it said.

A sense that the decision-making at the airline had slowed down seeped in. 'It's called glad handing' the same person said of Gangwal's view on this, 'like everyone makes everyone happy and no decisions are made? It's a very interesting phenomenon—one that we can do without.'

In the meanwhile, Gangwal had flooded the airline with expatriates to shake up the system.

'This business is very complex. Most of the complexity comes in the optimization part of revenue management, network planning, and scheduling, and that's where the big problem is. Unfortunately, in India we have never operated more than 150 planes and now we need an operation that can handle 300 narrow-body planes. This requires very sophisticated tools, so in that area we have brought in expats,' this person recalls Gangwal's words.

So, in 2016, Greg Taylor, who worked in lead roles in flight operations, financial planning and analysis, revenue management, and corporate planning in United Airlines with over 750 planes was brought in as a consultant to rejig the revenue management of the airline and add algorithms to the largely manual and excel driven revenue management and network planning system till then. Cindy Szadokierski—also from United Airlines– followed as vice president for airport operations and customer services. For network planning, Michael Swiatek was poached from Chile's LATAM Airlines. Jason Herter from United Airlines joined for operations control. In a significant move, Rohit Philip was brought in as CFO replacing Rahul's man Pankaj Madan.

IndiGo also hired William (Willy) Boulter who had been associated with Rahul previously. In another surprise induction in early 2017, IndiGo poached Go First CEO Wolfgang Prock-Schauer and made him Chief Operating Officer. Both were Rahu's choices.

Prock-Schauer's entry hurt Ghosh the most as his turf—pilot and crew operations—was under direct threat. Prock-Schauer started to conduct weekly pilot and crew meetings; he met with Rahul regularly. Ghosh was notably absent in such meetings.

'Wolfgang was fed with up Go First and one day he said something like can we think about something else? It was a God-sent opportunity for us. He is a very good person—a quality guy—and does a good job. I am shocked that Go First allowed him to go,' Rahul had explained to someone why he had hired him.

On 27 April 2018, Friday, at 1 p.m. Aditya sent a surprise note to the heads of the departments to meet him in the evening. He apologized for the short notice, especially it being the weekend. And more uncharacteristically, the message said that no preparations were needed for the meeting to be held at the Global Business Park headquarters of IndiGo.

The meeting started at 7.30 p.m. Rahul and Gangwal were present. Aditya was seated between the two of them. Rahul started by saying that it was a very sad day for the company as Aditya had decided to move on to do something of his own. Everyone—even those who knew things were not hunky dory—was shocked by the abruptness of the exit. They had expected Ghosh to remain on the board till a successor was found. However, he was eased out of not merely the IndiGo board but from that of all the other InterGlobe companies. Anil Parashar, a long-standing, low-key Rahul loyalist and chartered accountant, who has been with the family for years, now sits on most of the group's boards of directors.

Gangwal did not utter a single word—his face was impassive all through. After it was over, he shook hands only with one or two people, said thank you, and left the room. He did not chat up anyone in the room. Rahul, however, shook hands with everyone before he left. The three ladies in the leadership team—Summi Sharma who heads iFly, Suman Chopra, head of inflight services and Shalini Singh, head of administration—had tears in their eyes.

United's Greg Taylor—who had come as a consultant—was announced as the incoming CEO. Till he joined, Rahul was to be the interim CEO. 'Ten years is a long time on the treadmill. It's a tough business even if you are a chief people's officer,' the person aware of Gangwal's thinking recalled, 'Thoda break chahiye life mein.'

But picture *abhi baaki thi*. There was more drama to follow soon. A few years after the IPO, rumours started to make the rounds about the difference of opinion between the two co-founders. Although initially they were dismissed as products of the wild imagination of rival airlines, all hell broke loose the day Gangwal went public with the differences in the summer of 2019, accusing Rahul Bhatia of questionable related party transactions, violations of governance regulations and the company's code of conduct. He topped it off by claiming that IndiGo was being run like a 'paan ki dukaan.'

It was the biggest corporate shocker of that year. So, when did the relations between the two really sour? In my meetings with both Gangwal and Rahul, to get them to specify the point of divergence was rather difficult. It appeared that it had become too personal and I could not push beyond a point. Instead, I tried to find out more from other sources and marry that with what I got from the promoters to construct a more accurate picture of these times. Till 2016 everything appeared to be going swimmingly well—I found a less-viewed video of Rahul at the Graduation Day ceremony of The Indian School of Business, Hyderabad in which he was effusive in his praise for Gangwal.

'Rakesh Gangwal, the co-founder of IndiGo is someone I've known for almost 30 years. Early on in the planning phase of IndiGo, I had made one commitment to myself—if InterGlobe did ever launch an airline it would only happen in partnership with him otherwise we would simply not do it,' Rahul told a young crowd. Hero Moto's Pawan Munjal was seated behind him and even fetched him a glass of water when Rahul became very emotional and choked while speaking about IndiGo's success.

'The reason for this was quite elementary,' he continued, 'in all the years we have been involved with the airline industry I have personally not come across another individual and I mean this at a global level who is nearly as capable as Rakesh. The confluence of IndiGo's twelve and a half thousand employees, Rakesh is fundamental understanding of the airline business and

InterGlobe's unrelenting belief in the Indian opportunity in terms of commercial air transportation together with our resolve to contend with the challenges of doing business in our country is what makes the airline tick day in and day out.'

Changes, however, started to happen behind the scenes already. The first instance was the removal of Rahul's appointee Pankaj Madan as the CFO. And then Gangwal bringing in his own man Rohit Philip in 2016. That Madan is now back as InterGlobe's group CFO, after a hiatus, is indicative that Rahul would not have wanted him to leave IndiGo. He was merely meeting Gangwal's demands.

The relationship had not soured completely till July of 2017 too because Gangwal and Rahul surprised everyone and attended a call with analysts where only they spoke. They were talking about the privatization of Air India and why they had shown sudden interest in the state-owned airline.

'This is an interesting call with financial analysts and investors since we are only sharing our thoughts and vision and not numbers. It's like going to a corporate board meeting in a swimsuit,' Gangwal commented while replying to all the questions after Rahul made a brief introduction about the need to look at a loss-making Air India. The jocular tone showed Gangwal was still in fair control of IndiGo.

It is between the summer and the winter of 2017 that things hit a new nadir.

The CFO Philip had started making noises about related party transactions between Rahul's companies and IndiGo. Example were: IndiGo crew stayed at Rahul's InterGlobe-associated hotels such as Ibis; were trained at his Greater Noida simulator centre operated by InterGlobe and CAE; IndiGo itself operated from an InterGlobe property—Global Business Park; InterGlobe Air

Transport, led by former SpiceJet CEO Siddhanta Sharma, had control of IndiGo's sales and marketing and were paid 1 per cent of the ticket sales. At the peak, this would be around Rs 60 crore, according to a person in the know who did not want to be named.

Gangwal had raised objections and got the last one, prevalent since 2006, cancelled. The others, however, continued. Gangwal brought it up as a major governance issue in 2018 at the July board meeting. IndiGo was in the process of ordering 300 Airbus planes. As in the case with most other strategic matters, this was an area Gangwal led. However, an angry Gangwal said he would not touch the project.

'That left Bhatia very upset and totally at sea as there were clear responsibilities demarcated. After all, Bhatia had been taking everything on the chin here—from responding to the ministers' calls, to regulators, to investigation agencies to income tax offices while Gangwal did not even keep an official email id of IndiGo but was in India only quarterly to review performance. When the company became successful, he wanted a pie of everything,' said a Rahul aide.

In hindsight, when Gangwal tried to bring in his CFO, Taylor and other senior leaders, Rahul was alarmed. He brought in his own men–Wolfgang and Willy Boulter. Curiously even though Taylor was announced as the incoming CEO pending his security clearance from the home ministry, an area people close to Rahul monitored, his government approvals were never received.

Rahul felt that, after being allowed to take key decisions for the company throughout, Gangwal was now trying to take control of the company. In late May 2019, during a special board meeting of IndiGo, when Gangwal suggested a way out of the impasse—take in more independent directors on the IndiGo board and any related party transaction above Rs 50 lakh be approved by a full board – Rahul seemed to be convinced that was where things were headed, according to his aide.

As tensions escalated and legal opinions were resorted to, the two friends of 30 years landed up at Rahul's lawyer J. Sagar & Associates where Gangwal felt he was disrespected and became even more furious. For someone who had created IndiGo, to be asked pointed questions as if he was a criminal was infuriating.

He let it rip. 'Next question,' a furious Gangwal kept telling J. Sagar's lawyers. When they did not move on and persisted, 'But you haven't answered the question,' he went ballistic. 'English is neither my native tongue nor yours. Hindi *mein bolta hun: agla sawal*,' Gangwal snapped.

Rahul ended up calling his plan to expand board as 'nasty', and meet-the-lawyer effort drew to an unpleasant close. For three decades, there was no one between the two of them. Now, suddenly, there were a bunch of hard-nosed lawyers. This turned into a big fault line. There were also no sagacious men like HDFC's Deepak Parekh to broker a peace deal. The headstrong Gangwal possibly would not have listened to anyone.

Enraged, he wrote to markets regulator Securities and Exchange Board of India (SEBI), the prime minister, Narendra Modi, and to several cabinet ministers about governance issues at IndiGo. He launched his own website taking his governance concerns public. IndiGo had no idea until ten minutes after the letters had been shot off, that this was coming. The worst-case scenario in their minds was only a National Company Law Tribunal (NCLT)-driven process. Now IndiGo had to inform the stock exchange that a letter had indeed been written by Gangwal.

'Gangwal felt that he had not put his passion into this business to build a nationwide network to only have a situation where it became a private airline with public money,' said a person aware about Gangwal's decision to go to SEBI. 'It went beyond just peace between the promoters, he felt it needed a mature board if IndiGo was to go to the next level. 'When he was told he was not in control after all these years of being in control he could not take it lying down. 'What do you mean by one should not have control—he had a 37 per cent stake. *Mazak bana rakha hai*. Should one not blow up? Where does one draw the line? Can you be working for a year to fix the problem and still not blow up when nothing is being done?'

For Rahul, who resides in India and moves around in the top corporate and government circles, the taint that IndiGo was being run like a *paan ki dukaan* had an even more of a recall value than IndiGo staffers thrashing the passenger at the airport. At that time, Google top results showed IndiGo when one typed *paan ki dukaan*.

'Knowing Rahul, you may call him arrogant and that he keeps to himself or doesn't like media interactions, but that he has been called a thief, when he had mortgaged his own house to keep the airline flying, has hurt him no end,' the aide said. This was evident at the board meeting called to announce the first quarter results of the airline for 2019–2020. As if to cock a snook at Gangwal, Rahul asked his own restaurant, China Club, to serve food at the board meeting. He also asked them to serve paan with it. The Chinese restaurant—which Gangwal used to refuse in the early years and joke that he did not want to give IndiGo's money to Rahul's restaurant and ordered pizza instead –now served Indian food which Gangwal ate without any apparent discomfort and rounded if off with the *paan*.

IndiGo, and Rahul, heeded Gangwal all these years and even went for an IPO because Gangwal wanted it. Rahul was not in favour of it. And while the rationalization was that this would help the airline get better rates from lessors/banks because they can take higher exposure on a listed company, the feeling was that he was making his presence felt on the board of the company by shuffling it just before the IPO.

'Had Bhatia agreed to give control now, things would have flipped and today Bhatia would have been as powerless as Gangwal. This was all seen as a nibbling tactic,' the Rahul aide said. 'As far as the governance issues were concerned these were all joint ventures with top companies. For Rs 100 crore we will do all this?' this aide said of the JVs with French hotel group Accor S.A., Canada's flight training firm CAE etc.

The aide said Gangwal may have been instigated into going all out by a few people. One was a former finance minister—who is no more—and in recent years was not overly fond of Rahul. Another one was a top IndiGo official who had lost his throne.

Rahul too suddenly started to look at things very differently. He started telling people close to him that IndiGo was his brainchild; he had invested everything he had to start it, while Gangwal had even thought of selling the airline to Vijay Mallya when oil-crisis hit in 2008. On the other hand, Gangwal mocked this claim and said that when a crisis hits, one has to consider all options. As far as money was concerned, Airbus would have sent funds to IndiGo if he had made one phone call.

Rahul felt that although Gangwal had invested next to nothing to start IndiGo, he himself had been large-hearted and gave him nearly half the company. He also scoffed at Gangwal agreeing to pay Rs 35 crore to Taylor and Rs 100 crore to CFO Rohit Philip. 'Does even TCS (India's largest IT firm), give its top officials these kinds of salary packages?' he asked people close to him. Rahul replaced Philip and brought in Aditya Pande from GE Healthcare in 2019. Pande is now the CEO of InterGlobe Enterprises.

This paan ki dukaan jibe however also went on to haunt IndiGo's annual general meeting held in August of 2019. Rahul was present with all the board members, except Gangwal and Gangwal's friend and independent director, Anupam Khanna. Some shareholders asked Rahul why Gangwal and Khanna were not present to take questions from shareholders.

'*Main hoon na*,' quipped Rahul, to applause from the audience. He was perhaps also foretelling the future direction of the airline with those three words.

In a message aimed at showing Gangwal as dispensable perhaps, IndiGo announced a US$20 billion deal with engine-maker CFM International to power its next 280 Airbus A320neo and A321neo aircraft, switching from the glitch-ridden Pratt & Whitney engines that were selected by Gangwal. This was the airline's first mega deal announced since its inception in 2005, without Gangwal's imprint.

Rahul and Gangwal then fought in the courts. Eventually Gangwal decided to sell his entire stake in the airline by 2025. The 30-year-old friendship had finally ended in implacable animosity. Rahul had left Gangwal far behind in the race to take full control of India's largest airline –IndiGo.

What Next?

In 2009, IndiGo's then president, Aditya Ghosh, and chief commercial officer, Sanjay Kumar, landed in Patna to announce IndiGo's launch in the city. The announcement was received well—IndiGo was to introduce new flights connecting Patna to Bangalore, Mumbai, Kolkata, New Delhi, and Lucknow.

Back at their hotel, they were discussing that evening's upcoming meeting with local travel agents when their room door was flung open. Half-a-dozen trigger-happy youth stormed in with pistols and rifles in a scene that could have been out of any gangland movie. Ghosh and Kumar froze and then slowly rose from their seats with gun barrels being waved under their noses.

'Which one of you is Aditya Ghosh?' There was silence.

'He hasn't shown up for work today,' Kumar replied, realizing that the goons had not recognized Ghosh.

'Who is this guy?,' one of the gangsters countered.

'He is our sales head,' Kumar told them.

'This is not done. Tell him we will kidnap him even from Gurugram. We have our network everywhere,' the gang members threatened before leaving and banging the door shut behind them.

It turned out that the whoever had sent the goons was upset that the contract to handle IndiGo flights in Patna had gone to a rival company. No one was hurt; however, a terrified Ghosh and

Kumar fled from Hotel Chanakya to the airport. For months they did not return to Patna.

As IndiGo kept growing, it caught the attention of not just the 'Gangs of Patna' but of everyone in the industry. With over 350 aircraft, a 60 per cent plus market share and a whopping over Rs 1.3 lakh crore market capitalization already, the airline is now gearing up to double its size and ply a 600-aircraft fleet by the end of 2030. This new ambition and scale will bring even more attention and scrutiny, the likes of which IndiGo may have not seen before.

What would this journey be like? What are red flags that the airline should expect? Is there a reset needed?

Leadership arrogance

If you ask industry officials in private about IndiGo, 'arrogance' is the first word you will hear from them. The airline's success has given rise to overweening arrogance. This is manifested in multiple ways. IndiGo now believes it has the first right of refusal over any new aviation resource available or coming up in the country. It will do everything possible to appropriate it.

In the case of the new Noida airport, for example, while Tatas did build the airport, IndiGo clinched the deal to launch the inaugural flight in 2024. In return, it has won a package deal to get airport slots, parking bays etc. The airport was only too happy to get a major airline willing to park plenty of aircraft and open its second base on the outskirts of Delhi. Air India was late to the party.

Same was the case with Ayodhya. Riding the fervour over the new Ram Temple being built there, IndiGo offered to launch the first inaugural flight from the politically significant airport inaugurated by the Prime Minister Narendra Modi, and connect it to Delhi, Mumbai and Ahmedabad. IndiGo scored high on both asset-grabbing and mileage. Air India Express followed much later connecting the city from Delhi, Bengaluru and Kolkata.

IndiGo's aggression to get a government or regulatory policy to work in its favour has only grown in recent years. When Jet Airways went bankrupt in 2019, as per extant government policy, any available bilaterals were to be given, as the national carrier, first to Air India. The balance was to be distributed based on the domestic capacity deployed by the respective airline. The greater the capacity of the airline, the more the international bilateral rights they would be entitled to. At that time, nearly 50 per cent of the bilateral would have gone to IndiGo.

However, Ajay Singh, at that juncture leasing Jet Airways planes into SpiceJet, told an aviation ministry meeting convened to discuss the distribution that the government should avoid creating monopolies. He proposed that bilaterals should be given to those bringing in additional aircraft. More planes should mean more bilaterals. Go First's Ness Wadia supported him. He had five planes on ground and could get them up immediately too.

Rahul Bhatia was livid. He asked Wadia what his five planes were doing on the ground in the first place. Wadia snapped back saying he did not need Rahul's advice on how to run his business. He told Rahul and the other top airline and government officials present, 'Because I can afford it.'

I was told off the record that Rahul retorted that IndiGo had earned its dominance and had served the country for twelve years. He said his airline had followed route dispersal guidelines for regional connectivity and, most importantly, had 'played by the book'. When IndiGo was a small fry, it had accepted whatever was given and never had an issue with that. But an airline had failed, and Rahul pointed out that airlines build their presence over a long period of time. How could you artificially skew that presence,

Rahul demanded an explanation. He wanted to know why the policy had been made in the first place; might as well make it a fish market, he said.

He argued that if he increased the aircraft utilization of his 200 planes from twelve to fourteen hours, it amounted to a 15 per cent jump in productivity, equal to adding thirty additional planes.

Vistara's then CEO, Leslie Thng, pitched in with his own logic. As Jet Airways ran a two-class (economy and business class) service on its international routes, its bilaterals should be given to Vistara so, that the premium presence of Indian carriers does not diminish on those routes. Rahul snapped again, and said it was no big deal –he would get wide-body aircraft too and put a two-class configuration to London. Thng backed down.

Airline owners had never squabbled so openly in the ministry— an indication of how the industry had changed dramatically within a decade. Earlier, Vijay Mallya and Naresh Goyal ruled the roost in such meetings, while Rahul took the corner seat, quietly fiddling with his phone and departing quickly once the meeting was over, leaving, the two big shots to give bytes to the media. Nevertheless, by the end of this meeting, IndiGo had managed to get a fair, share of the bilaterals and airport slots. It mounted several flights to capitalize on the gap created by Jet's demise, especially in the lucrative Middle East market.

But this propensity to grab whatever possible creates a lot of bad blood and airports have started raising their voices. 'If someone is so dominant, they will start dictating–terms, like Tony Fernandes used to—make things here and there. Nobody wants IndiGo in a dominant position any more than they already are,' said a Delhi airport official. Reportedly, IndiGo not only demands changes in airport infrastructure but also that sometimes airport lifts should be reserved for their staff. They claim non-availability of lifts was resulting in delayed flight departures and affecting adversely the airline's on-time performance and aircraft utilization.

In the summer of 2023, a proposal to give unused slots of existing carriers to other airlines was placed on hold by the government because the airports protested that this will favour IndiGo. This was perhaps the first time that airports had come together in the open to oppose IndiGo's rise.

The fear of market domination is not unfounded though. In 2012, when the IndiGo was nowhere close to its current scale, it had a run in with India's largest online travel portal, MakeMyTrip. The portal was selling heavily discounted fares without naming the airline. This was unprecedented and perceived as a ruse to favour Kingfisher Airlines, which had run out of money, was desperate to get some revenue to run its operations, and, therefore, ready to sell cheap tickets.

IndiGo protested and pulled out all its inventory from MakeMyTrip. For three weeks, the travel portal could not offer IndiGo flights. With 20 per cent of the market then, IndiGo was still a significant player. As customers drifted off to other portals to book IndiGo tickets, MakeMyTrip scrambled, apologized and stopped selling opaque fares. IndiGo returned to MakeMyTrip and Kingfisher shut shop in a few months.

The anti-trust regulator Competition Commission of India (CCI) has also taken note of the airline's rapid market share growth. It has written to the aviation ministry in recent years but has not gone beyond that. Ashok Chawla, the former aviation secretary and former head of CCI, says that if a player's market share goes above 45–60 per cent it is a matter of concern, but the CCI may not have gone deeper because airline economics is too complex and does not lend itself to easy determination.

'There are two-three things on how to handle abuse of dominance,' he said, 'First, what are the competitive constraints—whether other competitors are able to compete with you. If not, then which are the city pairs where it is so? Then you go deep into it—which are these city pairs and then ask them to cut flights.'

Chawla says the telecom industry is a case in point. The government was concerned about Vodafone crumbling while Reliance Jio and Bharti Airtel grew dominant. Ironically, Air India was privatized in 2022, but in 2023, the government chose to buy a 33 per cent stake in Vodafone India.

'It raises red flag because a two-player aviation market is not good for economic activity—it tends to work against [the] consumer,' Chawla said. 'Cartelization concerns had come up when I was there saying that airlines are fixing fares, but I don't think much has happened. My advice to CCI would be to keep a close watch and keep this on their radar.'

Some work already appears to have begun. In its August 2023 report, the thirty-one-member Parliamentary standing committee on transport, tourism and culture has said that the aviation ministry should introduce 'reasonable upper fare caps' for all airlines to ensure accessibility of air transport for the common man. This came after a summer in which fares shot through the roof as Go First folded and IndiGo announced a record Rs 3,000-crore profit for the quarter ending June. Airlines will protest airfare regulation. Such measures, history has shown, also do not end up helping the passenger eventually. Government is therefore more likely to push for increased competition over time, many industry officials feel.

Dominated by IndiGo and the Air India group, a two-airline system is unusual and not heard of anywhere in the world. 'India is in a unique situation. The closest is Indonesia, where LionAir took away 60 per cent of the market share from Garuda. But Indonesia does not have enough population. If you look at any country anywhere else, you do not have this kind of problem where you have this kind of demand and growth. So India will have to handle its own issue,' former senior vice president of sales in Asia-Pacific and India at Boeing, Dinesh Keskar said. 'It is not going to change for a long time. Once you get to that position it is hard to lose (for IndiGo). The 500-plane order will seal their number one position over Air India.'

Even as the Indian market moves from around 700 aircraft and 144 million passengers a year to 1,000–1,200 aircraft and 260 million passengers by 2027, the dominant player will likely be IndiGo with a 450-aircraft fleet up from the current 350 plus planes. Air India with a likely 350 aircraft fleet will be the second largest but have a much bigger medium-haul and long-haul international presence.

This is in contrast to other aviation markets such as the US and China which have multiple carriers. In the US, the top four airlines—Delta, American, Southwest and United—carry nearly 60 per cent of the traffic. The market share is more or less evenly split between these four airlines while in India, Air India group's share is not even half of IndiGo's.

Similarly, China, where airlines are state-controlled, has a 600-million strong domestic market served by nine major airlines. Of these, with a 400-600 aircraft fleet each, Air China Limited, China Southern Airlines and Eastern Airlines are the largest. The balance six have 100-300 aircraft each. There are another eleven regional airlines and a few small operators too.

Air India

Despite its dominance, IndiGo is highly paranoid about competition and its key employees joining competition. Which is why, in 2021, following Air India's privatization and Akasa Air becoming a reality, IndiGo became even more protective of its key staff.

The aircraft finance team, for example, was ring-fenced, albeit using inducements and sweeteners. A few still opted for Air India.

Similarly, the airline asked its superannuating CEO, Ronojoy (Rono) Dutta, to sign a two-year non-compete agreement during which he agreed—in return for millions of dollars in payout—not to engage in any business that is similar or in competition with the company. Interestingly, the clause proscribed him doing this with any airline or potential airline within 4,800 kilometres of India. Dutta, 69, had been out of jobs for a long time, and his last full-time airline job was with Air Sahara in 2006 when he was brought to IndiGo by Rahul at the peak of his crisis with Gangwal. Dutta and Gangwal were once colleagues and both went on to head US airlines.

'Joining competition is their biggest insecurity. The AF team got very steep hikes, even till the manager level,' said an IndiGo executive. So far IndiGo officials did not have many local options to join a stable, well-paying airline. Vistara salaries were lower and Jet Airways was in bad shape. A rejuvenated Air India has completely changed the equation, raising fears of poaching.

Now many staffers are joining Air India from IndiGo. 'Our focus on employees is withering. They need to retain talent—many are going to Air India because of better working conditions. We are becoming a training institute for other airlines, for ground staff, crew, and sometimes even captains,' said a senior IndiGo official who did not want to be named.

Does it really matter? It does, this person explained. The new employees take time to adapt. However, there is much pressure on them and they start to falter. The recent episodes of delayed flights and of boarding and then offloading passengers from a flight are cases in point. On such occasions, experience counts.

Perhaps this is why the new CEO, Pieter Elbers, has brought in a new philosophy of employee engagements. This is not just monetary inducement (IndiGo paid a one and a half month's basic salary in bonus in May as it geared to announce record profits) but events such as IndiGo Superstar where IndiGo staff showcase their talents like singing, dancing and acting. Then there is IndiGo Cricket League for the airline's staffers to get together and play cricket. At the local stations, the airline encourages badminton and football tournaments. 'The focus is—keep them connected to you because you can't always give monetary benefits,' the IndiGo official said.

Would this be enough to keep its team intact when the competition is Air India? Its owners, the Tatas, are acknowledged as a benevolent employer while IndiGo is a known hard taskmaster. Air India also has the charm of having a much larger international network including long-haul locations. This is a big draw for employees who are entitled to free and subsidized tickets on the network.

However, people have not left in droves because IndiGo still is the best paymaster. It is well organized, has slick processes such as applying for leave from an app—when eligible, and there are no deviations. If it smells any move to poach, salaries are hiked. Because it is growing all the while, the promotions too come fast. Any valuable senior talent who may try to leave, it will grab back. In one recent case, a senior official who had left IndiGo and joined a rival airline and was set to again move out because of lack of promotion was snatched back and all the formalities of on-boarding him back were completed in just one day. In Air India, processes move at a glacial pace.

So will Air India really make a dent on IndiGo? At some point, when Air India group reaches 35–40 per cent of the market from the current 29 per cent, it will start hurting. Passengers will shift to a better product with possibly similar levels of on-time performance. This will be more on the metro routes where IndiGo has a very strong presence with hourly flights. This can potentially be challenged and then outsmarted as Air India and Vistara network combine.

Gangwal was very worried about this prospect and continues to be. He always felt that Air India under the combined might of the Tatas and Singapore Airlines will create a lot of trouble for them at some point of time. When the time comes, IndiGo will have to reduce airfares to be competitive—that is when its current 'super profits' will deplete.

'Only capacity addition can rock the boat for IndiGo,' another IndiGo official said, 'Continuous addition and for years.' Industry watchers expect Air India to start pinching IndiGo in two years. For IndiGo, 2024 and 2025 should have been even more golden years in the absence of serious competition. However, the airline has had the wind taken out of its sails to some extent by the faulty Pratt and Whitney engines which compelled it to ground nearly one-third of its fleet. People in the industry feel that retrofitting the engines with rectified spare parts will take most of these two years.

While the airline has wet-leased aircraft to make up for this lost capacity, the airline could have easily doubled its daily flights to 2,500–3,000 from 2,000 if it were not for these engine troubles.

Air India, which chose the more expensive CFM engines (which IndiGo too later switched to) for its Airbus aircraft, will not need such grounding.

Many in IndiGo feel if Gangwal had not broken up with IndiGo, and the engine problem had not cropped up, the airline's market cap would have gone way past the current Rs 1.3 lakh crore, since there was no competition worth the name.

The engine issue is also hurting the airline in other ways. The international crew on the wet-leased aircraft are not amenable to the airline management as much as the home-grown and trained staff are. The wet-leased planes which come with pilots and crew from other operators are also expensive. And therefore, IndiGo's own pilots, which are the most expensive workforce in an airline making up for nearly 70 per cent of the salaries or around Rs 5,000 crore annually in case of IndiGo, will be underutilized.

IndiGo has anyways been keeping dozens of extra pilots on its payrolls, which many in the airline say, is to ward off the possibility of a union.

The grounded aircraft are also keeping many other staff occupied in random work. 'Resources are getting distracted in doing non-productive work to keep those planes intact. Around forty planes had to be returned to lessors in 2024. Now what happens to them?' an IndiGo official asks. Their lessors claim that they had given IndiGo the planes in an airworthy condition; IndiGo has to sort out the engine problems and return the aircraft airworthy to them.

'And then, Air India is getting stronger day by day, they are adding fleet, they don't have OEM problems. We face more headwinds, but AI under the Tatas is a new organization and we have people and infrastructure—that is our advantage,' he adds.

For Elbers this will be a big challenge. His challenge will also be to break the multiple silos that have come up within the company over the years. An official who was in the airline's IT department told me that many now feel it is akin to a government job; to protect their turf, either they do not share critical information with other departments or they create problems. The IT department itself has gone through a lot of churn; the airline has had several network outages too.

Elbers has also started work on human resources and the succession plan for the top management. Most of the leadership at the airline is either past the retirement age or is close to it. They include head of engineering S.C. Gupta, head of operations Ashim Mittra, head of customer service Sanjeev Ramdas, chief aircraft acquisition officer Riyaz Peer Mohamed and head of in-flight services Suman Chopra. All these people, except Riyaz, were hired by Rahul and therefore have a great say in how things are run.

And given that Rahul keeps in touch with many of his hires also complicates matters for the new expat CEO. However people in the airline who deal with both Rahul and Elbers closely say that the new CEO holds a lot of sway on Rahul. While they give many examples, one that can clearly be seen is the people restructuring Elbers has carried out.

Engineering head Gupta and crew head Chopra will finally leave the airline this year making way for Parichay Datta and another new person who will be appointed in place of Chopra. This was unthinkable so far because many felt Rahul, who prefers loyalty, would not have allowed it. Similarly IndiGo has appointed Isidro Pablo Porqueras Orea, former chief operating officer (COO) of Spanish low-cost airline as chief of transformation (a designation that wasn't there earlier). Many expect Orea to fill the gap that will be created after the retirement of the current President and COO, Wolfgang Prock-Schauer. It remains to be seen whether Orea will be made President and COO too. Other senior officials could also make way for younger blood. However, some internally fear Elbers may be gradually filling top posts with expats at a time when the airline is on auto-pilot mode, with little competition and gushing record profits (which is keeping Rahul, who has also been busy buying hotels across the world and is launching a new hotel brand Miiro in Europe, happy).

But this change did not start in 2024 but after Elbers took charge and moved part of chief strategy and revenue officer Sanjay Kumar's portfolio to someone else. Kumar quit. That Kumar, another of Rahul's close aides, was allowed out of the airline showed that Elbers had begun stamping his authority. Rahul will allowing this but perhaps unnerved by the prospect of a trusted lieutenant joining competition like Air India quickly appointed Kumar as the CEO of his travel firm ITQ.

If one looks at the narrative Elbers, 54, has started pushing since his joining one can see that it clearly focusses on 2030 and what the airline needs to do to achieve the 600 plane fleet target. Interestingly this target dovetails very well with Elbers' retirement age and would potentially mean that he is looking at a second term at IndiGo when the current term that started in 2022 expires.

Elbers has also focussed on himself much more than the previous CEO Dutta and has channeled all external communication to go out largely via him, people at the airline say. This is clearly visible in his outings to meet the staff at various stations, showing himself enjoying various Indian festivals or even at the analyst calls which earlier used to include many leadership officials but has now largely been shrunk to include only the CFO and CEO.

'There was too much dependence on the old guard,' said a senior government official who has seen IndiGo's rise from close quarters. 'Jet too had the same issue. But when new blood was inducted without proper planning, many of them were from union backgrounds and they supported socialist ideas and did not allow policies that could help cut costs. That also contributed to the airline's downfall.'

That the airline is set in its policies and ways and nurses a fear that change would upset the applecart and skew the entire system is likely another problem that Elbers may face. Another challenge is to bridge the disparity that has crept into the rank and file of the airline employees. Some have been given a lot of shares by the airline and then there are the 'others' who have nothing.

Do the employee engagement events help? To some extent they do. But many feel they are staged and often those close to the management show up there. Many are youngsters. Others who avoid them find these shows, where pilots are dancing on stage with their uniform on, not in good taste. To his credit, Elbers has done a good job of asking the right questions and following up on them diligently—a practice that had been given the go-by during the Rono Dutta era as he preferred to keep everyone happy instead. Now if IndiGo COO Wolfgang Prock-Schauer says a certain number of aircraft will be up and running on a particular date, Elbers will remind him of the same on that specific date and drill down further if the planes are not ready. The level of questioning and foresight though is no match to what Gangwal brought, these senior IndiGo officials add.

Global Expansion

One of the KPIs of Elbers is to prepare the airline for its international growth on a scale heretofore unseen by the airline. IndiGo would be loath to let Air India dominate the international market and corner the entire domestic business class and corporate traffic pie left after Jet's demise.

International expansion is a more complex and risky process compared to domestic expansion where IndiGo did not have to contend with deep-pocketed players such as Emirates, Qatar, British Airways, Etihad, Lufthansa and Singapore Airlines. This fear is showing in how slow IndiGo has been to order wide-body aircraft. It has instead been running various experiments.

Using its narrow-body planes, IndiGo has conducted several internal exercises on long-haul flights with one stop en route. However, the results were not very encouraging. Passengers do not prefer to fly long distances in a narrow-bodied aircraft. Further, a one-stop flight will be a drag on the commercials since double take-offs and landings will use more fuel and lead to higher engine wear-and-tear costs.

These studies showed that while flights to Hong Kong or Istanbul may work, because IndiGo can consistently offer cheaper fares to rival the competition due to the economies offered by the more fuel-efficient A321neo, passengers may prefer to pay more for flights to say, London, on a wide-bodied Airbus A330 or A350 or Boeing 777 or 787.

This may have prompted IndiGo, since 2023, to experiment by using leased Turkish Airlines Boeing 777 planes and flying them to Istanbul from India using Turkish Airlines crew. Passengers are then allowed to travel further on Turkish Airlines's vast network. IndiGo's domestic services provide a strong 15–20 per cent feed to its international flights already.

With lessons from flying Turkish Airlines planes, IndiGo is working to bring special seats that are something between a premium-economy and business class seats on its A321XLR for the first time. The A321XLRs are also likely to have ovens, something the airline has avoided for nearly twenty years of its existence now. These planes which offer higher range are expected to arrive in 2025 and will help connect cities as far as Rome and Beijing. This will extend IndiGo's currently restricted market reach of the Middle East and Southeast Asia.

Partly to connect business class passenger onward through Istanbul and partly to take on Air India, IndiGo is adding business class seats on some of its A321neos. They will enter the service from 2024 and fly mostly on the domestic metro routes and nearby international destinations. The airline is also working on introducing a loyalty programme. It has also finally ordered 30 Airbus A350s in 2024 that will start arriving from 2027 and finally allow IndiGo to go long-haul on its own. In some ways, all this will complicate its simple business model and introduce complexities that have dragged down other mega airlines.

'There are many things that Air India does very well and there are certain things that we can improve upon,' Gangwal said, capturing it well when IndiGo first made a half-hearted pitch to buy Air India. 'In terms of time, how long would it take us to replicate or do something similar to what Air India does—I think it will be a long, long time. Air India has been able to acquire these routes through bilateral negotiations over a seventy-year-period. Back then, access to many large airports was much easier than what it is now—aviation was at its infancy. Most of these large airports like Heathrow, Kennedy, etc., are largely slot constrained. So, not for a moment do we believe that we will be able to replicate a network like Air India or a network like United in the near future. That is simply not going to happen.'

Safety

In scaling up, IndiGo will also have to ensure it does not take shortcuts in its safety standards—the kind DGCA discovered in 2023. DGCA fined IndiGo after many of its aircraft tails were found to be hitting the runway while landing.

To the airline's credit though, no passenger has been killed on an IndiGo flight in nearly twenty years now even as two crashes have killed 179 people in two Air India Express crashes during the same time period.

But fast growth, new recruits, quick turnarounds, and high productivity can be a deadly cocktail. Receiving DGCA notices and incidents like IndiGo staff manhandling a passenger are not good signs.

Gurdeep Singh Arora, who was a manager in IndiGo's airport operations and customer services (AOCS) from 2017 to 2022 says the airline needs to revisit its airport operations processes minutely. 'It was not a staff mistake,' Arora said of the manhandling incident, 'The staff was more concerned that this passenger batch (on the bus) leaves so that we can send flights on time. He would have shouted and the passenger would have not liked it. I, as an IndiGo airport staff, do not want a passenger to keep questioning me because every question will eat into my time. They have this "On Time Target" score; then there is competition between stations, which station did best on time, etc. All this pressure leads to such incidents.' Arora said the airline stipulates that the aircraft doors should close within thirty-two to thirty-seven minutes and the flight should be on its way.

'The stress on the staff is huge especially on the air side. Now they have huge ramp equipment and to push it to aircraft and to align it takes to two to three minutes. Then the doors open, but passengers can't be forced to disembark.'

Indeed, there have been multiple consumer complaints against IndiGo on social media too. Some stories have made it to mainstream media as well. In 2013, at the Kolkata airport, early in the morning at 3 a.m., an employee on duty whose job was to ensure the safety and maintenance of ramps, fell twenty-five feet to his death. His head hit the concrete on the tarmac.

Many airlines push for early departures, Arora said, but IndiGo has so many departures and, therefore, so many chances of being questioned. Even a minute's delay brings so much scrutiny that the staff gets frustrated. Airport staff are measured on a host of activities—from average passenger waiting time, average check-in time, average waiting time in the queue, average waiting in the security line, boarding time, time of arrival of the bus, time for baggage off-loading, first bag to last bag on the conveyor belt, time taken for first bag after first coach arrives, etc. All this keeps them on their toes all the time—and, therefore, highly stressed.

'Even with wheelchair passengers they will have to hurry, and then how will you treat them? The staff will give you an answer sometimes without listening to what you have said. What service can you expect?' he asked. The drivers and loaders at the airport are severely overworked. There are no DGCA guidelines on duty hours that applies to them as in the case of crew. Moreover, they constantly live under the fear of losing their jobs.

IndiGo's drivers at the Delhi airport are mostly from Rajasthan and from the scheduled tribe called Meena. Arora says that if they say they have a job at the airport, they receive fat dowries. So, it is a sought-after job even if it pays only Rs 18,000 a month and one has to stay in cramped quarters in areas like Mahipalpur, close to the Delhi airport.

'After this, if someone makes a mistake, he is treated shabbily. You punish him by making him wait for hours. Even if he has done night duty, you still call him at 7.30 a.m. and then meet him only at 2 p.m.,' said Arora.

IndiGo also insists that drivers wear seatbelts, which can be avoided as the driving speed is a mere 20 kmph. The drivers were also made to wear ties. But the gust from the AC blower would send them up into the drivers' faces affecting visibility and resulting in near accidents. Eventually, Cindy Szadokierski, the former vice president, airport operations and customer services, had to intervene and stop the practice.

'It is easy to sit in an AC room and say planes can turnaround in so many minutes. In real time, if someone checks CCTV footage of the turnaround, a lot of safety lapses would be visible. Some of them can be major,' Arora said.

IndiGo may not have had a deadly accident, but an airline official said it should reflect upon its processes and do an external audit to check if everything mandated in the operations manual is being followed or if some of it gets bypassed in the pressure to maintain efficiency to avoid being answerable in the questioning that can follow.

'The ratio of full-scope engineers versus category A engineers is critical in establishing the backbone of engineering. So, if full-scope aviation maintenance engineers (AMEs) are less, then critical jobs such as structural jobs, borescope jobs, etc., may get less attention. That is where the airline needs to focus on developing them,' a senior airline official said. Category A engineers are permitted to provide limited certification of inspection and maintenance tasks or carry out simple rectification only.

The big carriers in the Middle East, including the newcomer Riyadh Air, will keep poaching full-scope engineers from IndiGo. The airline thus will have three pain points—increasing fleet, Middle East airlines and Air India. For a fast-growing airline, any accident or major incident could bring in swift government intervention and the rivals will be only too keen to say: I told you so.

The airline also needs to find ways to keep the pilots on its side. Many pilots have formed social media groups to vent their growing frustration over salaries, excessive night or early morning flights, and rostering issues. A constant gripe is that they are treated as a 'mere number on the screen' and not given enough respect as they were in Kingfisher Airlines or Jet Airways.

'They are successful because they do not give power to the pilot. You get an email if you close the door late; one minute late and the fleet supervisor will call; you are always rushed. You can only survive if you put your head down and fly,' said one senior pilot who has left IndiGo.

The word 'union' spooks IndiGo. If anyone is heard talking about it or even criticizing the management, there are enough pilots in the cockpit who are friendly with the management who will quickly pass it on to the headquarters. Then the ordeal begins.

In 2022, a few pilots had said something on how they would not follow the fuel-saving guidelines since salaries had not been restored to the pre-Covid levels and that the airline needed a union. All this reached Gurugram in good time and the airline's management pilots came down hard on some of those pilots. Some pilots got so scared they left the airline soon enough.

While pilots have not been able to form a union yet or call in sick en masse, in 2022, the cabin crew was bold enough to surprise the airline by calling in sick in large numbers. They had decided to go for Air India's first big recruitment drive after the Tatas took over. Dozens of flights were delayed. A few months later, dozens of maintenance technicians went on sick leave in Hyderabad and Delhi to protest against their low salaries. Human resources will continue to be a big challenge for IndiGo. It is quite possible that it will be forced to better its working conditions and offer more perks to retain staff over the coming years.

Cultural Context

IndiGo will also have to reshape itself culturally. The airline has been built with a very US-centric approach and this reflects across the airline and in its cabin. Many say it is made for a high-context culture like India but functions like it is in a low-context culture.

A high-context culture relies on implicit communication and non-verbal cues, where a message cannot be understood without a great deal of background information on one-on-one relationships. Asian (including India), African, Arab, central European and Latin American cultures are generally considered to be high-context cultures.

On the other hand, a low-context culture relies on explicit communication, interpersonal connections are of shorter duration, is task-centred and decisions and activities focus on what needs to be done and have a division of responsibilities. Cultures with western European roots, such as the US, the UK, Australia etc., are generally considered to be low-context cultures.

Sometimes, when passengers complain about IndiGo's culture, this is probably the reason for it. This aspect will need the airline's attention. Perhaps IndiGo could learn something from Southwest Airlines founder Herb Kelleher, even though it was established in a low-context culture. In the fifty-six years of its existence, the airline—which now flies 815 planes and has around 17 percent domestic market share—is widely loved in the US.

Kelleher would often cite Southwest's success saying, 'A company is stronger if it is bound by love rather than by fear', and how, when 'someone comes to me with a cost-saving idea, I don't immediately jump up and say yes. I ask: what's the effect on the customer?'

Southwest, which has a heart as its logo and LUV (IndiGo's flight code is 6E which sounds similar to 'sexy') as its scrip code, consistently ranks among the top three most popular airlines in the US—above the traditional names like American, Delta and United. If you also ask people in the US, anecdotally they will say they love Southwest but may have a very bad opinion of an ultra-low-cost airline like Spirit Airlines.

This love is because of Southwest's policies. For example, Southwest's passengers do not have to fear losing money even if they miss their flight. The airline holds the money in reserve and passengers can book a flight whenever they want to, at a later date. It also does not have any change fees, unlike many other airlines which charge a bomb. It also allows one or sometimes two checked-in bags free, when other airlines insist on charging for checked-in luggage.

On top of that, it has a loyalty programme where, unlike most airlines which reserve very few seats for miles' redemption (2 per cent of total seats mostly), Southwest says if there is a free seat, it's all yours. Its schedule is also pretty much set a year in advance and rarely changes. It is happy to make its flights wait for its connecting passengers if needed and will not push back before time if it can afford to do so. In other words, Southwest does not pay mere lip service to customers, and people, therefore, flock to it.

An IndiGo official who has worked at the airport for a long time says that one of the reasons why some passengers get frustrated with IndiGo is because they are, all the time, trying to maximize profits by charging for everything from seat selections to food. Though most low-cost airlines follow that business model somehow by the time the passenger gets to the IndiGo aircraft, he or she is overwhelmed.

In a social media campaign in mid-2023, IndiGo came up with a slogan 'Love you too'. Therein lies a problem. It has assumed, taking its success as the touchstone, that it is loved. To become genuinely loved what it needs to do is to change its policies—while not losing sight of its profits—to be more accommodating, more friendly, show genuine concern towards the passengers and pivot towards a more Southwest-like approach as it grows bigger. As it thinks long-haul, where service matters more, it will need all those attributes even more. Similarly, one of its new campaign is called 'India by IndiGo'. The line reeks of domination rather than humility, many industry officials feel, something that it can do more with as the largest airline even as it gets ready to take on erstwhile national carrier Air India.

Still, what IndiGo has achieved in these years is truly amazing. Unless botched by often-cited arrogance, too many product tweaks and poorly-executed long-haul expansion to take on deep-pocketed Air India it is likely to be a long-term story which will have short-term bad patches but ultimately keep soaring, fuelled by India's economic growth which will drive volumes, profits, expansion and everything else. It is also the only 'Make in India' airline brand that has made its investors rich. At current market capitalization of around Rs 1.3 lakh crore or $15 billion, it is the fourth most valued airline globally after Ryanair ($33 billion), Delta Airlines ($30 billion) and Southwest ($17 billion) overtaking even United Airways ($14 billion). Interestingly, Gangwal first started his airline career at United and even when he launched IndiGo and became an entrepreneur, which most Marwaris pride being one, he was still a millionaire. But now as he exits IndiGo, he leaves as a multi-billionaire, proving even the legendary Richard Branson, 73, wrong. Branson once famously said: If you want to be a millionaire, start with a billion dollars and launch a new airline.

Both Rahul, 64, and Gangwal, 71, are now aviation legends themselves.

And importantly, between the time when Rahul had first dreamt of starting an airline in mid-1990s and now, thirty years later, he has not only made his reluctant father Kapil Bhatia proud by becoming the core of Indian aviation, but also ensured that globally too, IndiGo is Sky High.

References

3. Rakesh Gangwal

https://www.flightglobal.com/news/articles/where-next-for-the-gds-178095/Gangwal Wolf tutelage

Jain, Madhu. 2007. 'Living the American Dream', *Washingtonian*, 1 December, https://www.washingtonian.com/2007/12/01/living-the-american-dream/

MarketScreener 'Stephen M. Wolf', https://www.marketscreener.com/business-leaders/Stephen-Wolf-05DV7X-E/biography/

Moneylife Digital Team. 2015. 'IndiGo IPO: Promoters Flying High with Dividends to Themselves', 21 October, https://www.moneylife.in/article/indigo-ipo-promoters-flying-high-with-dividends-to-themselves/43765.html

Pais, Arthur J. 1999. 'Indian CEO pilots US Airways to dizzy heights', Rediff on the net, 24 April, http://m.rediff.com/business/1999/apr/24usair.htm

Shukla, Tarun. 2022. 'Jyotiraditya Scindia: I Would Like to See Many More Airlines Coming Onboard', 5 December, https://economictimes.indiatimes.com/prime/transportation/jyotiraditya-scindia-i-would-like-to-see-many-more-airlines-coming-onboard/primearticleshow/95985065.cms

Swoboda, Frank. 1998. 'US Airways President Promoted to CEO', 19 November, https://www.washingtonpost.com/archive/business/1998/11/19/us-airways-president-promoted-to-ceo/b249e8d3-d29c-4d35-a014-f7fb2715af47/

Zuckerman, Laurence, 'US Airways' Top Executive Is Leaving at a Critical Time', *The New York Times*, 28 November, https://www.nytimes.com/2001/11/28/business/us-airways-top-executive-is-leaving-at-a-critical-time.html

5. Rahul Bhatia

Thakur, Pradeep. 2005. 'DRI Drive Against Imported Cars Backfires', *The Times of India*, 5 December, https://timesofindia.indiatimes.com/india/DRI-drive-against-imported-cars-backfires/articleshow/1318153.cms

8. Lobbying

Mahapatra, Dhananjay. 2008. 'Jail Beckons Airport Duty Evaders', *The Times of India*, 29 January, https://timesofindia.indiatimes.com/india/Jail-beckons-airport-duty-evaders/articleshow/2739058.cms

Datta, Saikat. 2022. 'Whose Name On A Grain Of Rice?' *Outlook*, 5 February, https://www.outlookindia.com/magazine/story/whose-name-on-a-grain-of-rice/250566

ET Bureau. 2010. 'Govt Admits to Scam in Rice Exports', *Economic Times*, 20 November, https://economictimes.indiatimes.com/news/economy/foreign-trade/govt-admits-to-scam-in-rice-exports/articleshow/6957480.cms

Singh, Ajmer. 2010. 'Babus Ground Ethics for Aviation Jobs', 13 May, *India Today*, https://www.indiatoday.in/india/story/babus-ground-ethics-for-aviation-jobs-74121-2010-05-13

Sharma, Shantanu Nandan. 2017. 'Demitting Office with Full Sense of Satisfaction: Chief Election Commissioner Nasim Zaidi', *Economic Times*, 2 July, https://economictimes.indiatimes.com/news/politics-and-nation/demitting-office-with-full-sense-of-satisfaction-chief-election-commissioner-nasim-zaidi/articleshow/59404386.cms

Press Reader. 2017. 'Jet Airways Launches Bonus JPMiles Offer', 8 June, https://www.pressreader.com/oman/times-of-oman/20170608/281895888214766

Pandey, Munish. 2019. 'CBI Arrests Lobbyist Deepak Talwar in Aviation Scam Case', *Business Today*, 26 July, https://www.businesstoday.in/latest/economy-politics/story/cbi-arrests-lobbyist-deepak-talwar-in-aviation-scam-217041-2019-07-26

PTI. 2019. 'Praful Patel "Dear Friend" of Lobbyist Deepak Talwar: Enforcement Directorate', *Economic Times*, 10 June, https://economictimes.indiatimes.com/news/politics-and-nation/praful-patel-dear-friend-of-lobbyist-deepak-talwar-enforcement-directorate/articleshow/69728204.cms?from=mdr

Outlook Web Desk. 2022. 'Past Those Sand Traps', 5 February, https://www.outlookindia.com/magazine/story/past-those-sand-traps/282834 philmytummy. 2017. 'Saffron India Kitchen', 17 July, https://philmytummy.com/2017/07/17/saffron-indian-kitchen/

What Next?

PTI. 2022. 'IndiGo CEO Ronojoy Dutta Agrees to 2-Year Non-compete Curbs after Stepping Down in Sep', *Business Today*, 31 August, https://www.businesstoday.in/industry/aviation/story/indigo-ceo-ronojoy-dutta-pay-fixed-salary-non-compete-curbs-interglobe-aviation-346015-2022-08-31#:~:text=InterGlobe%20Aviation%20CEO%20Ronojoy%20Dutta,in%20competition%20with%20the%20company

About the Author

Tarun Shukla has been a business journalist for over two decades now, with work published in *The Wall Street Journal*, *The Economic Times*, *Mint*, *Hindustan Times*, *Financial Express* and *The Pioneer*. In 2010, his series of articles exposing India's air-safety gaps received a Society of Publishers in Asia gold award for investigative reporting.

HarperCollins *Publishers* India

At HarperCollins India, we believe in telling the best stories and finding the widest readership for our books in every format possible. We started publishing in 1992; a great deal has changed since then, but what has remained constant is the passion with which our authors write their books, the love with which readers receive them, and the sheer joy and excitement that we as publishers feel in being a part of the publishing process.

Over the years, we've had the pleasure of publishing some of the finest writing from the subcontinent and around the world, including several award-winning titles and some of the biggest bestsellers in India's publishing history. But nothing has meant more to us than the fact that millions of people have read the books we published, and that somewhere, a book of ours might have made a difference.

As we look to the future, we go back to that one word—a word which has been a driving force for us all these years.

Read.

   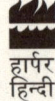